£4·25

D1420524

From the Ancien Régime
to the Popular Front

SHEPARD B. CLOUGH

President, Society for French Historical Studies, 1963-1964
President, Economic History Association, 1968-1969

From the Ancien Régime
to the Popular Front

Essays in the History of Modern France in
Honor of SHEPARD B. CLOUGH

Edited by
CHARLES K. WARNER

New York and London
COLUMBIA UNIVERSITY PRESS
1969

034326

Preface

WERE WE TO FOLLOW the precedent of a number of *Festschriften* this preface would be given over to a celebration of Shepard Clough's rich achievement as a scholar, the offices he has held, and the distinctions he has received. As former students of his, we cannot help contemplating such a prospect with pride, but we hope we are not too proud when we say we feel these things are well known. In turning from the more conventional appreciation, we are moved by the consideration that whatever broader appeal this volume may have, it is, in a sense, a very private tribute to a man whose human qualities we recognize along with his eminence as a scholar. To put it another way, in this preface and in the essays that follow, we would honor Shepard Clough as great teacher and good friend.

We would also like to record our gratitude that our seminar experience in that so well remembered study on the fifth floor of Fayerweather continues to live for us. To explain this fully would involve more encomiums and sentimentality than the Vermonter in our master might appreciate. One of our number, however, volunteered an explanation with more than a touch of Yankee forthrightness. "I'm writing something today," he said, "and I still think Shep Clough's going to be looking at it, that he's going to be tearing it to pieces next Tuesday. You know—*I'm glad* I feel that way!"

But our continuing experience operates on things more tangible than memories. Shepard Clough never stops giving of himself generously and convivially to us, whether it be on Morningside Heights, in Paris, or at professional meetings—places and organizations where we know he has more important responsibilities than furnishing the counsel we seek. Each of us carries his own debt of gratitude on this score. For many of us the magnitude of it did not become apparent until we took on academic and scholarly responsibilities of our own. From this remove, Shepard Clough's accomplishments as teacher and scholar seem to become equivalent to the legendary, a model for us to copy but perhaps never achieve. We acknowledge that we continue to be his pupils in many respects.

Several colleagues, not of our number, have called the attention of the present writer to our close and durable relationship with our mentor and remarked, not without envy, that it has probably produced a unique sodality. Many of us know that this is so. In presenting this volume, we would like Shepard Clough to know it, too.

The editor wishes to thank all those who contributed studies that would have found their place between these covers if space and exigencies of theme and balance had permitted. That determining the scope of this volume was a problem can be appreciated by anyone who knows Shepard Clough's wide-ranging interests. The editor is painfully aware, for example, that this collection of essays fails to do honor to his important contributions to Italian economic history and to the study of such problems as the definition of civilizations and the role of values in human behavior. But *est modus in rebus.* In place of a prodigal feast, the contributors to this volume hope they have presented a reasonably sufficient one. It is their wish that it will offer something of value to students of modern French history, meet with some approbation by Shepard Clough himself, and recreate, however imperfectly, some of the ambiance of his many memorable seminars.

The editor wishes to thank the Graduate Council of the University of Kansas for a grant to prepare the manuscript of this volume and the Department of History, Columbia University, for a grant towards publication from the William A. Dunning Fund. He also wishes to express his gratitude for the encouragement and support of Mr. Henry H. Wiggins, Assistant Director, Columbia University Press. Finally, he would like to acknowledge that the original inspiration for this volume belongs to Charles Freedeman, and that Charles Freedeman, Paul Beik, and Martin Wolfe have been constant and valuable collaborators in bringing it to completion.

CHARLES K. WARNER

Lawrence, Kansas
April, 1969

Contents

From the Ancien Régime
to the Popular Front

The Encyclopédie as a Business Venture

RALPH H. BOWEN

NORTHERN ILLINOIS UNIVERSITY
AND UNIVERSITY OF NANTES

IT HAS LONG BEEN RECOGNIZED that the *Encyclopédie* was a powerful agent of change in the realm of ideas and values. Among other things, the effect of this change was to facilitate the emergence of middle-class consciousness and to encourage the development of capitalist economy. Though one may say in general that the point of view of the *Encyclopédie* was that of liberal mercantilism, there were at least two major articles—"Fermiers" and "Grains"—by Dr. François Quesnay, the founder of the Physiocratic school, in which laisser-faire principles were expounded. Rationalism, hedonism, utilitarianism, and individualism, all of which have frequently been seen as essential components of the business mentality, permeated the seventeen volumes of the *Encyclopédie*'s text, and in the twelve volumes of illustrations there is enough exact information on industrial processes that if one set were to survive the destruction of our civilization, it would be possible (if the ability to read the French language also survived) to reconstitute the technology of eighteenth-century Europe. What is perhaps less well appreciated is that the publication of the *Encyclopédie* itself represented an economic achievement of considerable importance, marking some significant developments in the history of French publishing. At every stage of the enterprise, moreover, business calculations played a far from negligible role, and governmental policy toward the *Encyclopédie* was strongly influenced by economic considerations.

If Diderot was the chief architect and moving spirit on the editorial side, the chief entrepreneur of the "encyclopedic manufacture" was André-François Le Breton, a man who embodied a good number of the traits we are accustomed to associate with the modern businessman.[1] Energetic, shrewd, far-sighted, ambitious, harddriving, and unscrupulous, he had risen from modest beginnings to become the successful publisher of the *Almanach Royal*. When, late in 1744 or early in 1745, the young English bank clerk, John Mills, came to him with a proposal to translate Ephraim Chambers' *Cyclopaedia* (two volumes in folio) into French, Le Breton grasped the commercial possibilities at once and formed a partnership with Mills, who apparently let it be understood that he was in a position to put up part of the capital. Later, when the two partners fell out, Le Breton acted vigorously and decisively to eliminate Mills and secure full ownership of the *privilège* (royal letters-patent conveying an exclusive right to publish and sell the projected work).[2] Finding that the *Encyclopédie* (now expanded to five folio volumes, including one of illustrations) was too large an undertaking to finance alone, Le Breton formed a syndicate with three other booksellers, keeping a half interest for himself; the actual printing was to be done in his shop and was to be paid for before any profits were distributed.[3] Le Breton then proceeded

[1] Le Breton's personal qualities emerge from Diderot's correspondence, esp. from his letters to Sophie Volland (G. Roth, ed., *Denis Diderot, Correspondance* [Paris, 1955–65] 11 vols.). Much additional information is contained in the voluminous material relating to the lawsuit (1771–78) involving the publishers of the *Encyclopédie* and Luneau de Boisjermain; the bulk of these papers is in Bibl. Nat. MSS. Fr. 22,069 and 22,086.

[2] Bibl. Nat. MSS. Fr. 22,069, folios 263–67. In these "Pièces Justificatives" annexed to a *Mémoire pour P.-J.-F. Luneau de Boisjermain, souscripteur de l'Encyclopédie* (Paris, 1771) one finds copies of various "arrêts" of the Conseil d'Etat du Roi dating from 1743 to 1746 and relating to the *Almanach Royal*, the association between Mills and Le Breton, their subsequent quarrel, and the new *privilège* granted to Le Breton. For these episodes one should also consult F. Venturi, *Le Origini dell'Enciclopedia* (Rome, 1956) and "Le Origini dell' Enciclopedia in Inghilterra," *Itinerari*, Nos. 9–10 (Genoa, 1954), pp. 200–20.

[3] "Livre des Délibérations des sieurs Le Breton, David *l'aîné*, Durand et Briasson, Libraires à Paris, intéressés dans l'impression du Dictionnaire des Arts et Sciences de Chambers et Harris, traduit en français" (hereafter cited as "Délibérations"). This document (Archives Nationales U-1051) contains the record of decisions reached by the four associated publishers between 1745 and 1762. Along with some accounts it was apparently left behind by mistake in 1778 when the rest of the publishers' records (subpoenaed during their lawsuit against Luneau de Boisjermain) were returned. Discovered by Louis-Philippe May, these documents were published in the *Revue de synthèse* (XV, 1938; hereafter abbreviated as *Rs.*) and in the *Synthèse historique* (VIII, February, 1938). All subsequent references in this article are to the published texts. For details

to drive a series of hard bargains with his chief editors (of whom Diderot was the second in chronological sequence, the Abbé de Gua de Malves having proved to be a poor administrator during the year of his tenure), and with his other collaborators. In the end, overanxious about his good relations with the royal authorities, Le Breton did not even keep faith with Diderot by respecting the integrity of his text—though we now know that the damage was far less extensive than Diderot believed.[4] Poetic justice is perhaps satisfied by the fact that Le Breton, having made a handsome fortune from the *Encyclopédie,* went bankrupt when some of his other ventures came to grief. If not particularly attractive as a person, Le Breton deserves to be recognized as one of the outstanding entrepreneurs of eighteenth-century France.

For in material respects as well as in its cultural significance the publication of the *Encyclopédie's* twenty-eight massive volumes (thirty-five if we include the twelfth volume of plates, the four-volume supplement and the two-volume analytical table published by Charles-Joseph Panckoucke after Le Breton and Diderot had ceased to have any connection with the enterprise) was by any standards a noteworthy event.[5] No previous "inventory of knowledge" had been nearly as large; none had been the joint product of nearly 150 specialized contributors; none had enjoyed such strong financial backing; none was so expensive to produce; and probably none was commercially anywhere near as successful. Le Breton and his three associates may well have been substantially correct in their claim that the *Encyclopédie* was, up to that time, "the most important and extensive publishing venture ever undertaken."[6] The details of this business enterprise should be of considerable interest both to business historians and to students of the history of thought and culture.

---

of the agreement of October 18, 1745, constituting the syndicate, see *Rs.,* XV, 15–16; also the "Addition au Traité cy-dessus, en datte du 14e novembre 1745" (*Rs.,* p. 17).

[4] Douglas E. Gordon and Norman L. Torrey, *The Censoring of Diderot's* Encyclopédie *and the Re-established Text* (New York, 1947).

[5] Torrey, comparing the *Encyclopédie* with other major publishing ventures of the early modern period, called it "the biggest with respect to its bulk, the capital invested, the number and distinction of the contributors." Cf. "L'Encyclopédie de Diderot, une grande aventure dans le domaine de l'édition" (*Revue d'histoire littéraire de la France,* July–Sept., 1951) p. 306.

[6] "Réflections ultérieures . . ." [June 10, 1777] (Bibl. Nat. MSS. Fr. 22,069, fol. 431).

The history of the publication of the *Encyclopédie* falls naturally into three stages. First, there was a five-year period of preparation leading up to the distribution of the Prospectus of 1750 and the opening of the public subscription in October of that year. During this time a number of false starts were made, the plan of the work was revised and enlarged, and an adequate editorial staff, headed by Diderot and d'Alembert, was finally constituted. The second stage lasted until the "suppression" of the *Encyclopédie* in 1759. Despite the crisis of 1752, when the whole enterprise barely survived the *affaire* of the Abbé de Prades, and despite a continuing chorus of hostile criticism, seven volumes appeared. The number of subscribers grew far beyond the number originally hoped for, the government's attitude was generally benevolent, and from a commercial point of view the affair seems to have prospered mightily. A period of some anxiety must have followed the revocation of the *privilège* in March, 1759; but once again the support of public opinion and the connivance of sympathetic officials made it possible to survive the storm. Malesherbes, the Director of Publishing, gave permission for the opening of a new subscription for four supplementary volumes of plates, thus relieving the publishers of the obligation to refund money for the volumes of text as yet unpublished. After 1762 it was even possible to proceed quietly with the printing of the last ten volumes of text and to distribute these to the subscribers early in 1766 thanks to the willingness of the authorities to look the other way. No further difficulties arose and, with the delivery of the eleventh volume of plates in 1772, the original *Encyclopédie* of Diderot and Le Breton was finished. Each of these periods can be traced in considerable detail from the records available, and each has a special interest because of the changing character of the enterprise and the new kinds of business problems that arose.

The first five years of the *Encyclopédie*'s history are especially instructive for the student of the book trade in eighteenth-century France. The work had not yet assumed the ambitious proportions that its growing success and notoriety were to make possible after 1751. Thus, in the incubation stage between 1745 and 1750, it exhibits more faithfully than at a later stage the normal conditions and problems of the publishing industry in that period. In par-

ticular, the first projects and early arrangements reveal the extent
to which book publishing was bound up with governmental action
and with the system of corporative regulation maintained by the
Ancien Régime. Official good will and patronage were, from the
very beginning, indispensable: not only was it necessary to obtain
official permission to publish and to solicit subscriptions; it was
also necessary to cope with the complex problem of censorship,
involving (in addition to the Council of State and the Chancellor)
the Parlement of Paris, the Sorbonne, the archbishopric of Paris,
various prelates influential at Court, and the papacy itself. The
hostile influence of the Jesuits had to be counterbalanced. Official
and semiofficial bodies, notably the Academy of Sciences, needed
to be conciliated on occasion. Competitors bent on plagiarism or
outright piracy both inside and outside of France had to be dealt
with.[7] Finally, the guild regulations of the Communauté des
Libraires et Imprimeurs de Paris had to be complied with or cir-
cumvented. Operating within this intricate web of power and influence Le Breton needed all his abundant resources of initiative,
tact, and ingenuity to keep on good terms with all factions, some
of which might well be at loggerheads with others at a given moment.

As if this were not enough to tax the powers of an entrepreneur,
Le Breton—even after forming a syndicate with three other leading publishers—had to contend with a serious shortage of working
capital. Commercial credit was indeed available, but, as we shall
see, the prevailing interest rates were so high as to be virtually
prohibitive. This situation, which is no doubt traceable to the
underdevelopment of the French money market, seems to have
been a serious obstacle to expansion in the book trade as in other
branches of French economic life in the middle of the eighteenth
century. Le Breton's solution was to get the buyers of the *Encyclopédie* to put up the major part of the required capital; indeed,
the size and timing of payments was arranged in such a way as

[7] The publishers' "Délibérations" contain a resolution of October 28, 1751,
authorizing Briasson and David to go to London at the syndicate's expense to
negotiate with printers who had begun a pirated edition there; the two emissaries
were empowered to offer, in exchange for the abandonment of this project, a
certain number of copies of the Paris edition "at a very low price"; if this did
not work, they were to try to sell the London publishers sheets of the *Encyclopédie*'s illustrations (*Rs.*, pp. 25–26). Apparently the Londoners were
bought off, for we hear no more of this particular venture.

to build up a large interest-bearing surplus in the hands of the syndicate, thus greatly increasing the eventual net profits.

During the first five years, however, this solution was not available, and this period must have been extremely difficult from a business point of view, for no money was coming in and a great deal was going out. Before breaking with Mills, Le Breton had tied up some 5,000 livres in the venture. On the signing of the agreement with three other publishers (Briasson, Durand, and David *l'aîné*) on October 18, 1745, a total of 20,000 livres was paid in by the four members of the syndicate, half by Le Breton and the other half jointly by his three associates.[8] According to the code of regulations governing the book trade, no advance subscriptions could be solicited from the public until the entire manuscript of the proposed work had been approved by the official censor.[9] By 1751 the *Encyclopédie* had come to enjoy enough official favor that this rule was relaxed to permit each volume to be examined separately in advance of publication, but during the first five years there was no possibility of borrowing from the future purchasers of the work.

Yet heavy outlays had to be made, as the publishers' accounts show, to pay the editors, translators, consultants, contributors, and copyists, not to mention type founders, compositors, pressmen, engravers, papermakers, and the like. Consequently the syndicate was obliged to borrow, no doubt reluctantly, within a few months after its coming into existence; on February 28, 1746, a loan of 16,000 livres was obtained from the banker Valmalette for one year; the interest, amounting to 3,680 livres and 7 sols, was paid in advance, giving a rate of 30 percent per annum. This loan was repaid when it fell due on March 10, 1747, and thereafter the working fund was replenished by periodic assessments, with each associate paying in proportion to his share (one half for Le Breton and one

[4] "Traité de société, en datte du 18e octobre 1745" (*Rs.*, pp. 15–17).

[9] "Arrêt du Conseil d'Etat du Roi du 10 avril 1725 portant réglement sur le fait de la Librairie et Imprimerie," reproduced in "Pièces Justificatives," Bibl. Nat. MSS. Fr. 22,069, fol. 262. Art. III of this "Code de la Librairie," as it was unofficially called, provided that "There shall not be offered to the public any subscription except for the printing of very large works which could not be printed without this aid, unless permission has been granted by the Garde des Sceaux consequent to the approval which has been accorded to such works, in their entirety, by the censors whom he has appointed. . . ."

sixth for each of the other three).[10] By September 1, 1750, a month before the publication of the Prospectus and the first receipts from subscribers, the four associates had invested a total of 69,825 livres 18 sols and 3 deniers.[11]

Next to the problem of working capital the most troublesome of the publishers' concerns in these early years was that of finding a suitable editor. The first choice, the Abbé Jean-Paul de Gua de Malves, was a distinguished philosopher and scientist, a man who had many original ideas and a great deal of enthusiasm, but who proved to be deficient in organizing ability and practical sense.[12] His grandiose projects involved the publishers in ill-advised expenditures in such matters as the purchase of manuscripts from inept contributors. Not only was he paid a handsome salary (18,000 livres for an agreed period of two years) but he received during the year of his actual incumbency large additional advances which the publishers were able to recover only by legal action. Their books show that the Abbé de Gua was still paying off these debts as late as 1766. His contract with the publishers was dissolved by mutual consent on August 3, 1747.[13]

On October 16 of the same year Le Breton and his associates signed a new contract with Diderot and d'Alembert, who thus became joint editors, though the main administrative responsibility was to be Diderot's.[14] Both had been on the payroll since the beginning of the previous year, Diderot as translator and author,

[10] "Délibérations," *Rs.,* pp. 17, 20–21. Actually it is difficult to know whether they paid 8 percent or 30 percent because the entry in the "Délibérations" just cited gives the *amount* of interest, spelled out in words, as "trois mille six cents quatre vingt livres sept sols" (which works out to 30 percent per annum), while another ledger, the "Etat de la recette acuelle" showing receipts from all sources from 1746 to 1768, gives (under the entry of Feb. 28, 1746) the terms of the loan from Valmalette as "payable à un an à 8 percent d'interest" (*Rs.,* p. 99). There seems to be no way of reconciling this flat contradiction in the publishers' own records.

[11] "Etat de la recette actuelle" (*Rs.,* p. 101).

[12] Franco Venturi, "Le Origini dell'Enciclopedia," has collected the relatively few biographical facts available on this gifted but eccentric individual. One of his more ambitious (and no doubt costly) ventures was building and operating a machine for extracting gold dust from river sand.

[13] For the terms of his contract and the agreement *sous-seing privé* dissolving it, see *Rs.,* pp. 18–20 and 21. On Feb. 16, 1748, the company authorized Briasson to incur any legal expenses necessary to recover the sums advanced to the Abbé "jusques à parfait payement de ce qu'il nous doit" (*ibid.,* p. 22).

[14] *Ibid.,* p. 21.

d'Alembert as consultant on science and mathematics. (Contrary to what has long been believed, it was not Diderot who brought d'Alembert into the enterprise, for the latter's name appears for the first time in the publishers' accounts several months earlier than that of Diderot.)[15] Diderot did, however, recruit two friends, Eidous and Toussaint, who had helped him translate James's *Medicinal Dictionary* for Briasson. Little by little a group of writers was formed, most of whom received very low piecework wages, while a few were accorded lump-sum payments for articles on specified subjects.[16] Perhaps with their previous experience in mind, the publishers offered the new editors far less generous terms than the Abbé de Gua had enjoyed: each was to receive a monthly stipend of 144 livres. D'Alembert was to earn a total of 3,000 livres (of which he had already been paid 600); Diderot was to receive 1,200 livres upon publication of the first volume and a total of 6,000 in monthly payments.[17] This suggests that the *Encyclopédie* was still conceived on a fairly modest scale, for the period of d'Alembert's projected employment may be computed from the above data at a year and a half and that of Diderot at three and a half years.

It is not altogether clear when or by whom the decision was taken to enlarge the *Encyclopédie* from the five folio volumes contemplated by Mills's Prospectus of 1745 to the ten volumes promised by Diderot's Prospectus of 1750. Possibly there was no single decision and the manuscript simply grew, as was apparently the case between 1750 and 1772, when ten volumes became twenty-eight. The collaborative plan of work doubtless tended to produce such a result, for contributors who were specialists in their own fields may well have found it difficult to keep within the limited space assigned to them; indeed, Diderot seems actually to have

---

[15] *Ibid.*

[16] Cf. "Délibérations," *Rs.*, p. 22, under date of Oct. 19, 1747, for example: "It has also been decided that we will conclude an agreement with M. Le Roy *le fils* for the articles on clock-making, lock-making, description of mathematical instruments, and other subjects for a fee of 300 livres and a copy of *Chambers's Dictionary* when it is printed." This entry, incidentally, confirms that at the moment of Diderot's installation as chief editor the publishers were still thinking of their enterprise as a translation (with some expansion) of an existing work and not as a new and original publication.

[17] "Délibérations," *Rs.*, p. 21.

encouraged expansion in such cases.[18] Authors working on space rates had an obvious incentive to "pad" their articles, and the publishers, who planned to sell the completed work at so much per volume, had no special interest in keeping the work on a modest scale. On the other hand, there seems to be no conclusive evidence to support the subsequent charge of Luneau de Boisjermain, a dissatisfied subscriber, who accused the publishers of planning deliberately to circumvent their original promises in order to make a larger profit by selling a larger number of volumes.[19] Diderot

[18] See his article "Encyclopédie" in Vol. V (1755) of the *Encyclopédie, ou Dictionnaire raisonné des sciences, des arts et des métiers, . . . par une société de gens de lettres, . . .* (Paris, 1751–72; 28 vols. in folio). He explains that his method was to give each author a brief sketch of the article desired, often an article from Chambers, with a request to expand and improve; in this way, the author was less likely to be put off by the magnitude of the task (since apparently he was not being asked to produce an original piece of work) and was more likely to deliver his copy on time; in the majority of cases, moreover, the result was a new and far more substantial article because in the process of "revising" the author would little by little discard the unsatisfactory older material and add his own. Like all great editors, Diderot seems to have had a good grasp of the psychology of authorship.

[19] See notes 1 and 2 above. See also *Recueil des Mémoires composés par P.-J.-F. Luneau de Boisjermain sur le procès criminel que les sieurs Briasson et Le Breton lui ont intenté . . .* (Paris, 1770–72; 34 pièces); *Mémoires pour les libraires associés à l'Encyclopédie, contre le sieur Luneau de Boisjermain* (Paris, 1771); *Mémoire pour Luneau de Boisjermain* (Paris, 1777), MS. 4-bis, Cercle de la Librairie (Paris). Luneau de Boisjermain was an author and free-lance publisher as well as a forwarding agent for persons in the provinces wishing to obtain the books of Paris publishers more quickly and cheaply than was possible through normal channels of trade. Since his activities infringed a guild monopoly, Luneau was prosecuted in 1768 by the Syndics of the Communeauté des Libraires et Imprimeurs de Paris, who at that moment happened to be Briasson and Le Breton. To get revenge Luneau bought from one of the original subscribers a certificate that entitled him to receive the volumes yet to appear and then went into court in the role of a subscriber seeking a refund on the ground that the number of volumes was greater and the price per volume higher than originally promised. Technically his case was strong, for the conditions of the Prospectus had, indeed, not been adhered to, partly because acts of the public authority had intervened and partly because the publishers had used plausible pretexts for raising their prices, especially after 1765. Diderot, who had discovered Le Breton's treacherous tampering with his text in 1764, seems to have encouraged Luneau and to have given him much inside information; he later rallied to the publishers' side after Luneau had accused him of complicity in the "plot" to swindle the public by padding the *Encyclopédie*. The lawsuit dragged on through the courts until 1778, when Luneau, unable to prove bad faith on the part of the publishers, lost his final appeal to the Parlement of Paris. His many long legal briefs, which he had printed and distributed to the public, contain a vast amount of useful information, not only because of his knowledge of the book trade, which was exhaustive, but because he drew on Diderot's personal knowledge of the "secret history" of the encyclopedic enterprise. Finally, he was able

later explicitly denied that the publishers dictated the scale of the *Encyclopédie*. He also took upon himself the responsibility for determining the length of various articles and thus, by implication, the total size of the work.[20] It is perhaps a reasonable guess that Le Breton and Diderot were both ambitious to expand the *Encyclopédie*, one for commercial and the other for "philosophic" reasons.

In any event, the years from 1747 to 1750 must have been busy ones for Diderot and his associates. The best articles from Chambers and from similar compilations were translated, usually with substantial revision and expansion, and much new material was written. D'Alembert took charge of the scientific and mathematical articles, writing the most important ones himself, and he also busied himself with the "Discours préliminaire" which was to appear at the beginning of the first volume. Diderot solicited articles and edited those that were sent in, did research on industrial processes, and wrote descriptions to accompany the copperplate illustrations. He also drew up the Prospectus which, though dated 1751, was distributed to the European public in October, 1750.

By the middle of 1749, expenditures of all kinds had reached a total of about 60,000 livres.[21] With this capital investment at stake, it is not difficult to appreciate the publishers' consternation when Diderot, "the one man who holds the key" to the whole enterprise, was imprisoned in the Château de Vincennes on July 24, 1749, for having indiscreetly published—even though anonymously—his *Letter on the Blind*. Vigorous representations were immediately made to the authorities—not, as one might have ex-

---

to study the actual account books of the publishers when the court ordered these to be produced, and his later *Mémoires* make full use of this authentic information.

[20] In an open letter to Briasson and Le Breton dated August 31, 1771, apparently written at the request of the publishers, who were being sued for overcharges by Luneau de Boisjermain, Diderot exonerated his employers of any responsibility for the final length of the *Encyclopédie*: "The publisher thinks my long-windedness is hurting [*chasse beaucoup*] sales and complains to me. What is the result? I either pay attention or I don't, depending on my inclination. He insists and I threaten to resign. He persists and pleads with me; I beg him as politely as I can to get out of my office; so all he can do is carry on, at my discretion, an enterprise which he undertook without knowing where I would lead him." (*Oeuvres complètes*, ed. J. Assézat and M. Tourneux (Paris, 1875–77), XX, 31. Hereafter cited as A.-T.)

[21] The publishers' account books show total expenses of 62,395 livres 12 sols 6 deniers on January 24, 1750 ("Déliberations," *Rs.*, p. 21).

pected, protesting Diderot's innocence, but stressing his indispensability to a great national enterprise and foretelling financial ruin for the publishers if their editor were not promptly restored to his tasks. To the Comte d'Argenson, the minister who had ordered the arrest, they addressed a plea for clemency and a somewhat inflated claim that they had invested 80,000 livres in their undertaking and planned to invest 250,000 in all.[22] These *démarches* resulted in a marked relaxation of Diderot's prison regime —he was transferred from the *donjon* to the château itself, and he was allowed to work on papers brought to him by his employers and to receive other business visits. Still it must have been good news for all concerned when after two months of this relatively mild detention Diderot was finally released on September 3, 1749, and allowed to return to his desk in Le Breton's print shop.

A new phase in the *Encyclopédie's* business history opened with the publication of the Prospectus of October, 1750, which described the forthcoming work, gave sample articles, and fixed the conditions of sale. Broadly speaking, one may say that in this second stage the emphasis shifted from finance and production to marketing. Receipts from subscribers provided more than enough working capital and even permitted the syndicate to earn interest on the excess of funds deposited with them. Thanks to d'Alembert's reputation and connections in the world of science and to Diderot's dynamic qualities as general editor, there was no lack of enthusiasm for the new work among men of letters and before long it was possible to announce that Buffon, Voltaire, and other celebrities would lend the luster of their names. Diderot obtained a great deal of excellent publicity thanks to his sharp exchanges with Father Berthier, editor of the Jesuits' journal, the *Mémoires de Trévoux*; in this polemic he not only defended the *Encyclopédie* against the charge of plagiarizing older works but gave a clear indication that a "philosophic spirit" would guide the new compilation.[23] This was enough to label the *Encyclopédie* as a "con-

[22] Their letter is reproduced in A.-T., XIII, 113. For the fullest and most recent account of Diderot's imprisonment, see Arthur M. Wilson, *Diderot: The Testing Years, 1713–1759* (New York, 1957).

[23] *Lettre de M. Diderot au R. P. Berthier, jésuite* [Paris, 1751]. Father Berthier faithfully printed both of Diderot's letters (January and February) in his journal. In addition the two letters of Diderot were circulated as pamphlets.

troversial" work and hence to attract public interest. In addition, of course, it was a plea—and one that was heeded—for the support and cooperation of all those who were sympathetic to the general aims of the Enlightenment. From the commercial point of view, this meant that Le Breton and his partners could now count on a large number of unpaid promoters not only in France but throughout Europe and even in America, a sales force without precedent, unless we count the services rendered by the clergy to publishers of devotional literature.

It is probable that the publishers did not originally dare to predict anything like the success that the *Encyclopédie* quickly achieved. This would explain why they at first arranged for a modest initial printing of only 1,550 copies[24] and why they placed a fairly high price on their product; later, when the market proved capable of absorbing nearly three times that number, they not only did not lower the price but raised it for latecomers. At a time when wages for manufacturing workers probably averaged between one and two francs a day, the initial price of 280 livres (372 livres for those subscribing after May 1, 1751)[25] must have been prohibitive for all except the relatively well to do. It was planned that eight volumes of text and 600 plates (two volumes) would be published at the rate of two volumes per year; hence the entire work would be complete by December, 1754. Booksellers in Paris would be accorded a rebate of 12 livres per subscription, while those in the provinces would be allowed twice as much.[26]

    [24] *Encyclopédie, ou Dictionnaire raisonné . . . Dix volumes in-folio, dont deux de planches en taille-douce, proposés par souscription* (Paris, 1751). This Prospectus also contained an elaborate chart, based on Bacon's classification of human knowledge. Following the custom for titles issued in the final quarter of a year, it carried the date of the following year.
    [25] "Délibérations," *Rs.*, p. 17. This decision appears in a supplementary article dated November 14, 1745, annexed to the original contract of association. It was also provided that Le Breton would receive 25 livres per sheet (2 pages of the *Encyclopédie*) and that 75 copies would be printed *en grand papier*, presumably for bibliophiles and for presentation to the high and mighty. On July 3, 1751 (*ibid.*, p. 25), it was decided to print 2,050 copies on ordinary paper and 25 on special paper; to reflect the larger press run, Le Breton's price per *feuille* was increased to 33 livres.
    [26] Prospectus of 1751 (see note 24 above). At their meeting of November 21, 1750, just after the publication of the Prospectus, the four publishers formally incorporated its principal provisions in their "Délibérations." They also designated Briasson as bookkeeper and set up a system for issuing subscription certificates, for reporting (every two weeks) the number sold by each associate, and for the giving of rebates. ("Délibérations," *Rs.*, pp. 24–25.)

The response to this offer must have been highly gratifying. By April 29, 1751, 1,002 subscriptions had been sold and 60,120 livres had been paid in. The syndicate decided on July 3 to increase the printing of Volume I (which had appeared in the meantime, on June 28) from 1,550 to 2,050 copies. They also announced that they would continue to accept new subscriptions (at a higher price) for three more months and that (in order to tap provincial and foreign markets more effectively) the discount for dealers outside Paris would be raised to 36 livres per set. By the beginning of 1752 the number of subscribers had reached 2,000. The publishers had not only recovered all their original outlay but were able to share profits of 30,000 livres.[27]

In the interval between the appearance of Volume I and that of Volume II the *Encyclopédie* received a vast amount of free publicity thanks to the Jesuits' attacks and it gained notoriety from the condemnation of the young Abbé de Prades, one of Diderot's staff writers on theology, for the views expressed in his doctoral thesis, which was at first accepted with high praise by the Sorbonne and then repudiated under pressure when both Jansenists and Jesuits raised an outcry. An *arrêt* of the Conseil d'Etat du Roi dated February 7, 1752, forbade the further sale (and reprinting) of the two volumes of the *Encyclopédie* which had appeared—a prohibition which the publishers proceeded to ignore with impunity but which, contrary to the demands of the devout party, had placed no restrictions on the continuation of the work apart from tightening the arrangements for censorship.[28] When Volume III appeared, in 1753, the number of subscribers had grown so much that the total printing had to be raised from 2,050 to 3,100; moreover, since even this number soon proved insufficient, in February, 1754, it was decided to order a second printing of 1,100 copies; additional printings of the first two volumes (although illegal) were carried out at the same time, and Volume IV, which was issued in October of the same year, was printed in 4,225 copies. This was to be the press run for subsequent volumes of the first edition.[29]

The years from 1754 to 1759 were free of major crises. For

[27] "Délibérations," *Rs.*, p. 25.

[28] "Arrêt du Conseil d'Etat du Roi du 7 Février 1752," reproduced in "Pièces Justificatives" annexed to *Mémoire pour P.-J.-F. Luneau de Boisjermain* (Bibl. Nat. MSS. Fr. 22,069, fols. 268v–269r).

[29] "Délibérations," *Rs.*, p. 27.

Diderot and his coworkers this was a period of intensive work, as we may judge from the fact that Diderot wrote little else, apart from two plays and a few contributions to Grimm's *Correspondance littéraire,* during those five years. In all probability the bulk of the manuscript for all the remaining volumes was put together before 1759, and Diderot doubtless spent most of his time at his desk, for it was only later, as we shall see, that he undertook extensive firsthand research for the plates illustrating industrial processes. Diderot may have had a large part of his material in hand by the mid-fifties, and in later years both he and the publishers asserted that this was the case;[30] but even so there must have been a tremendous amount of editing to do. Though the sources do not permit us to be completely certain on this point, it seems very likely that by around 1755 Diderot had a fairly complete notion of the final dimensions and shape of the *Encyclopédie,*[31] and that the only major expansion in plans after that date was the decision taken in 1759 to increase the number of volumes devoted to illustrating the arts and sciences.

For the publishers the late fifties were a time of great prosperity. With 3,000 subscribers at the end of 1754, their gross receipts had risen to some 550,000 livres, as against total expenditures of 270,886 livres 15 sous;[32] net earnings were thus more than 270,000

[30] During the seven-year lawsuit with Luneau de Boisjermain (see notes 1 and 19 above).

[31] The Prospectus of 1750 had explicitly stated that the *Encyclopédie* "n'est plus un ouvrage à faire," and of course the law required that a complete MS. be in existence before subscriptions were solicited. If Le Breton and his partners (and his chief editor) are to be believed, they complied with this requirement; thus a MS. for at least eight volumes existed in 1750. We may note, by way of confirmation, that Vol. I only finished the letter "A"—so that even if we make allowance for the probability that Diderot and his staff would have concentrated on the first part of the alphabet, the fact that publication of the whole work was supposed to be complete by the end of 1754 suggests that they could not have neglected the later section of the alphabet completely in the early fifties. It is of course true that as more illustrious contributors (Montesquieu, Voltaire) were recruited, better articles were substituted for those already written. In any case, it seems irrefutable that Diderot knew by 1756 or 1757 that he was going to need at least twelve to fourteen volumes (instead of the eight promised in 1750) to complete his text; otherwise he would hardly have ended the letter "G" with Vol. VII.

[32] The figure for expenditures is given in Briasson's accounts under date of Dec. 28, 1754. ("Délibérations," *Rs.,* p. 27.) The income is calculated from the number of subscriptions and can be given only in round numbers because the records are not sufficiently detailed.

livres. The original investment of just under 70,000 livres[33] had been recovered four times over. Three years later, in November, 1757, just after the publication of Volume VII, there were 4,000 subscribers and gross receipts had risen to more than 960,000 livres.[34] The venture had succeeded beyond everyone's wildest hopes. The public was informed that there would eventually be more than ten volumes of text—Diderot now planned a total of fourteen volumes of articles—and that the number of plates would be increased from 600 to 1,000.[35]

But danger still lay ahead. The attempted assassination of Louis XV by Damiens in late 1757 and the ill-timed publication of Helvétius' *De l'esprit* in 1758 afforded pretexts to the reactionary party at Court, in the Parlements, and in the church; the *philosophes* came under intensified attack and the demand for stricter censorship of the press became impossible for the government to resist. Early in 1759 the *Encyclopédie*, along with a number of other works of advanced tendencies, was suppressed by decision of the Council of State.[36] On July 21 the associated publishers were ordered to refund to the subscribers all that the latter had paid in advance for volumes which would now not be delivered; this amount was fixed at 72 livres per subscriber.[37] The publishers

[33] The actual figure of 69,825 livres 18 sols 3 deniers is given in Briasson's "Etat de la recette actuelle" for Jan. 15, 1750 (*Rs.*, p. 101). From this date on, no further assessments for working capital are recorded. The first receipts from subscriptions are entered on Dec. 2, and by the end of the month a total of 7,428 livres was received. Another 2,424 came in during the first half of January (*Rs.*, p. 102). Thus the largest amount tied up in the venture could not have been more than 70,000 lives and was actually nearer 60,000, if we deduct from the investment total of Jan. 15 the 9,852 livres received from subscriptions by that date. Incidentally, if we assume that virtually all of these subscriptions were sold in Paris by the publishers themselves, as seems likely, given the fact that more time would have had to elapse for subscribers in the provinces to receive the Prospectus and remit their down payment of 60 livres through a provincial bookseller, then there must have been upwards of 165 buyers in the first six weeks, which suggests a certain enthusiasm on the part of the public.

[34] Income is computed from the number of subscriptions.

[35] "Avertissement" printed at the beginning of Vol. VII of the *Encyclopédie*, which was distributed in November, 1767. Each supplementary volume of text was to cost 24 livres and two additional volumes of plates were to add 90 livres to the total cost of the set.

[36] "Arrêt du Conseil d'Etat du Roi du 8 Mars 1759" reproduced in "Pièces Justificatives" annexed to *Mémoire pour P.-J.-F. Luneau de Boisjermain*, Bibl. Nat. MSS. Fr. 22,069, fol. 269.

[37] "Arrêt du Conseil d'Etat du Roi du 21 Juillet 1759" (*ibid.*, fols. 269v–270r).

would thus have had to pay out 288,000 livres on short notice; they were naturally reluctant to see such a large fraction of their profits disappear and immediately set up an outcry that they would be ruined if forced to make the reimbursement. We may well doubt, in the light of the figures already cited, whether they were threatened with bankruptcy as they claimed. Nor, in all probability, should we attach much importance to their hints that, unless ways were found to complete the *Encyclopédie* in France, they or their staff might accept an invitation to continue the enterprise in Holland, Prussia, or Russia.[38] But we may believe that the royal authorities, actuated by traditional mercantilist principles, were reluctant to destroy a business venture that was providing employment and taxable income to a considerable number of French workmen and businessmen as well as contributing to a favorable balance of trade (perhaps as many as half the purchasers of the *Encyclopédie* were foreigners).[39] There was also the international prestige of France to be considered. By stressing these considerations Malesherbes was able to turn the crisis to the advantage of the publishers by permitting them to launch a new subscription, this time for a four-volume collection of plates illus-

[38] Voltaire was particularly eager to see Diderot and his chief assistants emigrate; moreover, there were opportunities: Frederick II was apparently ready to provide facilities in Berlin. The chief obstacle seems to have been Diderot's solid sense of property rights: the manuscript of the *Encyclopédie* belonged to Le Breton and his partners, and it would be robbery to make off with it. Diderot also knew better than Voltaire that Malesherbes and the royal government wanted the *Encyclopédie* to continue; he was not, of course, unwilling to hint at the possibility of taking the *Encyclopédie* abroad in order to win better terms from Malesherbes.

[39] Le Breton later claimed that *three quarters* of the subscribers lived outside France, but he was then arguing against Luneau's claim that the subscribers should receive a sizable refund: always aware of the power of mercantilist arguments where the public authorities were concerned, Le Breton tried to make it appear that France would lose over a million livres to the foreigner if Luneau won his case. Fortunately Le Breton tended to be consistent in the degree to which he exaggerated the facts in his own interest: in other instances where his veracity can be checked, he seems generally to have added 12–15 percent to the truth; two thirds or five eighths, therefore, seems a reasonable adjusted figure. However, it is entirely possible, not to say probable, that neither Le Breton nor anyone else knew with any precision how many subscribers were Parisians, how many lived in the provinces, and how many were foreigners, for no lists were kept by Briasson, and the accounting system did not distinguish between foreign sales and those to provincial booksellers (the latter being the only ones who had a record of the names of subscribers outside Paris). See the various *Mémoires* cited in notes 1, 2, and 19 above, esp. *Mémoire pour les libraires associés à l'Encyclopédie* (Paris, 1772).

trating the arts and sciences; the down payment, covering the first volume, was fixed at 72 livres and the same price was to apply to each subsequent volume. The 4,000 old subscribers would each be credited with 72 livres, the exact amount of the refund to which they were entitled, and they would receive the collection of plates at a special bargain price of 28 livres per volume (instead of the 72 livres to be charged new purchasers).[40] Under these conditions it is hardly surprising that not a single subscriber chose to claim his refund in cash!

No sooner was this calamity avoided than a new threat loomed on the horizon. On November 23, 1759, there appeared in the *Année littéraire,* edited by Elie Fréron, a sworn enemy of the *Encyclopédie,* a letter signed by a certain Patte, an engraver who had worked for the celebrated savant Réaumur on the plates which the latter had been supervising for the Academy of Sciences for over thirty years preceding his death in 1757. According to Patte's allegations, which were extremely circumstantial, duplicate proofs of a large number of these plates had been abstracted by dishonest workmen and sold to the publishers of the *Encyclopédie.* Independent evidence exists to support the essentials of Patte's charge, and it is even possible to infer that Diderot had virtually completed the prose descriptions to accompany these illustrations before 1750 when the Prospectus appeared.[41]

Had this charge of wholesale plagiarism been sustained, the *Encyclopédie* would almost certainly have suffered a fatal loss of public confidence and prestige. In order to ward off this danger the publishers immediately demanded an investigation, whereupon a commission appointed by the Academy of Sciences made a visit to Le Breton's shop to inspect the drawings in Diderot's portfolios. We may assume that any incriminating evidence had already disappeared, for the official report gave the *Encyclopédie* a clean bill of health. Disaster had been avoided, but Diderot and the publishers were now faced with the necessity of producing new and original plates which would be able to stand minute comparison with those shortly to be published by the Academy. This meant

[40] "Privilège d'un Recueil de mille Planches. Du 8 Septembre 1759," reproduced in "Pièces justificatives," Bibl. Nat. MSS. Fr. 22,069, fol. 270.

[41] This whole episode has been exhaustively studied by Jacques Proust, "La documentation technique de Diderot dans l'*Encyclopédie*" (*Revue d'histoire littéraire de la France,* Juillet–Sept. 1957, pp. 335–52).

that Diderot and his helpers, including particularly the engraver Goussier, whose expense accounts for travel in the provinces are to be found in the business records of the syndicate, had to undertake the firsthand research which, up to that time, the editor of the *Encyclopédie* had done only occasionally. It meant also that the total number of plates had to be increased substantially in order to enhance the contrast between the two collections. Patte's denunciation thus led to a complete revision of the *Encyclopédie*'s visual and textual treatment of the arts and sciences, for Diderot was obliged to write new descriptions to accompany the revised plates, and this often led him to accompany his illustrator on his visits to various workshops in order to see with his own eyes how certain operations were carried out. This "field work" had not been foreseen in the beginning, at least not on this scale, but it turned out to be the source of one of the *Encyclopédie*'s most original and valuable contributions.[42]

Meanwhile, thanks to the benevolence of Malesherbes, the publishers had been granted a "permission tacite" to continue with the remaining volumes of text on the understanding that these would carry a foreign imprint and that final delivery would be made all at one time. Though the actual printing was done on presses which Le Breton had bought from the Jesuits after their order was suppressed in 1762, the title page of the last ten volumes attributed them to a Swiss printer, Samuel Faulche of Neufchâtel, and Diderot's name appeared as "Monsieur ***". All ten volumes reached the subscribers early in 1766 in a single bundle for which every recipient paid 200 livres in a lump sum. Le Breton was briefly imprisoned in the Bastille for failing to exercise enough discretion in distributing the work in Paris and Versailles.

If we now attempt to calculate the final balance sheet of the enterprise, we arrive at a theoretical income from the sale of subscriptions of at least 3.5 million livres by the end of 1771, when all seventeen volumes of text and nine volumes of plates had been published. Each of the thousand original subscribers would have paid 850 livres and each of the 3,000 subsequent purchasers would have paid 874 livres, which works out to 3,472,000 livres in receipts through the year 1771. Adding 452,000 livres, the pro-

[42] *Ibid.*

ceeds of the last two volumes of plates distributed in 1772, we reach a theoretical income of 3,924,000 livres for 28 volumes (the complete *Encyclopédie* of Diderot and Le Breton). Some allowance should be made, however, for discounts allowed to provincial and foreign booksellers: if we assume that two thirds of all subscriptions were sold outside Paris (which ought to be a generous estimate)[43] then the syndicate would have allowed rebates of 16,000 livres on the first thousand subscriptions and 72,000 livres on the remaining three thousand and we should therefore deduct a total of 88,000 livres for rebates. This leaves a net income from subscriptions of 3,836,000 livres. To this we should add the amount realized from the sale of the copper engravings to the publisher Panckoucke—this amounted to 230,000 livres, according to Luneau de Bois-jermain, who probably got the information from Diderot.[44] The net income thus comes to 4,066,000 livres.

In trying to estimate the costs of the venture we may take as a starting point the figure of 1,039,642 livres 7 sols and 3 deniers, which is the latest total given by the publishers' surviving account books as of the end of 1767.[45] For a later total, making allowance for the volumes of plates subsequently produced, we may accept the figure given in 1777 by Luneau de Boisjermain who, after examining all of Briasson's accounts, stated that 1,269,619 livres 9 sols and 3 deniers had been spent altogether, a reasonable total, given the 1767 total which we know to be authentic.[46] Even if we allow the publishers' claim that they suffered a loss of 30,000 livres as a result of a fire in their warehouse (the fact itself is confirmed by Diderot's correspondence),[47] their total commercial profits must have amounted to some 2,506,000 livres. This conclusion corresponds very closely with Diderot's statement to Catherine II:

I was the one who paid out all the money on behalf of the trades-men who had joined together to publish our work. When the whole

[43] See note 39 above.

[44] Moreover, in a *Mémoire* dated 1777, *after* he had examined the publishers' own books (Bibl. Nat. MSS. Fr. 22,069, fol. 397), Luneau continues to use this same figure in his computations.

[45] "État de la recette actuelle," *Rs.*, p. 102.

[46] Bibl. Nat. MSS. Fr. 22,069, fol. 397.

[47] *Précis pour les libraires associés à l'Encyclopédie contre le sieur Luneau de Boisjermain* (Paris, 1772), Bibl. Nat. MSS. Fr. 22,069, fol. 227v. Le Breton also claimed that Luneau failed to include some other "legitimate" costs, such as 100,000 livres in "presents," 85,000 livres in interest paid, 50,000 for warehouse expenses and 600,000 for accounts receivable (*ibid.*, fol. 228).

undertaking was finished, these expenses added up to 1,500,000 lives.
. . . They printed 4,500 copies, of which not a single one remains
these four years past and more.

They sold each set, on the average, at 900 francs each. Thus their
toal receipts were more than four millions and, after deducting all costs,
there remained 2,500,000 francs, which they themselves admit.[48]

In evaluating these profits we should of course bear in mind
that except for the first few years the publishers had no funds of
their own invested in the venture (except possibly for a brief interval in the early sixties, when they were printing the final volumes
of text and had not yet received any income from the illustrations);
indeed, it appears very probable that from about the middle of
1751 onward they were operating essentially with capital furnished
by the subscribers. Strictly speaking, therefore, we should make
some allowance for the interest accruing on the rather substantial
amount that was continuously in the syndicate's possession for a
period of some twenty years. This is impossible to compute exactly,
but Luneau de Boisjermain, who was thoroughly acquainted with
the economics of publishing, estimated that the total interest earned
probably amounted to at least one sixth of the costs of publication[49]—that is, to some 212,000 livres. Adding this to the commercial profits previously calculated, we arrive at a figure of just over
2,718,000 livres, which would represent total net profits. This
would be a profit of some 3,380 percent on the original capital of
just under 70,000 livres which had been invested by the end of
1750; that is, on the largest amount ever committed to the venture
(and that for only a fourth of its duration) by the publishers out of
their own pockets.

Profits of this magnitude were certainly not common in eighteenth-century publishing. The publishers of the *Encylopédie* were
exceptionally fortunate in that they reached the market at the
right time with a product that met an existing demand—indeed,
the effective demand proved to be three times as great as Le Breton
and his partners had originally foreseen. They owed a good deal
of their success to the publicity generated by the attacks of conservative critics, and the benevolence of the royal authorities (espe-

[48] Maurice Tourneux, *Diderot et Catherine II* (Paris, 1899), pp. 434–35.
[49] *Mémoire pour P.J.-F. Luneau de Boisjermain* . . . (Paris, 1771), Bibl.
Nat. MSS. Fr. 22,069, fol. 190r.

cially during the crisis of 1759) was worth a large amount in actual cash, not to speak of the personal security of the Encyclopedists themselves. Good management and dynamic business leadership doubtless contributed substantially to the final result, though one cannot, of course, give a quantitative estimate.

Nor should it be forgotten that the handsome profits realized by the *Encyclopédie*'s entrepreneurs reflect the fact that the cost of acquiring the manuscript was very low. Over a period of thirty years the total amount paid to Diderot came to less than 80,000 livres,[50] an average annual salary of only 2,600 livres—about one tenth of one percent of the net profits. The other authors either received trifling sums—like the 900 livres paid to the Abbé Mallet for his numerous articles on theology, church history, commerce, and money or the 300 livres paid to Toussaint for a series of articles on law[51]—or, like Voltaire and the Baron d'Holbach, donated their services. One, at least, the Chevalier de Jaucourt, who, next to Diderot himself, contributed the largest number of pages, even sold one of his houses to get money to pay the secretaries he employed to take dictation.[52] Luneau de Boisjermain believed that the total cost to the publishers of producing the text was not more than 150,000 livres. Even if this is somewhat too low, we can at least conclude that the true figure lies between this and the 400,000 livres claimed by Le Breton.[53] If we accept the latter figure, the literary property that constituted the *Encylclopédie* was acquired for less than half of one percent of the net profits.

Perhaps we may say in conclusion that in eighteenth-century

---

[50] Jacques Proust, *Diderot et l'Encyclopédie* (Paris, 1962), p. 59, citing MS. Cercle de la Librairie, 4-bis, pièce 5-bis, p. 7, which I have not had an opportunity to examine. The figure is presumably taken from a calculation made by Luneau de Boisjermain after he had seen the complete accounts of the publishers.

[51] *Rs.*, pp. 22–23.

[52] At least this is the tradition, probably originating with Diderot. There is a record in the "Délibérations," p. 108, of a loan of 12,000 livres from the Chevalier de Jaucourt (without mention of interest) dated Oct. 2, 1761, and a second entry dated Feb. 26, 1762, reaffirming the debt (*ibid.*, p. 29). This loan no doubt reflects the leanness of the years between 1759 and 1765 when the last ten volumes of text were being printed but could not be delivered; the plates were producing revenue after 1762, but there seems to have been a period of stringency during which it was necessary to borrow—how much, we have no way of knowing.

[53] *Réflexions d'un Souscripteur à l'Encyclopédie sur le Procès intenté aux Libraires associés à cet Ouvrage par M. Luneau de Boisjermain*, in Bibl. Nat. MSS. Fr. 22,069, fol. 368.

France, as at some other times and places, the idealism of intellectuals was good business, at least for some alert businessmen if not for the men of letters themselves. It is also perhaps not incongruous that fabulous profits were made from the literary and scientific work that may have been more effective than any other in advancing the public relations of modern capitalism.

The Meaning of the Revolution: Seven Testimonies

PAUL H. BEIK

SWARTHMORE COLLEGE

THE FRENCH REVOLUTION AS an overture to contemporary history has a secure place because of the richness of its forecasts of later problems. From old-regime France, biggest and most complicated of the highly developed countries of that era, the breakdown of political authority and the struggle for the succession brought forth a great variety of contending groups and competing programs, each with its assessment of what was happening and what was needed: in short, of what the revolution was about. These contemporaneous witnesses have their limitations but can never be rendered obsolete by accumulated evidence even when it is illuminated by other disciplines; at most, their testimonies will fluctuate in interest as we read them in awareness of accrued knowledge, problems of our own world, and current controversies among historians.

Since the Second World War there have been at least two major changes in perspective on the French Revolution, one of them a deepening appreciation of social content made possible by the work of Georges Lefebvre and his circle, the other the broadening bird's-eye view in comparative studies by Robert R. Palmer and Jacques Godechot. Both of these tendencies have been justly praised, and both have inspired critics. The Palmer-Godechot views have been opposed by persons who prefer to emphasize the undeniable uniqueness of what the French Revolution did rather than the general European or "Western" significance of the problems it was trying to solve. The Palmer-Godechot interpretations have also been disputed by those who point to difficulties of chronology caused by the uneven development of Europe and America at the end of the eighteenth century.

The Lefebvre circle associated with the *Annales historiques de la Révolution française* produced in the writings of Lefebvre himself going back to the First World War and in those of Labrousse, Reinhard, Soboul, Cobb, Rude, and others what is still the strongest tendency in French historiography, the search beneath the level of national politics into economic and social structures. The contribution of these men is not in dispute, but in recent years the Marxian inspiration toward analysis of social realities, which Lefebvre took from Jaurès and passed on to others, has been attacked as providing a misleading set of social categories and assumptions about social change. The English historian Alfred Cobban has been making this charge since 1954, and since the publication of his *The Social Interpretation of the French Revolution* (Cambridge, 1964), others have followed his lead.

The broadening and deepening of French Revolution studies and the controversies aroused thereby—and one must add twentieth-century revolutions and the problems of new nations—have reaffirmed the relevance of the French experience and added interest to the testimonies of its participants. What follows is a juxtaposition of some of the principal statements from the scene itself, representing major conflicts of opinion but with no pretension that they tell all or speak for measurable constituencies.

Of the seven testimonies to be presented here, the first will be that of Louis de Bonald, the most thorough, philosophical, comprehensive, and prophetic spokesman of the French Right, whose anonymously published book *Théorie du pouvoir politique et religieux dans la société civile, démontrée par le raisonnement et par l'histoire* (1796) was, intellectually, the high point of a revival of absolutism during the revolution. At the other end of the spectrum, which we shall cross from right to left, awaits François Noël Babeuf, whose socialist conspiracy also came in 1796, marking in a different way the maturing of the revolutionary crisis. Much of de Bonald's importance lies in the fact that his matured view of

the revolution would have spoken to the condition of scarcely anyone in 1789 but by 1796 represented the hardening of the counterrevolution.

De Bonald's metaphor for the French Revolution was the Tower
of Babel, presenting a spectacle of many particular wills where
there had once been a general will. The revolution in the terms of
de Bonald's sociology (the word is appropriate; he asked for a
science of society) was an attack by the "mixed professions" on the
"social professions" by turning against them the "natural professions"; in other words, men of arts and letters and the law had
aroused artisans and peasants against royal, sacerdotal, and noble
functionaries of what should have been a stable society of corporate
groups with largely hereditary professions.[1] What should have been
a "constituted" civil society had been wrenched from its natural
course, indicated by God via natural laws knowable to human
reason, and had become thereby a "non-constituted" society, outside the law and given over to the clash of private interests. Without religious power to repress wills and political power to repress
exterior acts, there was bound to be an anarchy whose conflicts
could be abated only by turning energies outward into foreign
wars. The French Republic meant anarchy and war, the European
republics that the French were trying to encourage meant anarchy
and war on a larger scale, and the outcome could only be a weaken-
ing and disorganization that would mean a decline of Europe and
its conquest by barbarians from the East just as Rome had declined
and been conquered by barbarians from the North.[2]

What de Bonald saw happening was a dual revolution from
Christianity to atheism and from monarchy to republicanism. In a
great reversal of the role of the early Christian missionaries a sect
of atheistic philosophers had been reducing European civil society
to a savage state. It was more than a simple plot; it was a great
historical aberration, in the deepest sense providential, for God
must be using France to teach mankind a lesson.[3] But de Bonald,
who wrote independently of Joseph de Maistre and emphasized

[1] Louis de Bonald, *Théorie du pouvoir politique et religieux dans la société
civile, démontré par le raisonnement et par l'histoire* (3 vols.; n.p., 1796), I, vii–
viii, xix–xx, 531–33; II, 174n.; III, 29, 183.
[2] *Ibid.*, I, 1–17, 49–50, 52, 132, 309, 311–14, 318–19; III, 316–18.
[3] *Ibid.*, I, 315, 321, 322, 532–33.

the providential much less, was given to economic, social, and demographic explanations of European history and of the revolution.

For commerce, considered as the one religion of societies ever since money became the one God of men, by displacing the means of subsistence, by piling up in Europe the grains of Africa and the rice of Asia, contrary, perhaps, to the views of nature, disarranges its system of population and prepares the causes and instruments of revolution by fostering the birth of men through the agency of foreign foodstuffs, as one causes fruits to be born and to ripen by means of artificial heat.[4]

De Bonald related political ideas such as separation of powers to the rise of commerce and saw an affinity between Protestant ideas, trade, the money economy, and democracy.[5] It is clear that he associated the long-term causes of the revolutionary crisis with intellectual and social individualism and with the rise of Protestantism and the middle classes since the great discoveries. Thinking of 1789, he described something like a revolutionary situation: a society with new needs, industry, commerce, and an expanded population suffered a catastrophe that could be taken advantage of by the *philosophes* and the politically ambitious.[6]

De Bonald's political philosophy at its heart was a defense of absolutism and the old social order, which he fused together into an ideal that he called civil society and described as a God-given norm expressive of the general will. Reading his testimony, one might conclude that he was simply condemning the revolution for violating well-established principles. In fact he organized those principles under the stimulus of the revolution and was himself as much creator as defender. His synthesis was indeed old-fashioned in that it defended old-regime society, but in making the old regime worth defending de Bonald produced a kind of utopia, surprisingly modern in its parts and already suggesting the giant nineteenth-century systems of Comte and Marx more than any philosophies of the era he was defending.

When we move leftward from de Bonald to the leading Anglophile statesman Jean-Joseph Mounier, we enter a different atmosphere, for Mounier believed in representative government in an

[4] *Ibid.*, I, 315.
[5] *Ibid.*, I, 477, 527; III, 312, 313, 315, 322.
[6] *Ibid.*, III, 316–18.

individualistic society with social movement and distinctions available to merit and service as well as to birth. Yet there were elements of traditionalism in Mounier's thought. Especially after the disorders of July, 1789, he tried to save as much tradition as possible, warning that the French were not savages just beginning their history. Mounier feared the awesome constituent power invoked by Sieyès (who will be discussed below); in spite of his austere personality, he was fairly close to Mirabeau politically, although he never wanted to work with the great disreputable tribune. Both were trying to set the brakes before the crown's authority was dissipated, but Mounier the draper's son was more conciliatory of the aristocracy than Mirabeau the alienated noble. Mounier, like Mirabeau, was unable to overcome the intransigence of the court and the aristocracy and the public's suspicions of them. Both the absolute royal veto and the legislature of two chambers in which he hoped that nobles and clergy would sit with commoners were voted down in September, 1789.

Mounier emigrated in 1790 and lived until 1806, serving as director of a school in Weimar and later as a Napoleonic prefect. There can be no question of reviewing all of his writings here, but two of his books are especially useful: *Nouvelles observations sur les États-Généraux de France* (February, 1789); and *Recherches sur les causes qui ont empêché les François de devenir libres, et sur les moyens qui leur restent pour acquérir la liberté* (1792). From the one to the other there is some evolution in the author's thought, but in essentials Mounier remained faithful to his program of 1789. He wanted, by ending special privileges for the nobles, to make it possible for well-to-do, enlightened commoners to trust them and cooperate with them in manning representative institutions that would respect the king's authority and grant equality before the law to the multitude without allowing them to tyrannize over their betters.

After having destroyed all pecuniary privileges, abolished exclusions that have been in operation against non-privileged citizens, and subjected all of the prince's subjects equally to the authority of the laws, we must, if we wish to enjoy liberty for any length of time, renounce this unfortunate mistrust that divides the orders. . . .[7]

[7] Jean-Joseph Mounier, *Nouvelles observations sur les États-Généraux de France* (n.p., February, 1789), p. 269.

Finally, the French will not have a beneficial and durable constitution until the time when there will no longer exist any differences of interest between the nobles and the other citizens; when the people will be able, without inconvience, to call upon gentlemen to represent them. . . .[8]

These aspirations of February, 1789, amounted to an interpretation of the revolution that Mounier wanted. They were not repudiated by his historical reconstruction of 1792.

From the observations that I have been presenting, it is evident that in France before the revolution nothing was regulated in any precise manner, neither the rights of the crown nor those of the people, nor those of the courts; that the aristocracy had too much influence in the government; that personal liberty was frequently exposed to infringement by various arbitrary authorities; that political liberty was almost completely lacking; that the legitimate power of the king, of the sort necessary to the public welfare, was not firmly enough established; that the remonstrances of the parlements, however useful, being full of dangerous maxims and often written in a menacing tone, were by degrees accustoming the subject to lose all respect for the throne. . . .[9]

In 1792 Mounier described the point at which the revolution might have been stopped in 1789.

Consent to taxation reserved for the Estates General, the necessity for them to agree to all laws, their periodic meetings, the responsibility of ministers; these four principles thus effected a revolution in the French government. . . .[10]

This four-point program, with its mention of the Estates General, could be misinterpreted as backsliding toward the aristocratic politics of 1789—a position on the revolutionary spectrum between absolutism and Mounier's original Anglophile doctrine.[11] This was not the case, however. In 1792 Mounier condemned the old Estates General and advocated what he had come to favor in the

---

[8] *Ibid.*, p. 278.

[9] Jean-Joseph Mounier, *Recherches sur les causes qui ont empêché les François de devenir libres, et sur les moyens qui leur restent pour acquérir la liberté* (2 vols.; Geneva, 1792), I, 25–26.

[10] *Ibid.*, I, 57–58; see also pp. 60, 62.

[11] The aristocratic position, to which Louis XVI consented at the royal session of June 23, 1789, is not represented in this essay. It faded away during the revolution, eroded on one side by the absolutist revival and on the other by defections to the Anglophile position. See my *The French Revolution Seen from the Right* (Philadelphia, 1956).

summer of 1789: a bicameral legislature elected by propertied citizens, with nobles eligible to the lower house and the upper house accessible to commoners of merit. The purpose of this policy was to keep the nobles in politics, both to safeguard the crown against the new representative institutions and to help well-to-do commoners guard those institutions against the multitude.[12]

Mounier's plans presupposed a social revolution because he wanted equality before the law, which meant depriving the nobles of most of their privileges and making nobility chiefly a sign of merit. It is true that he still tried to conciliate the aristocracy by minor concessions, but the price the aristocracy had to pay to be accepted in the representative institutions was abandonment of most of their privileges and the opening of careers to talent.

Mounier's program, after failing in 1789, retained the loyalty of moderate liberals and persons longing for stability. Under the Directory it had a renewed appeal, but by that time the absolutist revival to which de Bonald gave intellectualized expression was full-grown and had the allegiance of Louis XVIII and the leading *émigrés*. With the monarchists hopelessly split and the influence of the army in politics increasing, the Anglophile kind of compromise had to wait until 1814.

Antoine-Pierre Barnave was at first a young lieutenant of Mounier, but broke away in 1789, taking a position to the left of the Anglophiles, and with his friends Duport and the Lameth brothers played a leading part in the making of the Constitution of 1791. In the revolutionary spectrum he belongs, therefore, with the Feuillants, defenders of the '91 settlement who, fearful that the revolution would go beyond that point, came to be secretly desirous of making the constitution somewhat more conservative. Barnave was one of the commissioners sent by the Assembly to return the royal family to Paris following the flight to Varennes. Thereafter he gave confidential advice to the king and queen in an effort to strengthen their position. After the close of the Constituent Assembly, he returned to Grenoble where, after August 10, 1792, he was imprisoned because of compromising papers found in the Tuileries. While in prison he wrote the remarkable manuscript called *Introduction à la Révolution française*, first published

[12] *Recherches sur les causes,* vol. I, chs. XII, XIII, XIV, XV.

with his *Oeuvres* in 1843.[13] Barnave was taken to Paris for trial before the Revolutionary Tribunal in November, 1793, and executed on November 29.

An astonishing impression of modernity is made by Barnave's *Introduction,* not only because Lefebvre and his circle have interpreted early modern history in much the same way, but also because of Barnave's demand for comparative history. "One would try in vain," he wrote, "to form an accurate idea of the great revolution that has been shaking France if one were to examine it by itself . . ." [14] He took the view that those who had control of the sources of power—armed force, property, and opinion—were able to make the laws; but the combinations varied from place to place.

The same cause, that is, the progress of movable property that is in Europe the natural milieu for democracy and the cement for the unity of states, has successively modified all the political regimes. According to whether it has been more or less favored by geographical location, it has established a variety of governments; where the people found themselves to be very strong in a small state, it established republics; where, in a large region, it had ony sufficient force to uphold, by means of taxation, the monarchical power against the aristocracy, common enemy of the prince and the people, it gradually established absolute monarchies; where it was able to develop further, after having served for a long time as accessory to the throne against the great nobles, it caused an explosion and, making a place for itself in the government, it established limited monarchy. . . .

This progression, common to all the European governments, is what prepared the way in France for a democratic revolution and made it break out at the end of the eighteenth century.[15]

Barnave related economic life to intellectual progress.

With the arts, which enrich us and which increase the number of men by multiplying the means of nourishing them, is born that most sublime knowledge that directs the light of reasoning upon all matters of credulity. . . .[16]

He had—thanks to Montesquieu—a sociological understanding of

---

[13] Antoine-Pierre Barnave, *Introduction à la Révolution française.* The edition used here was edited from the original manuscript by Fernand Rude (Paris, 1960). See his "Présentation."
[14] *Ibid.,* p. 1.   [15] *Ibid.,* p. 14.   [16] *Ibid.,* p. 23.

the relations of the parts of society to each other. Further, he created a metaphor that accounted for revolutions.

One can, from a certain point of view, consider these things—population, wealth, moral standards, enlightenment—as the ingredients and substance making up the social body, and one can see in the laws and the government the fabric that contains and encases them. Under all conditions it is necessary that they be related to each other proportionally in force and extension; if the fabric expands to the extent that the substance increases in volume, the progress of the social body will be able to take place without a violent commotion; but if, instead of an elastic force, it opposes a brittle rigidity, there will come a moment when their harmonious relationship will cease entirely and the substance will either be absorbed or break its casing and spill out.[17]

Applying these principles to European history,[18] he wrote that England had developed a fine constitution for a maritime island with a flourishing town life and industries, but that the English constitution was not suitable for export to the Continent, for any country with powerful nobles and less commerce would—under a bicameral system like the English—fall prey to the aristocracy.[19] In France Montesquieu with all his talent had not understood that the tempered absolutism of his time would not last; that the middle classes and the ideas of the Enlightenment would grow stronger and the aristocracy, entrenched in provincial estates, clergy, and judicial bodies, would engage in a suicidal contest with the crown, so that there would come a "democratic explosion."[20] For its part, the crown in its struggle with the parlements used methods that lost it the public's respect, and then compounded its errors.

If there was a way to forestall the explosion of the popular power, it would have been to associate it with the government, such as it was at that time, and to open all careers to the Third Estate; the exact opposite was done . . . the Third Estate was accustomed to seeing an enemy power in the throne that it alone could uphold or overturn, and the aristocracy was encouraged in that madness that, later, when the time came to discipline it, led it to provoke a revolution whose victim it has become.[21]

Although Barnave viewed the revolution as the outcome of the

---

[17] *Ibid.*, p. 24.   [18] See, for example, *Ibid.*, pp. 24, 25.
[19] *Ibid.*, pp. 24, 25, 35–47, 49.   [20] *Ibid.*, pp. 39–40, 47–49, 52–53.
[21] *Ibid.*, p. 53.

"natural march" of the people toward the assumption of "its place in the government,"[22] his view of the suffrage, expressed in an important speech of August 11, 1791, opposing radical courses of action after the king's flight to Varennes, was that electoral assemblies should have enlightenment, interest in public affairs, and independence of fortune. With exceptions, "a certain fortune, a given tax contribution, is up to a certain point ◆pledge of more extensive enlightenment." And "the final guarantee is that independence of fortune which, by placing an individual above need, more or less protects him from the means of corruption that might be tried on him."[23] In his *Introduction à la Révolution française* Barnave regretted the lost opportunity to reconcile the main social forces as the Anglophiles had tried to do.

If the government, cutting short the debates that arose between the orders, had come to the aid of the commoners before they had learned their own strength; if, from the first days, its influence had obliged the orders to deliberate in common, it is probable that . . . the work of the Assembly would never have been influenced during its whole course by the inflammatory atmosphere of a people in a state of revolution; that all the old elements of society, working in concert to give it a new form, not being divided by open hates, and still appearing to be invested with all their respective strengths, the result of the labor would have been some kind of compromise among the various parties, a new arrangement of what existed rather than a complete reshaping.[24]

This was in the spirit of his former chief, Mounier, and was something of a *mea culpa*.

Even more than Barnave, Emmanuel Joseph Sieyès represents two perspectives shared by many revolutionaries—the view upward toward the old-regime establishment and the view downward toward the people. Unlike Barnave, he disdained any return to the traditional even after he had become aware of the people's potential for getting out of hand. His reputation as the leading political scientist of the revolution was founded when he directed the laser beam of the constituent power against the traditional

---

[22] *Ibid.*, p. 51.
[23] *Journal des états-généraux convoqués par Louis XVI, le 27 avril, 1789; aujourd'hui Assemblée nationale permanente, ou Journal logographique . . . par M. Le Hodey* (Paris, 1791), XXXI, 377–84 *passim*.
[24] *Introduction à la Révolution française*, pp. 58–59.

claims of the first two estates to have an Estates General with vote by order.

Let us repeat: a nation is independent of all forms; and whatever the manner in which it wills, it is sufficient that its will make itself known in order that all positive laws give way before it as before their source and supreme master.[25]

These dangerous words were published in January, 1789, in what was to be the most famous pamphlet of the revolution: so famous that there is a real possibility of our being blinded by the author's repertoire of political means and forgetting about his ends.

To suggest to his readers what was at issue in France, Sieyès wrote that "the night of barbarism and feudalism" was ending.

The empire of reason is extended further every day; more and more it requires the restitution of the rights that have been usurped. Sooner or later it will be necessary for all classes to be included within the boundaries of the social contract.[26]

One would close one's eyes in vain upon the revolution that time and the force of things have brought about; it is no less real. Formerly the Third was in serfdom; the noble order was everything. Today the Third is everything; the nobility is a word. But beneath this word has glided a new and intolerable aristocracy; and the people has every reason to want no more aristocrats.[27]

The reference to a "new and intolerable aristocracy" was aimed at the events of the year just ended, 1788, when the common front of the aristocracy and Third Estate against "ministerial despotism" had broken up and the leaders of the aristocracy had begun to insist on vote by order in the Estates General.[28] Sieyès had written in his *Essai sur les privilèges* in 1788 that when the king admitted anyone to a privileged category,

he opens the soul of this citizen to a particular interest and more or less closes it to the inspirations of the common interest. The idea of the *patrie* becomes, for him, restricted; it becomes associated with the caste into which he is adopted. . . .[29]

---

[25] *Qu'est-ce que le tiers état? par Emmanuel Sieyès. Précédé de l'Essai sur les privilèges. Édition critique avec une introduction par Edme Champion* (Paris, 1888), pp. 69–70.

[26] *Ibid.*, p. 54.   [27] *Ibid.*, p. 79.   [28] *Ibid.*, pp. 73–74.

[29] *Essai* . . . , p. 9.

In a note to his second edition of *Qu'est-ce que le tiers état?* (also published in 1789) Sieyès observed that

it is neither differences of profession nor of enlightenment that divide men; it is differences of interest. In the present circumstances there are only two of these: that of the privileged and that of the non-privileged.[30]

He attacked the "triple *aristocracy* of Church, Sword, and Robe" as having a special interest in giving the historical Estates General the legislative power, since it was "a *clerical-noble-judicial* assembly." [31] The monarchy had almost always been a shield for the aristocracy,[32] and the current crisis concerned the aristocracy.

Moreover, it is no longer a question, for the Third Estate, of being better off or remaining as it was. Circumstances permit no calculation; one must advance or fall back, abolish or recognize and legalize iniquitous and unsocial privileges. Now, one must be aware how senseless the project would be of consecrating, at the end of the eighteenth century, the abominable remains of feudalism.[33]

Two illustrations of the social concern accompanying Sieyès's political views may be added. His central argument about the nature of representative government was built on a theoretical model of an individualistic society in which individuals willed an association, the associates willed in common as a community, and the community began to use representatives when it became too big to exercise its own common will. In this way he explained the nature of a constitution, which was a set of rules for the exercise of the "representative common will," and the nature of the "constituent power" flowing from the nation. In this exposition the "nation" was defined to exclude the nobles or any groups having special laws to protect their interests.[34]

What is a nation? A body of associates living under one *common* law and represented by the same *legislature*.[35]

The Third embraces therefore everything that belongs to the nation; and everything that is not of the Third cannot be regarded as belonging to the nation. What is the Third? Everything.[36]

A second illustration of the social assumptions accompanying

---

[30] *Qu'est-ce que le tiers état?* Champion ed., pp. 42–43, n. 2.
[31] *Ibid.*, p. 35.   [32] *Ibid.*, p. 36.   [33] *Ibid.*, p. 78.
[34] *Ibid.*, pp. 64–68.   [35] *Ibid.*, p. 31.   [36] *Ibid.*, p. 32.

Sieyès's political views may be seen in his remarks about the English constitution, which he regarded as admirable for a product of the seventeenth century but rather out of date and generally overrated. Real representative government would be much more efficient than the wasteful conflict and balancing of the English institutions, but with all their faults they worked fairly well precisely because English society was afflicted with scarcely any privileged corporate bodies such as the French. "The Lords of the upper chamber do not even form a distinct *order*. There is in England only one order, the nation." In France, given its social structure, the English system would be "vicious." In France even a unicameral legislature would not work properly unless all privileges were first abolished.[37]

> It will be necessary for nobles and clergy to have no other interest than the common interest and for them to enjoy, under the law, only the rights of plain citizens . . . Let no one accuse me of upholding the distinction of the orders, which I regard as the worst possible creation from the point of view of the good of society. There would only be one thing worse: to amalgamate the orders *in name* while leaving them *really* separate by the maintenance of privileges. That would be to consecrate forever their victory over the nation.[38]

Space is lacking for details of Sieyès's further development, but he may be glimpsed on three other occasions. In a pamphlet of July, 1789, he took a position between the aristocracy and the still immature people and fended off both. Introducing a distinction between civil rights, which were "passive rights" possessed by everyone, and political or "active rights" possessed by persons "who have interest and capacity for public affairs," he at the same time wrote that there must be equality of political rights if the society was to be kept free of privileges.[39] What he was doing was forestalling any reservation of political functions for an aristocracy of birth. He was saying that there had to be *equality among those who had political rights*: the political revolution would not work without a social revolution. There could still be "passive citizens," and they would, in effect, be represented by the "active citizens." According to the leading student of Sieyès's thought, Paul Bastid,

---

[37] *Ibid.*, pp. 59–64.   [38] *Ibid.*, p. 60.

[39] *Préliminaire de la constitution. Reconnaissance et exposition raisonnée des droits de l'homme & du citoyen, par M. l'Abbé Sieyès* (Versailles, July, 1789), pp. 14, 19, 20–21.

he never wanted a crude plutocratic screening to separate out the active citizens but was a democrat who intended for everyone eventually to be an active citizen and in the meantime wanted from voters only a small voluntary contribution as a test of political consciousness and responsibility.[40]

The National Assembly ignored the nuances of Sieyès's thought and established a property qualification for voting and holding office. After the Terror the Thermidorian Convention prepared to do the same. In a speech of July 20, 1795, Sieyès affirmed that representative government had to be made to work, since all else was "usurpation, superstition, and madness," but he urged that stability would be served by recognition that "the sovereignty of the people is not unlimited," since, when forming the community, individuals gave up a minimum of rights. Sieyès now wanted to filter the popular will through a number of specialized representative agencies performing a division of labor. His emphasis was on expertness and on keeping authority from being concentrated in the hands of any one political body.[41] The Convention rejected these proposals, but four years later Sieyès elaborated them into the scheme that was appropriated in slightly altered form by Napoleon. Playing down the *constituent* power and emphasizing the organization of the *constituted* power in its various specialized aspects, now clothed (including the executive) with all the dignity of the representative function, Sieyès reduced the people's role to the election of lists of candidates from which the constituted authorities could coopt governmental personnel.[42] The laser beam was supposed to be reduced in intensity at its origin by the natural rights of the individual and split, at the government level, into separate rays, but Napoleon seized it and focused it to suit himself.

Sieyès in his search for order rearranged the theory of representation in a dangerous way that contributed to a modern theory of dictatorship. It remains true that for him the meaning of the revolution was the establishment of representative government linking the state to an individualistic society.

The Marquis Jean-Antoine-Nicolas Caritat de Condorcet belonged to the social and intellectual elite of the old regime, but he

[40] Paul Bastid, *Sieyès et sa pensée* (Paris, 1939), pp. 347–48.
[41] *Réimpression de l'ancien Moniteur*, XXV, 291–97.
[42] Bastid, *Sieyès . . .* , pp. 398–404.

became a democrat who would have none of the thesis that political action was a specialized function and not a right: an idea that has persisted in our spectrum up to this point. Condorcet is most famous for his *Esquisse d'un tableau historique des progrès de l'esprit humain,* written while he was in hiding during the Terror, before he was captured, to die a mysterious death in prison in 1794. He was also a superb theoretician of representative government. His speech to the Convention on February 15, 1793, presenting the constitutional project of which he was principal author, is one of the most formidable political science lectures of all time. The project was shelved during the Girondin-Mountain struggle and Condorcet, who bitterly attacked the Mountain's constitution, became increasingly associated with the defeated Girondins and thus became a casualty of the Terror.

In Condorcet's view the French Revolution came to

a country that was at once the most enlightened and the most enslaved of lands, a country that possessed at the same time the most enlightened philosophers and the most crassly and insolently ignorant government, a country whose laws were so far below the level of public intelligence that not even patriotism or prejudice could attach the people to the ancient institutions. . . . It was inevitable, then, that the revolution should begin in France.

The maladroitness of her government precipitated it, her philosophers guided its principles and the power of her people destroyed the obstacles which might have stood in its way.[43]

But the revolution was more than French. The Enlightenment, an international movement with cosmopolitan, humanitarian, secular ideals, had told man "to submit all opinions to his own reason and to use in the search for truth the only instrument for its recognition that he has been given."[44] In view of the progress of opinion and the backwardness of institutions, "nothing could now protect the enemies of reason or the oppressors of freedom from a sentence to which the whole of Europe would soon subscribe."[45] Eventually there would be a world revolution; with liberty and equality and self-determination for all societies, there would be international peace, economic and scientific cooperation, and material abundance

[43] *Sketch for a Historical Picture of the Progress of the Human Mind,* tr. by June Barraclough (London, 1955), p. 146.
[44] *Ibid.,* p. 136. See also pp. 141–42.   [45] *Ibid.,* pp. 141–42.

for all. The key was liberty, to release the creative energies of men and nations, but equality and education were also essential to all men and all societies; otherwise only a small proportion of mankind would be productive. The "social art" of bringing institutions into harmony with nature could also reconcile people's interests and make them more considerate of each other, thereby bringing about moral progress.[46] Condorcet's optimism drew a famous reply from Malthus. Saint-Simon and Comte were to acknowledge his influence and try to improve on his "social art." Condorcet himself acknowledged that "we still see the forces of enlightenment in possession of no more than a very small portion of the globe, and the truly enlightened vastly outnumbered by the great mass of men who are still given over to ignorance and prejudice." [47]

From its place in this world-historical process the French Revolution derived its meaning. Politically it was the shift to representative government, the more representative, the better. Condorcet was a partisan of statistics both for finding social laws and for organizing the political process. He thought that there was greater probability in a large assembly of smothering special interest groups. He rejected the contrived separations and restrictions of the Anglophiles and Feuillants. The will of the people should pour through clear and unobstructed, by means of manhood suffrage (ideally, universal suffrage), a unicameral legislature, legislative supremacy, proportional representation, frequent elections, local self-government, and the use of petitions and the referendum. There should be an end to the "astute and false policy" of allotting rights "unequally between men, according to birth, fortune, or profession" and to the age-old division of humanity "into two races, the one fated to rule, the other to obey, the one to deceive, the other to be deceived." [48]

In February, 1793, when he presented his constitution to the Convention, Condorcet was concerned about interference with the democratic process by local insurrections and by demagogues professing to speak for the people, and he took pains to show how to prepare for and conduct a proper referendum. In private he may have had nightmares in which the sovereign people denied what was scientifically valid. In his public career his answer was to make

---

[46] *Ibid.*, pp. 129, 169, 184, 192, 194.   [47] *Ibid.*, p. 169.

[48] *Ibid.*, p. 129, for quotations. For Condorcet's presentation of his constitution, see *Discours prononcé dans la séance du vendredi 15 février, par Condorcet, au nom du comité de constitution, Réimpression de l'ancien Moniteur*, XV, 456–72.

sure it was really the sovereign people whose opinions were being expressed; he did not falsify the principle of democracy on grounds of the immaturity of the multitude. He was aware that the revolution entailed economic and other burdens as well as rapid changes in opinion, and he said rather prophetically that the people would have to be appeased and disciplined without damage to their public spirit.[49]

The social side of the revolution was very real to Condorcet.

The revolution in France was more far-reaching than that in America and therefore more violent: for the Americans, who were content with the civil and criminal code that they had received from England; who had no vicious system of taxation to reform; and no feudal tyrannies, no hereditary distinctions, no rich, powerful and privileged corporations, no system of religious intolerance to destroy, limited themselves to establishing a new authority in place of that which had been exercised up till then by the British. None of these innovations affected the ordinary people or changed the relations between individuals. In France, on the contrary, the revolution was to embrace the entire economy of society, change every social relation and find its way down to the furthest links of the political chain. . . .[50]

Like most of the revolutionaries he emphasized the need to remove unnatural obstacles to a free economy and society.

It is easy to prove that wealth has a natural tendency to equality, and that any excessive disproportion could not exist or at least would rapidly disappear if civil laws did not provide artificial ways of perpetuating and uniting fortunes; if free trade and industry were allowed to remove the advantages that accured wealth derives from any restrictive law or fiscal privilege. . . .[51]

Little government intervention would be needed once the basic free society had been attained. Social (not absolute) equality was within reach, for the sources of inequality were known.

These differences have three main causes: inequality in wealth; inequality in status between the man whose means of subsistence are hereditary and the man whose means are dependent on the length of his life, or, rather, on that part of his life in which he is capable of work; and finally, inequality in education.[52]

[49] *Réimpression de l'ancien Moniteur*, XV, 456, 459.
[50] *Sketch for a Historical Picture of the Progress of the Human Mind*, p. 146.
[51] *Ibid.*, p. 180.   [52] *Ibid.*, p. 179.

The first cause, as noted, could be remedied largely by abolishing unfair laws. For his time Condorcet was surprisingly sensitive to the second category; he could see no way of eliminating it, but he thought that the insecurity of the great majority who possessed little or no capital could be largely removed by social insurance for the aged and unfortunate based on actuarial tables; and he suggested that by similar methods capital could be provided for young people founding families.[53] Education would reduce though not eliminate class differences.

From such time onwards the inhabitants of a single country will no longer be distinguished by their use of a crude or refined language; they will be able to govern themselves according to their own knowledge; they will no longer be limited to a mechanical knowledge of the procedures of the arts or of professional routines; they will no longer depend for every trivial piece of business and every insignificant matter of instruction on clever men who rule over them in virtue of their necessary superiority; and so they will attain a real equality. . . .[54]

Condorcet's aspirations were not as far removed from those of Robespierre, our next subject, as the reputations of the two men would lead one to expect but, because they differed greatly in personality and no doubt because Robespierre came to hold more power and responsibility, they now seem worlds apart in what the revolution meant to them—or perhaps one should say in what the revolution did to them.

Maximilien Robespierre's most famous speech, that of February 5, 1794, on political morality[55] was an effort, as he said, "to indicate clearly the aim of the revolution and the destination at which we wish to arrive." In developing this subject Robespierre linked together four ideas: democracy, "a condition in which the sovereign people, guided by laws of their own making, do for themselves everything that they can do well, and through delegates everything that they cannot themselves do"; equality, for "the French are the first people in the world who have established true democracy by summoning all men to equality and to full rights as citizens . . ."; the practical value of virtue, for whereas an executive can be re-

---

[53] *Ibid.*, pp. 180–81.   [54] *Ibid.*, p. 183.
[55] *Sur les principes de morale politique qui doivent guider la Convention dans l'administration intérieur de la république, Réimpression de l'ancien Moniteur,* XIX, 401 ff.

strained by representatives, "who will restrain the representatives themselves if not their own virtue?" And to cement together the others he added patriotism, for "this virtue . . . is simply the love of the *patrie* and its laws." [56]

What the revolution meant to Robespierre seems, therefore, to have been its great innovation of linking government to society and making it do society's will and thereby cease to be an oppressor. In another major speech, about religious and moral ideas and republican principles, on May 7, 1794, he spoke to the Convention of its mission.

Yes, you can show the world the unprecedented spectacle of democracy solidly established in a great country. . . . Until our time the art of governing has been the art of deceiving and corrupting men: it must now become the art of enlightening them and making them better.[57]

If the French Revolution was the maker of the first legitimate government, it followed that France's opponents were illegitimate. Robespierre called them "organized hordes of savages and disciplined brigands." [58]

Robespierre's democracy was founded on the conviction that the people were good and could be more or less equal. In his pamphlet of 1791 on the suffrage he rejected property qualifications for voting.

Was it to fall back under the yoke of an aristocracy of the rich that they broke, along with you the yoke of the feudal aristocracy?

In support of my position I call to witness all those whose nobility of soul and sensibility have drawn them into close contacts with the people and made them worthy of knowing and loving equality: I call upon them to bear witness that in general nothing matches the people in justice and goodness so long as they are not irritated by excesses of oppression. . . .[59]

Like other radical democrats of his time, he believed in the ideal of laissez faire in a society of small property owners, a society that

[56] *Ibid.*, XIX, 401–3.

[57] *Rapport sur les rapports des idées religieuses et morales avec les principes républicains, Discours et rapports de Robespierre*, ed. by Charles Vellay (Paris, 1908), p. 351.

[58] *Ibid.*, p. 352.

[59] *Sur le marc d'argent* (Avril, 1791) *Oeuvres de Maximilein Robespierre, édition préparé sous la direction de Marc Bouloiseau, Georges Lefebvre, Albert Soboul*, VII (Paris [1950]), 167 (first quotation), 166 (second quotation).

would shape itself more or less spontaneously if special privileges were abolished, and would foster a state of mind conducive to democracy.

And if we wish to emphasize this idea, what is the source of this extreme inequality of fortunes that concentrates all the wealth in a few hands? Is it not bad laws, bad governments, in the last analysis all the vices of corrupted societies?

These heroes were aware, and we ourselves sometimes reiterate, that liberty can only be solidly based on moral standards. Now what moral standards can a people have whose laws seem calculated to stimulate a feverish quest for wealth?[60]

Robespierre's political revolution had moral and social prerequisites and required, first, an attack on old-regime society and, second, efforts to assure justice in the newly emerged social order. In his proposed Declaration of Rights he wrote that society had the obligation "to provide for the subsistence of all its members, either by procuring work for them or by assuring the means of existence to those unable to work," and also to encourage the "progress of the public reason and place instruction within the reach of all citizens." [61] It is evident that both tactically, in the crisis of the revolution, and as a result of the long-term needs of the French people Robespierre was drawn into more state action than he had originally contemplated. Certainly by the time of his speech of May 7, 1794, relating religious and moral ideas to republican principles he was looking for ways to overcome the lag of moral ideas behind the arts and sciences.

The idea of the Supreme Being and of the immortality of the soul is a constant reminder that we must be just; it is therefore social and republican. Nature has given man the sensations of pleasure and pain, which make him avoid the physical objects that are harmful to him and search out those that are helpful to him. Society's masterpiece would be the creation in him for matters of morality of a quick instinct which, without the tardy aid of reasoning, would lead him to do good and avoid evil; for the individual reason of each man, distracted by his passions, is frequently only a sophist pleading their cause, and in man authority can always be attacked by way of self-esteem. Now what produces or

[60] *Ibid.*, pp. 165 (first quotation), 170 (second quotation).
[61] *Sur la nouvelle Déclaration des Droits, Oeuvres*, IX, 461, 464–66.

replaces this precious instinct, what makes up for insufficiency of human authority, is the religious sentiment, which imprints in people's souls the idea of a sanction given to precepts of morality by a power superior to man. And so I do not know that any legislator would ever be well advised to nationalize atheism. . . .

You will feel the necessity to make it [education] universal and equal for all the French. It is not a question of forming *messieurs*, but citizens: the *patrie* alone has the right to bring up its children; it cannot confide this trust to the pride of families or to the prejudices of individuals, always nourishment for aristocracy and for a domestic federalism that narrows souls by isolating them and destroys, along with equality, all the bases of the social order.[62]

The moralist in Robespierre was very strong and the success of everything he stood for depended on very high moral standards that he must have come to realize were beyond the capacity of most of his countrymen in their everyday lives: this fact seems to have been central to his career and to his ultimate perplexity and failure; it is more important than one or another social measure such as the Ventôse decrees. The crises of the Terror period actually postponed, for Robespierre and others like him, the facing of the discrepancy between their standards and the aspirations of ordinary people, or for that matter, of ordinary deputies to the Convention. On December 25, 1793, in his *Rapport sur les principes du gouvernement révolutionnaire*, Robespierre made a very significant statement to the Convention:

The foundation of the French Republic is not a child's game. It cannot be the product of caprice or recklessness, nor the chance result of the collision of all individual claims and of all revolutionary groups.[63]

Spontaneity, compromise, and liberalism were for the moment too dangerous. The revolution, whose enduring meaning he saw as the ending of oppression by governments, took on a second, subsidiary meaning during the Terror.

Constitutional government is concerned principally with civil liberty, and revolutionary government with public liberty. Under the consti-

---

[62] *Discours et rapports*, ed. Vellay, pp. 361 (first quotation), 369 (second quotation).
[63] *Ibid.*, p. 316.

tutional regime it is almost enough to protect individuals against abuses of the public power; under the revolutionary regime the public power is obliged to defend itself against all the factions that attack it.[64]

Robespierre's original concern—"it is almost enough to protect individuals against abuses of the public power"—eventually encountered two great obstacles, backwardness and counterrevolution. Yet terror against these made virtue all the more necessary, and as he said on February 5, 1794, in his speech on political morality, the purer the revolution became, the more numerous were its enemies. "From that situation comes the defection of so many ambitious or greedy men who, since the point of departure, have abandoned us along the way because they did not set out on the voyage with the same end in view." [65] Robespierre then made one of his most famous statements. "The revolutionary government is the despotism of liberty against tyranny." There is no reason to believe that the ultimate meaning of the revolution had changed for Robespierre, but its requirements were multiplying and its means had become a revolutionary dictatorship that he and his associates could define but not direct toward agreed ends.

To pass from Robespierre's revolution to Babeuf's is to move from one climate of conviction to another, from one egalitarianism to another, from one program of liberation and education of the lower classes to another, from one search for an epochal mutation of society to another; but there is a limit to the similarities. Babeuf's words express an alienation from his society far more profound than Robespierre's; his moral demands, although infused with greater warmth and more emotion than Robespierre's, and seeming to come from among the people instead of from a vantage point above them, are even more remote from the conceptions of everyday men and women than Robespierre's.

The "Conspiracy of the Equals" for which Babeuf was arrested in 1796 and executed in 1797 was aptly named, for equality was his guiding principle, his obsession; he became a socialist by transmuting into a new form of equality the products of his autodidactic studies of the Enlightenment and the moral fervor of his rebellion

[64] *Rapport sur les principes du gouvernement révolutionnaire* . . . 25 *décembre, 1793*, in *Discours et rapports*, ed. Vellay, p. 312.
[65] *Réimpression de l'ancien Moniteur*, XIX, 404.

against poverty. From the revolution he took for socialism the idea of dictatorship and thus became something of a prophet; but he did not need the revolution to teach him about equality but on the contrary could see the revolution only in terms of equality and was full of saintly illusions on this subject. There is a recurrent formula in his writings that may be quoted as an important part of his testimony. Here is an early example from his first important work, his *Cadastre perpétuel*, a book on taxation published in 1789:

Everything that we have been expressing leads to the conclusion that it is illegitimate for any man to enjoy well-being disproportionately greater than that stemming from his share in the advantages accruing to each inhabitant when the country's product is divided by its population. Such a disproportion leads to disorder, for nature, economical of her gifts, provides little more than what is needed by the beings she has created; and if some enjoy a superfluity, others must lack necessities.[66]

In a letter of August 20, 1791, to the curé J. M. Coupé, Babeuf again expressed his key idea.

The Constitution must be a national patrimony in which may be found both bread for the spirit and bread for the bodies of the people, and in which a covenant for both intellectual and material life should be not only clear, precise, and positive, but also immediately sanctioned by the placing in common of all resources indefinitely multiplied and accrued by means of a carefully constructed organization and wisely directed labor.[67]

If we now turn to No. 35 of Babeuf's newspaper *Le Tribun du Peuple*, November 29, 1795, to that portion which Babeuf proposed as a Plebeian Manifesto, we find him in the maturity of his career asserting

That, to be more specific about this, it is necessary to *enchain fate*; to make the fate of each coassociate independent of chance and circumstances, fortunate or unfortunate; *to assure to each and to his posterity, however numerous they may be, sufficiency but nothing except sufficiency*; and to close to everyone every possible way of ever obtaining more than an individual share of the products of Nature and labor.

That the only way to achieve this end is to establish a *common administration*; to suppress private property; to attach each man to the

---

[66] Maurice Dommanget ed., *Pages choisies de Babeuf* (Paris, 1935), p. 81. Babeuf had a coauthor but was able to insert many of his own ideas.

[67] *Ibid.*, p. 107.

aptitude, to the industry that he knows; to oblige him to deposit its product in kind in the common warehouse; and to establish a simple administration of distribution, an administration of subsistence, which, keeping a register of all persons and things, will distribute the latter with the most scrupulous equality and have them delivered to the homes of all citizens.[68]

What the revolution meant to Babeuf was, in short, the purest, most extreme, most fervently moral egalitarianism, leading at first to the ideal of partitioning the fruits of the earth,[69] and later, with the same premise of society's obligation to care equally for all of its members, to common ownership and social distribution of all commodities produced, still viewed largely in terms of the peasant and artisan economy of his time, but with an ideal of planning to bring production into line with needs, and with confidence that the benefits of scientific advances could best be shared under this system.[70]

Babeuf insisted on judging the revolution in terms of these ideals. "They are mistaken," he wrote, "who think that I am agitating only with an eye to substituting one constitution for another . . . Every constitution that allows the ancient dehumanizing and abusive institutions to go on existing will cease to excite my enthusiasm."[71] He went on to say that the "perfect equality" dictated by nature and the social contract had been violated by the growth of absurd conventions that permitted concentration of wealth until finally the suffering of the majority had brought about a revolutionary period "when a general overturn of the property system becomes inevitable, when the revolt of the poor against the rich is an unconquerable necessity." And he concluded: "since '89 we have been at this point. . . ."[72] Earlier in the month he had written: "What is the French Revolution in particular? A war declared between the patricians and the plebeians, between the rich and the poor." The French Revolution was only the open declaration of this war, which had been waged continuously since the growth of institutions enabling the few to expropriate the many.[73] He con-

[68] *Ibid.*, pp. 261–62.   [69] *Ibid.*, p. 127.

[70] Letter to Charles Germain, July 28, 1795, *Ibid.*, pp. 212–14 (and the quotations already cited from the Plebeian Manifesto).

[71] *Manifeste des Plébéiens,* in *Le Tribun du Peuple,* No. 35, November 29, 1795, *Ibid.*, p. 250.

[72] *Ibid.*, p. 251.

[73] *Le Tribun du Peuple,* No. 34, November 5, 1795, *Ibid.*, pp. 236, 238.

sidered the degradation of the majority to have been in large part achieved by the withholding of education from the people, and he believed that "equal distribution of knowledge to the whole people would make all men almost equal in capability and even in talents" and that "since acquired knowledge is in the public domain it must be equally distributed." [74] Cultural deprivation as a means of exploitation was one of his most persistent themes. In 1789 he addressed the upper classes: "You are these unworthy tutors; the people, today arrived at their age of reason, were until now carefully kept in a state of perpetual adolescence and fatal inertia which kept them from recognizing their rights." [75] At this time he was rather optimistic about the diffusion of enlightenment among the people[76] but by 1795 he warned a confidant that if their full program for making men equal were known, the frightened and horrified crowds whose educations had been stunted by the ruling groups would turn on the reformers.

We would be condemned to centuries of execration because the clique of the powerful would have left no stone unturned to ensure that the purity of our intentions would never be understood or even presumed. Ah! if there were the good fortune to be understood by the masses. . . .[77]

Later in the year he became bolder when he wrote in the Plebeian Manifesto (already cited) what socialism should mean. Throughout the year 1795 he had been aware of a struggle between factions within the republic, one "bourgeois and aristocratic" representing the wealthy minority, the other "popular and democratic." In early November he warned that the revolution had been losing out to the wealthy since Thermidor, and said that leaders who wished to counteract this tendency would have to call on the plebeians.

But note, too, that you cannot mobilize them for great services unless you assure them of possession of the promised land, showing it to them at not too great a distance: the promised land which, if you fail, they will soon set about conquering under some other Moses.[78]

In December, 1795, he wrote:

The revolution has given us proofs on proofs that the French people, for

---

[74] *Le Tribun du Peuple*, No. 35, November 29, 1795, *Ibid.*, p. 261.
[75] *Cadastre perpétuel, Ibid.*, p. 82.   [76] *Ibid.*, pp. 87, 89–90.
[77] Letter to Charles Germain of July 28, 1795, *Ibid.*, p. 218.
[78] For the names of factions, see *Le Tribun du Peuple*, No. 29, December 21, 1794–January 8, 1795, *Ibid.*, 192–93; for the quotation, *Le Tribun du Peuple*, No. 34, November 5, 1795, *Ibid.*, p. 241.

all that it is a great and old people, is by no means incapable of adopting the greatest changes in its institutions, and of consenting to the greatest sacrifices in order to ameliorate them. Have they not changed everything since '89 except this single institution of property?[79]

In the end, as is well known, Babeuf tried to act without waiting for the people; he tried to keep going a revolution that to him was more urgent than making the people understand.

With precautions this seven-man spectrum may be found useful in reconsidering the meaning of the revolution. Make of the seven what you can is the first rule, but remember to start with what is there, not supposing that they speak for all strata or all parties or even for all aspects of their own thought. Do not expect them to be the whole revolution: they are merely examples of consciousness interacting with it, juxtaposed here because they represent major differing points of view.

De Bonald and Babeuf placed themselves, by their actions, at opposite ends of the conventional spectrum and, by their words, in a contest of traditional, organized inequality with extreme equality; of hereditary property rights in everything, including status and functions, with the abolition of property. De Bonald the Catholic Christian and Babeuf the atheist humanist were both rationalistic worshipers of the natural order, opponents of representative institutions dominated by the wealthy, and, at their respective extremes, if one includes Babeuf's last position, elitists. Their aspirations were so far removed from those of ordinary men that they seem about to fall off the extremities of the spectrum; and yet in their understanding of the revolution, as distinct from their evaluations of it, they were not at a great distance from each other.

From de Bonald to Mounier is a long step, and at the other end of the spectrum it is also a long step from Babeuf to Robespierre. Admittedly the steps would be shorter if between de Bonald and Mounier there had been included a representative of the "aristocratic" position, someone endorsing representative government adapted to old-regime society, and if between Babeuf and Robespierre there had been placed in this study some *enragé* expressing the confused aspirations of the sans-culottes. Although Mounier conceded something to the old aristocracy, he nevertheless de-

---

[79] *Le Tribun du Peuple,* No. 37, December 20, 1795, *Ibid.,* p. 271.

manded representative government based on a society without significant privileges, and since everyone to the left of Mounier amplified his view that this kind of social revolution was essential to the political shift to representative government, the meaning of the revolution for everyone on the spectrum is highlighted here: even de Bonald in rejecting the revolution agreed on what it was about.

Without reviewing details, it may be observed that the shift from Mounier to Barnave on the way toward the center of the spectrum is not great; nor is the shift back toward the center from Robespierre to Condorcet. To be sure, it is difficult to evaluate the momentous endorsement of revolutionary government in the case of Robespierre, which sets him somewhat farther apart from the less deeply engaged and earlier sidelined Condorcet than Mounier is from Barnave. If we think about Mounier–Barnave on the one side and Robespierre–Condorcet on the other, we have a confrontation between liberal monarchists and democratic republicans; to both pairs the revolution was an attack on old-regime society as well as a turn to representative government, but there were real differences over who was to control the representative institutions, and this matter had social implications: roughly, classical liberalism versus a more egalitarian social ideal. Sieyès, at the center of the spectrum, divided his attention between those to the right and left of him on the social question and eventually tried to reconcile their political views by combining the appearance of democracy with the reality of management of politics from above, insuring liberty by distributing powers and functions. He did not differ as much from the others in the fact of his failure as in the element of disingenuousness in his theory that abetted dictatorship.

For they all failed, and each can be criticized for impracticality, and not one (alone or with associates) could dominate events except temporarily, and nobody got what he wanted. Yet it seems that they all agreed in general terms on what the revolution was about; the spectrum resulted from differing evaluations of what was possible and desirable as the old corporative society was deprived of its legal supports, and plans were made for representative government. These, at least, are the most visible issues; there are also some striking assessments of class relationships, the Enlightenment, religion, and the international character of the revolution, but these, while legitimately notable in some of our testimonies, are not present in all. The same is true of the problem of the people's readiness or unreadiness for responsibility; if there is anything we know more about than the revolutionaries did, it is the peasants and sansculottes; the problem of the people seems to have provoked surprise and dismay among the revolutionary leaders and contributed, unexpectedly, to the idea of dictatorship. With the single qualification that only de Bonald lost out altogether on the social question, it may be said that no one on the spectrum succeeded during the revolution or was without influence afterward. Their condition spoke to the nineteenth and twentieth centuries.

French Doctors Face War, 1792–1815

DORA B. WEINER

MANHATTANVILLE COLLEGE
AND COLUMBIA UNIVERSITY

AT THE TURN of the nineteenth century modern clinical medicine was born in France, and Paris became the center of world medicine for a generation,[1] during which France also waged war against most of Europe for twenty-three years. French doctors had to cope with the sick and wounded of fourteen armies, under the challenging climatic conditions of Italy, Egypt, the Antilles, Spain, Germany, and Russia. These far-flung expeditions brought the French army doctor massive experience in surgery, and with diseases now diagnosed as malaria, typhus, typhoid fever, gonorrhoea, syphilis, scurvy, and dysentery. Treatments also had to be devised for little-known illnesses, sometimes prevalent in epidemic proportions: conjunctivitis and trachoma in Egypt (in addition to tetanus, hepatitis, leprosy, elephantiasis), bubonic plague in Syria, and yellow fever in the Antilles. The devotion and self-sacrifice of the French army doctors—led by the famous physician Desgenettes[2]

Research for this paper was made possible by a grant from the National Library of Medicine, whose generous support is here gratefully acknowledged.

[1] See E. H. Ackerknecht, "La médecine à Paris entre 1800 et 1850," *Conférences du Palais de la Découverte*, Série D, N. 58 (Paris, 1958); "Paris Hospitals around 1800—A New Era in Medicine," *Ciba Symposia*, VII, No. 3 (August, 1959); "Die Therapie der Pariser Kliniker zwischen 1795 und 1840," *Gesnerus*, XV (1958), 151–63; and especially the same author's excellent recent book *Medicine at the Paris Hospital, 1794–1848* (Baltimore, 1967).

[2] Trained at Montpellier and Paris, N. R. D. Desgenettes (1762–1837) took part in all of Napoleon's wars, beginning with the first Italian campaign where he served as physician-in-chief. Decorated with the Legion of Honor in 1804 and made an imperial baron in 1809, he was elected to the Academy of Medicine in 1820 and to the Academy of Sciences, as a corresponding member, in 1832.

and the surgeons Percy[3] and Larrey[4]—were universally acknowledged. And yet the French army medical service, after a brief and brilliant existence, was deprived of all autonomy and the doctors were henceforth treated like "the bakers and butchers." [5] Ruled by the quartermaster, subordinated to the Office of War Administration, army medicine was put on a level with food supply, sanitation, and prisons. The French Army Medical Corps did not attain importance and autonomy until the early years of the Third Republic.[6]

These puzzling developments—and indeed the history of medicine during the French Revolution and under Napoleon—do not seem to have been of interest to many historians. One searches in vain, in the pages of such classics on this period as Georges Lefebvre's *La Révolution française* and *Napoléon*, Mathiez's *La Révolution française*, Thompson's *Napoleon*, Lachouque's *Napoleon's Battles*, or indeed in the 1,170 pages of Chandler's recent *Campaigns of Napoleon*, for an informed discussion of medicine as it affected history.[7] The *Revue des études napoléoniennes*, for example, contains but one long study concerned with health.[8] Conversely, the historians of medicine tend to focus on the scientific and technical advances achieved by such men as Bichat, Corvi-

---

[3] P.-F. Percy (1754–1825) graduated from the Faculty of Besançon at twenty-one and enlisted in the army as surgeon in 1776. Named surgeon-in-chief of the Rhine army in 1792, he served continuously from then on, except when prevented by a serious, recurrent ophthalmia. Elected to the Academy of Sciences in 1807, he too was decorated with the Legion of Honor, and made an imperial baron by Napoleon in 1809.

[4] D.-J. Larrey (1776–1842) began his career as a naval surgeon and also enlisted in the Rhine army in 1792. He served without interruption until Waterloo, as surgeon-in-chief to the Consular—later the Imperial—Guard. He too received the Legion of Honor and was made an imperial baron and a member of the Academies of Medicine and of Sciences. On Saint Helena Napoleon said of him: "Larrey is the most virtuous man I have ever known."

[5] A. G. Chevalier, "Physicians of the French Revolution," *Ciba Symposia*, VII, No. 11 (February, 1946), p. 250.

[6] Laws of November 28, 1876, and March 16, 1882.

[7] G. Lefebvre, *La Révolution française* (Paris, 1951) and *Napoléon* (Paris, 1965); A. Mathiez, *La Révolution française* (Paris, 1922); J. M. Thompson, *Napoleon Bonaparte, His Rise and Fall* (Oxford, 1958); H. Lachouque, *Napoleon's Battles* (London, 1954); D. Chandler, *The Campaigns of Napoleon* (London, 1967).

[8] L. Houdard, "Le service de santé à l'armée d'Egypte," *Revue des études napoléoniennes*, XXXVIII (1934), 84–96, 160–68, 214–26; XXXIX (1934), 37–50, 180–95; XL (1935), 153–68, 236–46; XLI (1935), 16–27. See also her brief "La situation sanitaire au siège de Mantoue," *Ibid.*, XXXI (1930), 101–10.

sart, Laënnec, Louis, and Pinel, leaving their relevance for social history to the imagination and learning of the reader.[9]

True, the medical history of the French Revolution and Napoleon fills two booklets of *Ciba Symposia*[10] and there are a number of excellent articles on special aspects of the topic under study.[11] The history of the French Army Medical Corps has been outlined by several of its members.[12] Some recent studies by Richard Cobb emphasize the relationship of high prices and misery to morbidity and mortality during the Terror.[13] Numerous, in many languages, are the papers dealing with Napoleon's health, his illnesses, his agony, and his prejudices against physicians.[14] But the fate of the army medical service during the French Revolution and under Napoleon remains to be studied.

The published sources are plentiful.[15] Many army doctors kept

[9] See, for example, M. Laignel-Lavastine, ed., *Histoire générale de la médecine, de la pharmacie, de l'art dentaire, et de l'art vétérinaire,* vol. 3 (Paris, 1949); A. Le Pelletier de la Sarthe, *Histoire de la révolution médicale du 19ème siècle* (Paris, 1855); H. Guiart, *Histoire de la médecine française* (Paris, 1947).

[10] See Vol. III, No. 6 (1941) and Vol. VII, No. 11 (1946). As always, these booklets are beautifully illustrated but have no bibliography.

[11] Apart from the work of E. H. Ackerknecht, already mentioned, see especially G. Rosen, "Hospitals, Medical Care and Social Policy in the French Revolution," *Bulletin of the History of Medicine,* XXX (1956), 124–49; "The Philosophy of Ideology and the Emergence of Modern Medicine in France," *Ibid.,* XX (1946), 328–39, and "Problems in the Application of Statistical Analysis to Questions of Health, 1770–1880," *Ibid.,* XIX (1955), 27–45; O. Temkin, "The Philosophical Background of Magendie's Physiology," *Ibid.,* XX (1946), 10–35; "The Role of Surgery in the Rise of Modern Medical Thought," *Ibid.,* XXV (1951), 248–59; and A. Berman, "The Heroic Approach in Nineteenth-Century Therapeutics," *Bulletin of the American Society of Hospital Pharmacy,* XI (1954), 321–27; and "Education for Hospital Pharmacy," *Ibid.,* XII (1955), 248–53.

[12] P.-J. Gama, *Esquisse historique du service de santé militaire en général et spécialement du service chirurgical depuis l'établissement des hôpitaux militaires en France* (Paris, 1841); L. J. Bégin, *Etudes sur le service de santé militaire en France* (Paris, 1849); Dr. Brice and Captain Bottet, *Le corps de santé militaire en France, son évolution, ses campagnes,* 1708–1882 (Paris, 1907); J. Des Cilleuls, "Le service de santé militaire des origines à nos jours," *Revue internationale des Services de santé des armées de terre, de mer et de l'air,* 1951, pp. 1–130; S. L. L. Kouchnir, *Considérations sur l'évolution du service de santé militaire de 1789 à 1814.* Thesis (Paris, 1955).

[13] R. Cobb, *Terreur et subsistances, 1793–1795* (Paris, 1964).

[14] The most comprehensive medical bibliography concerning Napoleon will be found in J. Kemble, *Napoleon Immortal: The Medical History and Private Life of Napoleon Bonaparte* (London, 1959).

[15] For laws and decrees, see *Le moniteur universel,* 1789 ff., and *Journal militaire officiel* (1790–1830), 84 vols. For Napoleon's orders and opinions, see *Correspondance de Napoléon Ier publiée par ordre de l'Empereur Napoléon III* (Paris, 1858–70), 32 vols., and *Correspondance militaire de Napoléon Ier ex-*

diaries[16]—often so well written that it is hard to stop reading; some educated lay officers did the same.[17] (All of these authors were thus practicing a new genre of historical writing, the history of military medicine.[18]) Many of them sent or read memoirs on medical problems to the Egyptian Institute,[19] the Mathematics and Physics Sec-

traite de la correspondance générale (et publiée par ordre du ministère de la guerre) (Paris, 1878–97), 10 vols. See also Pelet de la Lozère, *Opinions de Napoléon sur divers sujets de politique et d'administration recueillies par un membre de son conseil d'état* (Paris, 1833), and J. Locré, *Napoléon au conseil d'état* (Paris, 1963).

An officially sanctioned journal of military medicine existed only under the monarchy. See *Recueil d'observations de médecine des hôpitaux militaires* (1766–1772), R. de Hautsierck, ed.; *Journal de médecine, chirurgie, et pharmacie militaire* (1782–88), D. R. Dehorne, ed., 7 vols., and (1815–16), Biron and Fournier, eds., 2 vols.; *Recueil des mémoires de médecine, chirurgie et pharmacie militaires*, 1st series (1817–45), 61 vols., 2d series (1845–58), 23 vols. Continued under various titles.

Some of the medical reports sent by the chief military physicians and surgeons to the National Health Council in Paris have been published: see, for example, "Les rapports originaux de Larrey à l'armée d'Orient," Paul Pallary, ed., in *Mémoires de l'Institut d'Egypte* (1936).

It has not yet been possible to explore the much more abundant archival sources, some of which are located at the Chateau de Vincennes, in Paris. See France, Ministère de la guerre, *Inventaire des archives conservées au service historique de l'état-major de l'armée* (Chateau de Vincennes), M.-A. Fabre, ed. (Paris, 1954).

The vast possibilities of studying the French soldiers' physical and medical history from primary sources can be gauged from a perusal of A. Corvisier, *L'armée française de la fin du 17ème siècle au ministère de Choiseul: Le soldat* (Paris, 1964), 2 vols., with its astounding documentation.

[16] N. R. D. Desgenettes, *Histoire médicale de l'armée d'Orient* (Paris, 1802); D.-J. Larrey, *Clinique chirurgicale exercée particulièrement dans les camps et les hôpitaux militaires depuis 1792 jusqu'à 1829* (Paris, 1829–36), 5 vols.; P.-F. Percy, *Journal des campagnes du baron Percy, chirurgien-en-chef de la grande armée* (1754–1825) (Paris, 1904).

[17] A. Moreau de Jonnès, *Monographie historique et médicale de la fièvre jaune des Antilles et recherches physiologiques sur les lois du développement et de la propagation de cette maladie pestilentielle* (Paris, 1820).

[18] The novelty of this genre is somewhat debatable: in France, the *Apologie and Treatise Containing the Voyages Made into Divers Places* (Paris, 1585) of Ambroise Paré might claim precedence as might the *Rêveries of the Maréchal de Saxe* (Paris, 1738). In England, some influential books had been published on the subject, for instance J. Lind, *Essay on the Hygiene of the Sailors* (London, 1757); R. Brocklesby, *Observations on Military Hospitals* (London, 1764); and J. Pringle, *Observations on the Diseases of the Army* (London, 1772).

[19] For example, L. Bruant, "Notice sur l'ophthalmie règnante," *Mémoires sur l'Egypte, publiées pendant les campagnes du général Bonaparte* (4 vols.; Paris, 1799–1802), I, 95–102, and "Observations sur les maladies qui ont règné en Fructidor, An IV, dans l'armée d'Orient," *Ibid.*, II, 315–29; N. R. D. Desgenettes, "Notice sur l'emploi de l'huile dans la peste," *Ibid.*, I, 321–26; G. N. Renati, "Topographie physique et médicale du Caire," *Ibid.*, II, 353–67.

tion of the French Institute,[20] to various rival medical societies in Paris[21] and, after the fall of Napoleon, to the revived Academy of Medicine[22] or to public-spirited journals such as the *Annales d'hygiène publique et de médecine légale.*[23] The French medical press of the early nineteenth century abounds in reviews of dissertations, manuals, and monographs concerning medical problems[24] which

[20] This "section" corresponds to the Academy of Sciences under the Bourbons. The close connection between the Egyptian and French Institutes is exemplified by a paper on chemical affinities which the chemist C.-L. Berthollet (1748–1822) began to read to the Egyptian Institute in 1799 and continued to read to the French Institute after his return to Paris with Bonaparte (*Mémoires de l'Académie des sciences de l'Institut de France,* III [1799–1800], 1).

[21] The most important of these, each with its own publication, were, in chronological order of their foundation: the Société de santé de Paris, founded on March 22, 1796, renamed Société de médecine on February 15, 1797, which published the *Recueil périodique de la société de médecine de Paris* (14 vols., 1796–1802), continued as *Journal général de médecine, de chirurgie et de pharmacie* (96 vols.; 1802–30); the Société médicale d'émulation, founded later the same year (5 Messidor, Year IV), publishing *Mémoires* (1797–1826), under the empire quite irregularly (V [1803], VI [1806], VII [1811], VIII [1817]; and the semiofficial Société de l'Ecole de médecine de Paris, founded on 9 Vendémiaire, Year IX, on the suggestion of the Minister of Interior, Lucien Bonaparte, which published the *Journal de médecine, chirurgie, pharmacie, etc.* (1800–17). (A journal by the same name had existed during the old régime under the editorship of Vandermonde [95 vols., 1754–93].)
Examples of important papers relevant to this study, read to the Société de médecine de Paris are: N. R. D. Desgenettes, "Sur les maladies qui ont régné à l'armée d'Italie," *Recueil périodique de la société de médecine de Paris,* II (1797), 427–56; M. Laubri (physician-in-chief of the army in Holland), "Les maladies qui ont régné dans l'armée de Hollande," *Journal général de médecine, de chirurgie et pharmacie,* XVI (1803), 20–28; D.-J. Larrey, "Notice sur la fièvre jaune considérée comme complication des plaies d'armes à feu . . . ," *Ibid.,* XVII (1804), 141–51; A. J. Renoult, M.D. (surgeon of the *gendarmerie d'élite*), "Notice sur l'hématurie qu'éprouvent les Européens dans la haute Egypte et la Nubie," *Ibid.,* 366–70.
Relevant papers read to the Société d'émulation médicale are: J. Cassan, "Mémoires sur le climat des Antilles et sur les maladies qui sont particulières à la zône torride," *Mémoires de la société médicale d'émulation de Paris,* V (1803), 25–180; A. Moreau de Jonnès, "Essai sur l'hygiène militaire des Antilles," *Ibid.,* VIII (1817), 175–241; P.-F. Briot, "Sur les avantages que la chirurgie théorique et pratique doit retirer des observations et des opérations faites aux armées dans les dernières campagnes," *Ibid.,* VIII (1817), 243–442.

[22] Abolished in 1793, the Academy of Medicine was not reopened until 1820, was closed and purged in 1822 and reopened in 1823.

[23] Beginning in 1829, these *Annales* published highly interesting work by men in many professions who shared a concern for public health.

[24] Examples of inaugural dissertations are: M. G. Lachese, *Essai sur l'hygiène militaire* (Paris, 1804); H. Millioz, *Essai sur le scorbut qui a régné à Alexandrie, en Egypte, pendant les blocus de cette place, en l'an XI* (Paris, 1804); F.-C. Pouqueville, *Sur la fièvre adéno-nerveuse ou sur la peste d'Orient* (Paris, 1804).
Examples of manuals on military hygiene are: J. J. Martin, *Manuel de l'officier de santé* (Paris, 1802); F.-V. Pallois, *Essai sur l'hygiène navale ou*

the wars kept urging on French physicians and competent laymen.

The evidence suggests that the beginning of the Consulate marks a dividing line between eight years of republican rule when the welfare of citizens and soldiers—including their health—was of genuine concern to the government, and fifteen years of Napoleonic autocracy when the needs of strategy, administrative efficiency, and economy gradually gained ascendance over humanitarian and medical considerations. The first period is marked by official gratitude toward the maimed and wounded, by some deference toward the competence of medical men, by idealistic experiments in medical education and in prompt assistance to casualties on the battlefield. Even in this early period there is evidence that, despite the enlightened tenor of the law, the traditional prejudice against doctors was already reasserting itself and that the military resisted the intrusion of professionals with a higher allegiance than to the god of war.

In the Napoleonic era only "battle surgery" (the phrase is Percy's) met with any kind of success. Other medical assistance was gradually rendered impossible. Indeed, from Austerlitz to Leipzig, the battlefields lay far from home, problems of logistics became insuperable, supplies were scarce, many soldiers were foreigners (making communication with French doctors difficut and often eliciting less dedicated efforts than French patients), the army "health officer" was of increasingly doubtful competence since the army medical schools had been abolished, until finally, in the merciless Russian winter of 1812, mere survival remained the only aim of the hale, and the wounded died in the snow, of cold and starvation. It is therefore the eight years of republican rule, rather than the fifteen years of Napoleon's reign, that arrest the attention of the student interested in the fate of medicine during these wars.

France declared war against the "King of Hungary and Bohemia" in April, 1792. Soon she faced a coalition including most of Eu-

---

l'hygiène appliquée à préserver du scorbut les équipages des vaisseaux pendant les voyages de longcours (Paris, 1801); E. B. Revolat, *Nouvelle hygiène militaire ou Préceptes sur la santé de l'homme de guerre considérée dans toutes ses positions: comme les garnisons, les, cantonnements, les campements, les bivouacs, les ambulances, les hôpitaux, les embarquements, etc.* (Lyon, 1804).

Examples of monographs are: F. Boussenard, *Essai sur la peste* (Paris, 1802); J. F. X. Pugnet, *Mémoires sur les fièvres de mauvais caractère du Levant et des Antilles . . .* (Lyon, 1804); F. Ruette, *Essai sur l'éléphantiasis et les maladies lépreuses* (Paris, 1802); L. Valentin, *Traité de la fièvre jaune d'Amérique* (Paris, 1804).

rope. The young medical men who marched off to heal, amputate limbs, or bury their comrades found the French army medical service in a "state of utter confusion." [25] As in so many other branches of French economy and society, piecemeal efforts at reform had resulted in bewildering discrepancies. Louis XVI had inherited an arc of well-built military hospitals planned by Vauban around France's periphery. The excellent hospital regulations still excited the admiration of a British captain in 1856.[26] Also, in 1775, several army hospitals had been ordered to offer courses in anatomy, physiology, surgery, pharmacology, chemistry, botany, and first aid, in order better to educate the lower echelon medical personnel.[27] It is in these classrooms, the military "amphitheatres," that the famed French clinical tradition has its roots.

Clinical teaching [writes Bégin] . . . began in the "amphitheatres" of military medicine where it was organized and practiced in a manner still followed in the best European medical schools. This was years before Desbois de Rochefort and after him Corvisart introduced it into the curricula of the medical faculties.[28]

But when it came to staffing and supplying the army hospitals, the king encountered intractable difficulties. A law of 1708 provided for a doctor, a surgeon, an apothecary, and their aides to staff each of the hospitals. In time of war these men were to join the troops and be replaced *pro tem* by local practitioners. This blueprint remained just that, for inducements to join the army were slight, especially after 1747, when an Office of War Administration (*commissariat de guerre*) was created. Its ambition, during an irregular but persistent 140-year history, was to limit the role of army doctors to medical care only. A three-cornered tug-of-war among army doctors, professional soldiers, and administrators forms an ever-present backdrop for any study of French army medicine. As late as 1872 an army surgeon was still denouncing "the one im-

[25] L. J. Bégin, *Etudes sur le service de santé militaire en Franc,* 104.

[26] Th. J. Thackeray, *The Military Organization and Administration of France* (2 vols.; London, 1856), ch. XII "Hospital service."

[27] Royal ordinances of December 22, 1775, February 26, 1777, May 2, 1781. Until 1781 the assistants to surgeons and pharmacists were still hired and paid by hospital administrators or even by civilian suppliers (Bégin, pp. 11–12).

[28] *Ibid.,* p. 42. Louis Desbois de Rochefort (1750–86) was famous for his lessons in clinical surgery at the Charité hospital in Paris. Jean-Nicolas Corvisart (1755–1821), famous for his expertise in anatomy and surgery, taught at the Ecole de santé in Paris (1795–97) and at the Collège de France (1797–1804). He introduced percussion into France and served as Napoleon's First Physician.

pediment to progress: the subordination of military medicine to the commissariat . . . contrary to all the rules of reason, truth, and justice. . . ." [29]

On the eve of the French Revolution, regimental hospitals were being planned.[30] In order to implement the change, many of Vauban's military hospitals were abolished and 61 doctors and 58 pharmacists dismissed. Morale among army medical personnel was low.[31]

In the first 18 months of fighting the republic lost 600 medical men. Where to find replacements? True, the doctor draft law of August 7, 1793, made all physicians, surgeons, and pharmacists from eighteen to forty liable to military service, and the army medical schools at Strasbourg, Metz, and Lille—and, later, Paris[32]—still trained lower echelon personnel. But the need for doctors was soon rendered desperate because France had no more medical schools.

Indeed, during the early egalitarian and destructive phase of the republic, medical acadamies, faculties, and societies seemed to republican hotheads—the painter Jacques-Louis David, the doctor Jean-Paul Marat—typical of the privileged professional corporations, those superannuated centers of reaction with which a young country could dispense.[33] Thus the medical profession became a target for revolutionary zeal. On August 8, 1793—one day after the doctor draft—there disappeared 18 faculties of medicine, 15 colleges of surgery, the Royal Society of Medicine, and the Royal Academy of Surgery. All Frenchmen were now equal to their doctors. But the number of doctors was dwindling.

The absurdity of this situation and the national need were clear. A law of December 4, 1794 (14 Frimaire, Year III) therefore created three "Health Schools"—the democratic reincarnation of the Faculties of Paris, Montpellier, and Strasbourg—where 550 "national scholars" (*élèves de la patrie*) were to be trained annually,

[29] L. Lefort, *La chirurgie militaire et les sociétés de secours* (Paris, 1872), p. 2.
[30] Decree of May 18, 1788.
[31] See, for example, the impassioned protest of M. Coste, First Surgeon of the royal armies and medical director of the French forces in America: *Du service des hôpitaux militaires rappelé aux vrais principes* (Paris, 1790).
[32] The medical school at the military hospital of the Val-de-Grâce in Paris was established by a decree of 30 Floréal, Year IV. Schools for naval medical personnell were opened at Brest and Toulon.
[33] See J. Fayet, *La Révolution et la science, 1789–1795* (Paris, 1960), chs. III and V.

free of charge.[34] The criteria of selection included a "loyalty oath": "The candidate chosen for this career must carry in his heart love of freedom, hatred of tyranny, and whole-hearted devotion to the Republic." [35] Instructions to the regional selection committees urged that:

preference be given to the candidate capable of clear thought, quick and accurate judgment, keen analytic observation, able to understand, at a glance, the relationship of complex facts and to draw valid conclusions, who is filled with dedication to science and eager to devote himself unreservedly to his medical studies.[36]

Even if 550 such paragons could have been found annually, historic reality provided neither the time nor the facilities for turning them into doctors.

The army medical council very urgently demanded surgeons. Many students were drafted soon after their arrival at medical school. . . . Percy found them untrained, weak, easily homesick, and susceptible to typhus and dysentery. . . . They quickly memorized many facts, learned some technical skills, and then were sent off to complete their apprenticeship on the battlefield.[37]

The Health Schools were at first so democratic that no examinations were held nor diplomas granted: a true republican would know when he had learned enough and was ready to be a "health officer"—the democratic equivalent of "physician" or "surgeon." By 1798 "protests arose everywhere against the quackery and incompetence that endangered the health and lives of the citizenry." [38] Egalitarian enthusiasm, useful in sweeping away outmoded institutions, was threatening to eradicate professional competence.

Yet, at first, this revolutionary enthusiasm had been creative for French medicine. When the *patrie* was to be defended by armed citizens marching under the red, white, and blue flag to the sound of the *Marseillaise,* doctors flocked to the colors so that every possible service and care might be offered the nation's sons.[39] Decree

---

[34] This system worked for only three years. Scholarships were discontinued in Floréal, Year VI (May, 1798).

[35]. A. Prévost, *Les études médicales sous le directoire et le consulat* (Paris, 1907), p. 5.

[36] *Ibid.*   [37] *Ibid.*, pp. 7 and 21.   [38] *Ibid.*, p. 21.

[39] In 1792, 1,400 physicians and surgeons joined the army; their number had risen to 2,570 by January, 1793, and to 4,000 by the end of that year. A max-

followed decree regarding stationary and field hospitals; the duties of physicians, surgeons, pharmacists, and their helpers (including the cutler, tinsmith, and cooper to accompany each ambulance division); aid to invalids, veterans, widows, and orphans; the military honors due casualties carried into a hospital; the special seats reserved for disabled veterans at public celebrations; the neutral status of the enemy's wounded.[40]

The decrees of April and June, 1792, ushered in the brief golden age of French military medicine. They gave the army doctor officer's rank, a free hand in making medical decisions, and the decisive voice in planning medical care on the battlefield.[41] All medical personnel would be treated free of charge in the military hospitals. The government would assume the provisioning, thus putting an end, it was hoped, to graft and profiteering. A central supervisory health council of nine—later fifteen—members was to sit permanently in Paris.

The problem was overwhelming. Between 1791 and 1813 France drafted 4,556,000 men. In 1793 she had 650,000 men under arms, and by February, 1794, their numbers had risen to 1,200,000. Usually ten percent of the soldiers were sick.[42] Whenever the medical personnel were given a free hand by the military much was achieved; witness the spectacular innovations in ambulance service: the stretcher-bearers, the "flying ambulance," and the "wurst."

The stretcher-bearers were first organized in the Rhine army of 1792 by Percy. They seemed essential

for, at the time, it might happen that several men would leave the firing line to carry a wounded comrade to the dressing station, some

---

imum of 8,000 was attained in 1794. See the Report by Frauvel to the Council of Five Hundred, 12 Brumaire, Year VI.

[40] The chief relevant decrees are dated April 21 and 27, 1792 (with a *"Règlement d'exécution"* of June 20, 1792), December 21, 1792, and August 7, 1793.

A typically French note was struck in the *Instruction* of 16 Ventôse, Year III: "The Republic wants to spare no expense for the cure of its defenders. But funds shall be used only for the recovery of patients. Excessive economy and unnecessary expenditures are equally condemned."

[41] Actually, the wording of many decrees was less than clear, and thus the source, as will be seen, of disputed authority. For example, article III of the decree of June 20, 1792, stipulated that decisions regarding the site, healthfulness, and supervision of field hospitals were to be made by the war commissioner *"together with and according to* the observations of the chief health officer" (italics mine).

[42] G. Morache, "Hygiène militaire," in *Dictionnaire encylopédique des sciences médicales*, A. Dechambre, ed. (Paris, 1864–89).

considerable distance from the battlefield. . . . [Those with less de-voted friends] might not receive medical attention till the outcome of the battle was decided, and even then those of the victorious army received first care.[43]

The "flying ambulance," sometimes compared to our medical heli-copter, was also first tried in the Rhine army, and was perfected in the Italian army in 1796–97 under Larrey. His ambulance was light and mobile, able to pick up casualties during battle, admin-ister first aid, travel back to a field hospital, and return quickly into the melee to retrieve more wounded. The "wurst" was used by Percy during the German campaign of 1799–1800. Longer and more cumbersome than Larrey's vehicle, it could accommodate more men and supplies, up to ten doctors could bestride it and thus save their energies for the hard work that awaited them. Percy recounts—as dispassionately as possible—what were his experi-ences, and they were no doubt typical.

I had proposed to our generals that my collaborators in all divisions, and especially in the vanguard, should have this kind of light and manoeuverable carriage on which ten men can easily ride. I had ex-plained the remarkable advantages for the safety, speed, and improve-ment of medical service. They were so pleased that several such "wurst," minus the horses, were immediately put at my disposal by the command-ing artillery officers. But the horses became the stumbling block of our project. They were never refused, but such were the obstacles, pre-texts, and excuses that the "wursts" were returned to the arsenal whence they had been taken for the relief of the surgeons and the well-being of the wounded. Some thought that it might have been a dangerous spectacle to see medical officers ride, since a system full of ill-will, op-pression, and humiliation had long condemned them to walk and be covered with dust and dirt: they *should* walk and be miserable, other-wise, some administrators said, they would become too cocky.[44]

While the first medical innovations were made on the European fronts, new challenges awaited the French army doctors in more far-flung expeditions, notably in Egypt, Syria, Guadeloupe, Mar-tinique, and Santo Domingo.

When Dominique-Jean Larrey, chief surgeon of the Eastern

---

[43] H. P. Bayon, "Napoleon's Egyptian Expedition: Brilliant Military Victories—and Ultimate Disaster Through Disease," *West London Medical Journal*, XLVIII, No. 2 (1943), p. 39.

[44] Percy, *Journal des campagnes du baron Percy . . .* , p. 3.

Army, set foot on Egyptian soil on July 1, 1798, he eagerly looked forward to the exotic adventure on which his admired commander Bonaparte, then aged twenty-nine, had bidden him embark. Egypt and Syria were unknown from the medical point of view—except for light shed by ancient texts: Hippocrates, the Old Testament, Hellenistic doctors, and accounts of the Crusades. Larrey kept a diary. At first, he wrote,

the troops were bothered only by fatigue, diarrhoea, and slight dysentery caused, it seems, by the cool nights and the excess of watermelon and not—as some doctors thought—by the Nile water which has never bothered anyone. (Footnote: This water tastes good, is definitely safe and easy to digest. An analysis has been made which proves that it is of better quality than the waters of European rivers.) [45]

Soon Larrey had to treat

a persistent ophthalmia which made several of our soldiers absolutely desperate and many of them blind. . . . [It] spared few during the winter of 1798–9 . . . within two and a half months more than three thousand persons had to be hospitalized. . . .[46]

A modern observer has diagnosed this "ophthalmia" as "the very contagious but not dangerous conjunctivitis caused by the Koch-Weeks bacillus, doubtless frequently complicated by genuine trachoma." [47] But Larrey had no such bacteriological wisdom at his disposal. It is pitiful to watch him struggle with the etiology and therapy of the disease.

The causes of ophthalmia include the burning heat, the sunshine refracted by the many white objects, which tire and irritate the sensitive part of the eye; the abuse of drink and women; the windblown dust which penetrates under the pupil and irritates the eyeball; especially the stoppage of perspiration by the sudden change from heat to cold; the cool and humid nights for the soldiers who camp out. . . .

I have noticed that blond men are more subject to this disease than dark; I have also noticed that the right eye is more susceptible to the illness than the left; for whenever only one eye is affected, it is the right one. This is perhaps because most persons sleep on their right

[45] D.-J. Larrey, *Relation historique et chirurgicale de l'expédition de l'armée d'orient en Egypte et en Syrie* (Paris, 1803), pp. 13–14.

[46] *Ibid.*, pp. 19, 32.

[47] M. Meyerhof, "A Short History of Ophthalmia During the Egyptian Campaigns of 1798–1807," *The British Journal of Ophthalmology*, XVI (March, 1932), 131, 132, 145. (They may, of course, also have suffered from sunstroke or some sort of solar conjunctivitis.)

sides so that the humidity emanating from the soil affects that part of the body first.[48]

For remedies he advised the following:

When the ophthalmia is inflammatory, begin by bleeding at the veins of the neck, arm, or foot . . . then use leeches, applied at the temples, as close as possible to the eye. . . . Later prescribe footbaths, emollient and soothing fumigations, lotions made with linseed, poppy, or oriental saffron. . . . To soothe pain at night, cover the eyes with a salve made of beaten egg whites with a few drops of rose water and several grains of alum. . . .[49]

While Larrey and his staff thus struggled with "Egyptian ophthalmia," a much more serious disease made its first appearance. In the winter of 1798 in Cairo Larrey diagnosed his first case of bubonic plague.

He put the patient in isolation. When the man died, Larrey had the body, belongings, and bedding burnt, and the room fumigated. He informed the chief medical officer, Desgenettes, and also "addressed a circular to all surgeons, inviting them to continue their solicitous care for these patients and at the same time to take all possible precautions against contagion." [50] When, during the siege of Jaffa in March, 1799, he lost up to fifteen men a day, he "spoke of them to General Bonaparte." [51] But the general pressed on northward and besieged Acre. There the plague reached its most destructive period. Larrey multiplied his work. As precautions he could advise only "cleanliness, frequent ablutions of the whole body with cold water and vinegar, fresh linen and clothing, exercise and moderation. . . ." [52] No doubt such hygienic measures were helpful to some extent.

In the Antilles French army doctors had to struggle with yellow fever. When peace was made between France and England in 1802, the British returned Martinique and Guadeloupe to its owners. "Our soldiers were quartered in the very barracks and hospitals where this disease had attacked so many of the English troops," writes an excellent observer; "most of the beds where we slept had been theirs. . . ." [53] The French had landed in the fall of

[48] Larrey, *Relation historique et chirurgicale* . . . , p. 24.
[49] *Ibid.*, p. 26.   [50] *Ibid.*, pp. 87–88.   [51] *Ibid.*, p. 97.   [53] *Ibid.*, p. 106.
[53] Moreau de Jonnès, *Monographie historique et médicale de la fièvre jaune des Antilles* . . . , p. 92.

1802; an epidemic was soon unleashed. In the first three months the French lost over half their men. "In the hospitals almost all the doctors and surgeons died; we lost forty of them in succession. Of all the persons employed near yellow fever patients only a few aged negroes survived." [54] Everyone was terror-stricken and most turned superstitious. The etiology of the disease remained unsuspected, though Moreau de Jonnès was convinced that the weather was closely connected with yellow fever. To contract the disease, it was enough, he writes

to expose oneself at length to the hot sunshine, be caught in a draft when perspiring, neglect to change one's rain-drenched clothes, undertake a taxing journey on foot or on horseback, breathe the burning air in churches during the great religious ceremonies, be bled needlessly, take excessive baths or drugs, be frightened, depressed, homesick, agitated by a passion such as rage or love, or simply experience some strong stimulation that might favor the development of the sickness.[55]

His therapy is as eclectic as his etiology, and he adds that "the number and variety of remedies show only too clearly that they are useless." [56] His conclusion: "It is only through a system of public health adapted to local, meteorological, and human factors that yellow fever can be eradicated from the Antilles and prevented from invading Europe." [57] Moreau reports mainly on Martinique. The ravages of yellow fever in Guadeloupe and in Santo Domingo confirm his findings. Between January and August, 1802, over half the medical personnel died in Santo Domingo, and during the whole ill-starred expedition the French lost 35,000 men, including the leader, General Leclerc, Bonaparte's brother-in-law.[58]

It has often been said that the French ignored the phenomenon of contagion whereas the English—afflicted by the same diseases in Egypt and in the Antilles—were aware of it. This is, of course, not true. Moreau de Jonnès writes: "No one doubts the contagiousness of yellow fever. . . . Several doctors assured everyone that the disease was not communicable . . . but . . . [even] those who voiced this opinion took all possible precautions." [59] When Larrey had diagnosed the outbreak of bubonic plague, he

[54] *Ibid.*, p. 100.   [55] *Ibid.*, p. 98.   [56] *Ibid.*, p. 129.   [57] *Ibid.*, p. 138.
[58] Dr. P. Bonnette, "Le calvaire médical de St. Domingue et de la Guadeloupe," *Hippocrate*, 6th year (1938), pp. 484–85.
[59] Moreau de Jonnès, *Monographie historique. . .* , p. 100.

wrote: "One cannot deny that the plague is epidemic and contagious." [60] When the plague spread in Syria during the spring campaign of 1799, Larrey, having alerted Bonaparte, issued a circular to the medical officers: "When this disease reaches a certain point, it is contagious; all necessary precautions should be taken by the medical personnel and recommended to the soldiers. . . ." [61] No one, of course, knew how to differentiate between the phenomena of contagion and infection, the terms "miasma" and "pestilential virus" were loosely used, and no one suspected lice or mosquitoes. The hopes of the scientific and medical community were buoyed by the spectacular success of vaccination, introduced into France in 1800 despite the war, and accepted in fast increasing circles. [62] Yet smallpox remained the only disease thus conquered.

In order to discredit belief in contagion, Bonaparte went to great lengths: hence his much-discussed visit to the Jaffa pesthouse and his fearless physical contact with infected patients. When Desgenettes inoculated himself with the pus from an open bubo, he was gallantly assisting his commanding general, not conducting a scientific experiment. For reasons of morale, Bonaparte was quite ruthless in holding his medical personnel to their duties; witness the well-known order of the day of January, 1799:

Any health officer abandoning a first-aid station in battle, or refusing to care for patients who might carry a contagious disease, shall be arrested, tried by a military tribunal, and judged according to the law dealing with deserters. Whatever his station, no Frenchman shall fear death.

Citizen Boyer, surgeon at Alexandria, coward enough to refuse his services to patients who had had contact with supposedly contagious cases, is unworthy of being a French citizen. He shall be dressed as a woman, paraded through the streets of Alexandria on a donkey with a sign on his back saying "Afraid to die, unworthy of being a Frenchman." After that, he shall be sent back to France . . . and deprived of his citizenship. [63]

[60] Larrey, *Relation historique et chirurgicale* . . . , p. 140.

[61] *Ibid.*, p. 106.

[62] *Rapport fait au nom de la commission nommée par la classe des sciences mathématiques et physiques de l'Institut pour l'examen de la méthode de préserver de la petite vérole par l'inoculation de la vaccine* (Paris, 1803), and R. G. Dunbar, "The Introduction of the Practice of Vaccination into Napoleonic France," *Bulletin of the History of Medicine*, X (1941), 635–50.

[63] J. Lasserre, "A l'armée d'Egypte: discipline, récompenses diverses, et armes d'honneur," *Revue des études napoléoniennes*, XXX (1930), 106–7.

Larrey had a much higher opinion than his chief of the French soldier's moral fiber:

Let no one think [he wrote] that our soldiers were frightened by the word *plague*. . . . They had become morally and physically toughened by the hardships they had already undergone. It would have been desirable to inform the military, at the first appearance of the plague, and to explain, in a reassuring way, the true character of the disease.[64]

In Egypt as in the Antilles, the doctors cured whenever they could, and comforted and reassured the men to the best of their ability. They won everyone's respect and admiration.

With the end of the Egyptian campaign and the defeat of the Second Coalition, a tenuous peace was established between France and her European foes. Bonaparte had put an end to republican government in France: the eight-year-old experiment in democracy was over. Within a year or two the First Consul managed to centralize and modernize French finances, justice, administration, education, and religion. Would he reform army medicine as well?

It may be worthwhile quickly to pinpoint the main issues on which a decision was needed at the beginning of the Consulate. These included the recruitment and training of doctors, their rank and role in peacetime and wartime, the staffing of permanent and field hospitals, and training for battle surgery. From the point of view of morale among army doctors, two issues were vital: the clarification of their relationship to the ministry of war, and permanent commissions. Would the military health council continue to have consultative functions only? This was a vital point for physicians and surgeons. Their freedom of action depended on it, in their relationship with hospital administrators, pharmacists, local city authorities, and police. The question of rank was equally crucial. Army doctors had never been accepted as equals by military officers. The literature abounds with requests for *l'épaulette*, a recognizable status symbol, and for permanent commissions. None of these problems was new, of course. But controversial issues had slowly crystallized as a result of the idealistic legislation issued in the first republican war years.

Indeed, the laws of the Year I had proclaimed principles as if they were a reality: the equality of physicians and surgeons; the

---

[64] Larrey, *Relation historique et chirurgicale* . . . , pp. 136–37.

"assimilation" of army doctors to the officers' corps. But principles were not the knife with which to cut the cake of custom: traditionally physicians formed an intellectual and social élite, whereas "barber-surgeons" plied a trade and pharmacists kept shop. Physicians were therefore esteemed far above surgeons. In the army, on the other hand, surgeons had long been honored and doctors scorned. So "battle surgery" was regarded as essential in the field and its demands honored by the seasoned soldier—in contrast to hospital medicine which was neglected.

Did army officers consider "health officers" as their equals? Legislation recurs during this period admonishing the army that health officers should be "assimilated." In fact army doctors tended to be ignored every time a decree concerning officers did not specifically mention them.[65] All the traditional prejudices were thus reasserting themselves as the idealistic revolutionary legislation of 1792–93 was applied by thousands of laymen—erstwhile civilians or professional soldiers—now dealing with the administration of medical matters. Napoleon was no exception. Given his decisive voice in French affairs during the first fifteen years of the nineteenth century, his opinions on medicine loom large.

Napoleon disliked doctors and distrusted medication. His experiences in Italy and Egypt had convinced him that most drugs were worthless. This confirmed his view that clean water, fresh air, moderation, and will power were the best therapeutic agents. He had also found that doctors tended to have minds of their own and this, as his power grew, he increasingly resented. Once First Consul, he muzzled the "Ideologues," those "idea-mongers," many of them physicians, who believed in observation, experiment, and the power of the individual mind.[66] While one might attempt to portray Napoleon as a patron of science, one could not possibly depict him as encouraging medicine.[67] Once emperor, he sur-

---

[65] One of the first instances of this unfair treatment occurred when officers' horses were captured by the enemy; the owners were to be indemnified. The law of May 7, 1793, did not specifically mention health officers—they received no indemnity. On many occasions officers were to get pay raises, bonuses, retirement or fringe benefits. Again and again health officers were bypassed. (Bégin, *Etudes sur le service de santé militaire*, pp. 93 ff.)

[66] See G. Rosen, "The Philosophy of Ideology . . . ," *Bulletin of the History of Medicine*, XX, 328–39; and O. Temkin, "The Philosophical Background of Magendie's Physiology," *Ibid.*, XX, 10–35.

[67] In an excellent recent study of the Société d'Arcueil, the author attempts to show that Napoleon furthered science. A more convincing case could be made

rounded himself with medical courtiers such as Corvisart who had independent judgment but was a therapeutic skeptic like His Majesty.

As for his own health, Napoleon was unconcerned. He *knew*, from boyhood on, that because his father and grandfather had died of cancer of the stomach this would be his fatal illness as well. He would therefore die of nothing else. He participated fearlessly in sixty major battles; he had nineteen horses shot from under him. He thought himself invulnerable. He died of cancer of the stomach.[68]

Napoleon's attitude toward medicine was thus solidly rooted in prejudice. His *Correspondence* and his remarks to the Council of State suggest that he gave medicine little attention. His directives for the soldiers' well-being emphasized preventive and hygienic measures: healthful encampments, adequate rest, solid shoes and warm clothing, sound food, fresh air, and good spirits—these were his preferred medications. One can hardly quarrel with these precepts. High casualties depressed him. As for the wounded, his main concern—like any general's—was their return to active duty. He had little sympathy with men who, like Percy, urged the creation of an Army Medical Corps with career officers, special schools, a distinctive uniform, and appropriate salaries.

Lest one be tempted to condemn too categorically Napoleon's shabby treatment of his army doctors, it should be remembered that the Imperial Guard had a medical service which was judged excellent by contemporaries. Each battalion of infantry or squadron of cavalry had its surgeon; the Guard had its own hospital, its light maneuverable ambulances, its special personnel, uniformed down to the male nurses. Morale was high, to the end, at Waterloo. True, this medical service was the work of Larrey, but it was not only Larrey's work: the chief physician, surgeon, and pharmacist of the Guard's medical service were paid 9,690 francs a year, more than three and a half times the salary of the highest paid army doctors with thirty years' service.

Much could have been done with money, a little time, and

for Napoleon as a champion of technology. See M. Crosland, *The Society of Arcueil: A View of French Science at the Time of Napoleon* (London, 1967).

[68] See, for example, A. Braun, "Napoleon I und die Medizin," *Zeitschrift für ärtzliche Fortbildung*, XXX (1933), 628–29; B. Sokoloff, *Napoleon: A Doctor's Biography* (New York, 1937); and J. Kemble, *Napoleon Immortal*.

a will. It is true that excellent improvements in battle surgery were planned and, had the plans been carried out, French soldiers would have received prompt and efficient succor on the battlefield. Given the opportunity offered Napoleon Bonaparte in the Year VIII, subsequent legislation concerning army medicine comes as a shock.

By a succession of decrees from 1800 to 1804 [69] hundreds of medical officers were discharged with a small sum of money as their only reward, the army medical schools were abolished, and the staffs of the army hospitals sharply reduced. The health council was replaced by six inspectors and the authority of doctors strictly limited to medical matters. The administrative officials of the war department would make the decisions regarding army medicine. As a result of these measures, "the entire medical corps of the army gradually disintegrated." [70] The number of army physicians declined from 210 doctors and 1,665 surgeons in 1800 to 62 doctors and 842 surgeons in 1802. "As far as any other health personnel was concerned the situation was very much worse, indeed, such personnel practically no longer existed," [71] and the army medical services were seething with "discouragement, rage, and revolt." [72]

Why did Napoleon Bonaparte choose to face fifteen years of warfare without an adequate medical service? Chevalier argues that he anticipated "a long peace." [73] This theory is hardly tenable. Some aver that his medical service was adequate. The evidence is meager indeed.[74] He may have thought that, in case of war, he might work another miracle of 1793 and assemble another Army Medical Corps by an appeal to patriotism. How wrong he was, if

[69] The main relevant decrees were dated: 4 Germinal and 24 Thermidor, Year VIII; 16 Frimaire and 15 Nivôse, Year IX; 18 Vendémiaire, Year X; 20 Vendémiaire, Year XI; 9 Frimaire, Year XII; and 14 Fructidor, Year XIII. The decree of 15 Nivôse, Year IX, ended by stating: "The army medical service is based on temporary commissions only and . . . strictly speaking, *there is no medical corps*" (italics mine).

[70] A. G. Chevalier, "Hygienic Problems in the Napoleonic Armies," *Ciba Symposia*, III, No. 6 (Sept., 1941), p. 974.

[71] *Ibid.*, p. 975.

[72] Brice et Bottet, *Le corps de santé militaire* . . . , p. xviii.

[73] Chevalier, "Hygienic Problems in the Napoleonic Armies," p. 113.

[74] S. Haendcke, "Beiträge zur Hygiene in der Armee Napoleons I," *Sudhoff's Archiv für Geschichte der Medizin*, XXVI (1933), 47–64; F. Helme, "Napoléon et la médecine: La prophylaxie et le service de santé," *La Presse médicale*, XXIX Annexe (June 15, 18, 1921), pp. 853–55, 177–80; R. Lacronique, "Mesures d'hygiène et de prophylaxie prescrites à l'armée d'Allemagne, 1810–1812," *La France médicale*, 51st year (October 25, 1904), pp. 377–84.

he considered the campaign of Austerlitz a mere sequel to the victory of Valmy! The stark truth is that army medicine under a military dictator is really a paradox, since warfare and healing serve diametrically opposed purposes: generals court death; doctors preserve life. Napoleon would have composed his differences with Russia and England had the true welfare of his men been his paramount concern.

Perusal of the numerous medical accounts of the Spanish campaign of 1808 and the Russian campaign of 1812 soon makes it clear that medical care gradually became an irrelevant luxury. The heat and drought of Spain, the cold and snow of Russia, the poor logistic preparation resulting in lack of food and supplies were more effective killers than battle wounds or sickness. The diaries of Blaze[75] and Percy[76] in Spain, of Larrey,[77] de Kerckhoffs, and Roos[78] in Russia are heartrending documents. The hunger, thirst, cold, and pain were indescribable. Out of an army of over half a million men which invaded Russia in 1812, 350,000 died or "disappeared." A doctor of the Imperial Guard complained that "there was a drastic lack of transportation, food, medical supplies, and drugs. Several days after a battle one could still find wounded men who had not been helped. They would die of hunger rather than of their wounds. . . ."[79] In the frenzied retreat from Moscow casualties were a handicap: "Everyone had the same idea: get rid of the wounded. Whenever the soldiers stopped to camp or to rest and these unfortunates needed to get out of the carriage or to have their dressings changed, they were abandoned."[80] One history of the French Army Medical Service comments:

[75] S. Blaze, *Mémoires d'un apothicaire sur la guerre d'Espagne pendant les années 1808 à 1814* (2 vols.; Paris, 1828). In one of his lighter moods, Blaze classified military personnel as follows: First class, glory and wealth (imperial marshals and generals); second class, glory without wealth (most officers); third class, wealth without glory (war commissioners, employees of the treasury, the supply corps, the hospitals . . .); fourth class, neither wealth nor glory (health officers, doctors, surgeons, pharmacists). Vol. II, pp. 220–28.

[76] Percy, *Journal des campagnes du baron Percy.* . . .

[77] Larrey, *Clinique chirurgicale.* . . .

[78] J. R. L. de Kerckhoffs, *Histoire des maladies observées dans la grande armée française entre 1812 et 1813* (Anvers, 1836); H. Roos, *Souvenirs d'un médecin de la grande armée* (Paris, 1913).

[79] M. Bouvry, "Services de santé et ravitaillement de la grande armée pendant la campagne de 1812," *La Presse médicale*, LXIV (1956), 1804. (This is a review of a Paris thesis [1955] by Pierre Blouin, which I have not yet been able to examine.)

[80] *Ibid.*

The Empire scorned humanity. . . . The abandonment and disdain of the wounded was the rule in its armies. The decadence of the medical service is one of its major faults. Though this service included the most famous doctors and surgeons, they were hampered by changing and incoherent laws; they lacked encouragement and support and could act only as individuals. How remarkable would their work have been if the all-powerful Emperor had supported them, if their prescriptions of drugs and hygienic measures had been acted on by well-trained assistants! They could thus have curtailed the horrendous expenditure in French lives extracted by the Great Epic! [81]

Many French army doctors, it would seem, would gladly have followed Napoleon into battle, had the Army Medical Service been better organized.

Civilian French medicine reaped considerable benefits from Napoleon's disdain and neglect—albeit benefits of a negative nature. Physicians were not drafted into the army in huge numbers. The medical schools and the hospitals suffered relatively little interference. And it is in these medical schools, especially in Paris and in the Parisian hospitals, that clinical medicine now blossomed. Born of the ideas held by the reformers of the late eighteenth century (Condillac, Helvétius, and their circle), freed from the shackles of tradition by the bold destructive blows of the Revolution, channeled into creative teaching by the imaginative reforms

---

[81] Brice and Bottet, *Le corps de santé militaire en France* . . . , p. XIX.

The following statistics need no comment: "Of the 4 1/2 million soldiers engaged in the Revolutionary and Napoleonic Armies during 1792–1815 about 2 1/2 million died in hospitals and 150,000 were killed in action. . . . In the Egyptian campaign Bonaparte lost 4,758 out of 30,000 in action and 4,157 from disease, of whom 1,689, including 40 medical officers, died from bubonic plague. In the Russian campaign his total forces, increased to 533,000 by reinforcements, had shrunken to 95,000 when he reached Moscow, although there had been only two battles. . . .

"The losses in the principal battles from Austerlitz to Waterloo were:

Austerlitz: 12,000 French killed and wounded out of 94,000;
Jena-Auerstadt: 6,000 out of 96,000;
Eylau: 15,000 out of 79,000;
Friedland: 12,000 out of 86,000;
Aspern: 8,000 killed, 24,000 wounded out of 70,000;
Wagram: 23,000 killed and wounded, 7,000 missing out of 181,700;
Smolensk: 20,000 out of 180,000;
Borodino: 32,000 out of 130,000;
Leipzig: 30,000 out of 145,000;
Waterloo: 30,000 killed and wounded, 6,000 prisoners, out of 72,000."
From F. H. Garrison, *Notes on the History of Military Medicine* (Washington, D.C., 1922), pp. 169–70.

of Pinel, Hallé, Thouret, and other professors at the new Paris "Health School," enlivened by clinical conferences in the various hospitals, and enriched by laboratory work, the new French medicine made Paris the medical center of the world. The new methods of percussion and auscultation were taught; mass autopsies were performed. Laënnec's stethoscope was used. Medicine had emerged into the modern world.

While official disdain and neglect thus gave medicine much needed freedom, the wars entailed more positive stimuli. The benefits to surgery are obvious. Newly developed methods included the ligation of blood vessels, the tourniquet, the extraction of foreign bodies in gunshot wounds through a counter-opening, the dipping of bandages in water (Percy) or in camphorated hot wine (Larrey).[82] According to an experienced army surgeon, the most valuable lesson was speed, and simplicity of instruments and medication.[83] The large number of available cases stimulated the use of statistics in medicine. The government had applied them to problems of health and population since the seventeenth century.[84] Now they were increasingly used by doctors—who were led to view diseases as entities and to subject them to statistical analysis.[85]

Statistics were also applied to public health and hygiene.

The Napoleonic wars . . . , [writes Ackerknecht] seem to have increased rather than stifled knowledge and understanding of hygienic problems, private and public, and their application. Former and active army medical officers supplied a considerable contingent of . . . hygienists. . . .

When the "veterans" of 1815 started their study of hygiene, they found in Paris the unparalleled institution of a regular chair of hygiene, one of the many creations of the revolution in the medical field.[86]

[82] A. G. Chevalier, "The Physicians and Medical Service of the Revolutionary Armies," *Ciba Symposia*, VII, No. 11 (1946), p. 254.

[83] P.-F. Briot, *Histoire de l'état et des progrès de la chirurgie militaire en France pendant les guerres de la Révolution* (Besançon, 1817), pp. 4–5.
Cf. also Biron, "Discours sur les progrès de la médecine militaire en France depuis un demi-siècle," *Journal de médecine militaire*, I (Paris, 1815).

[84] G. Rosen, "Problems in the Application of Statistical Analysis of Questions of Health," *Bulletin of the History of Medicine*, XIX, 31.

[85] See, for example, the use of statistics by Philippe Pinel (1745–1826) in his *Résultat d'observations et construction des tables pour servir à déterminer le degré de probabilité de la guérison des aliénés* (Paris, 1807).

[86] E. H. Ackerknecht, "Hygiene in France: 1815–1848," *Bulletin of the History of Medicine*, XXII (1948), 119.

These "veterans," with their solid and varied experience and their new interests were a major influence, of course, on French medicine after 1815. It may be sufficient to mention that both Larrey and Desgenettes became inspectors general in the army medical service, that the great hygienists Fodéré[87] and Réveillé-Parise[88] as well as the despotic Broussais[89] had years of military duty to their credit.

Most subtle, but perhaps most lasting, was the effect of the Napoleonic wars on the feelings of the French public concerning its medical men. Although, among the military, discrimination against army medical personnel continued for two generations longer, the attitude of the public at large toward physicians changed. Gone from French literature are Molière's pompous robed doctors who speak Latin, quote Galen, and would not deign to touch a patient. The physicians of Balzac and Flaubert, of Beyle and Sainte-Beuve are knowledgeable, respected, kindly men like Dr. Benassis, Balzac's "Country Doctor." Many Frenchmen owed their lives to the selfless dedication of physicians such as he. The wars of the Revolution and Empire had won for French doctors the respect and admiration of their countrymen.

[87] F. E. Fodéré (1764–1835).   [88] J. H. Réveillé-Parise (1782–1852).
[89] F. J. V. Broussais (1772–1838).

The Growth of the
French Securities Market, 1815–1870

CHARLES E. FREEDEMAN

STATE UNIVERSITY OF NEW YORK
AT BINGHAMTON

"La Bourse est le monument par
excellence de la société moderne."
— P. J. PROUDHON

EVEN BEFORE INDUSTRIALIZATION was well under way in France,
there existed nascent capital markets, encompassing both small
rural moneylenders, often notaries, and urban bankers. These individuals either employed their own capital or acted as intermediaries for a small number of other persons. Paris also possessed a
rudimentary securities market. Although the Paris Bourse expanded
in the 1780s, it involved only a small number of speculators.[1]
The Revolution interrupted its growth and it was still in its in-
fancy at the time of the Restoration. Only four securities were
quoted on the Paris Bourse in 1815. The capital market achieved
its next stage of development with the proliferation of negotiable
securities, which was dependent upon government borrowing and
the rise of joint-stock companies. This essay is concerned with the

I am indebted to the Dean's Fund at Northern Illinois University for financial
assistance in the preparation of this essay and to Professor Rondo Cameron for
suggesting improvements in its content.

[1] George V. Taylor, "The Paris Bourse on the Eve of the Revolution, 1781–
1789," *American Historical Review*, LXVII (July, 1962), 967. The Paris Bourse
was founded in 1715.

growth of that portion of the capital market in which savings were mobilized by the purchase of public and private securities.

The development of the securities market was determined by financial intermediaries—banks, brokers, and the Bourse—the growth, dispersion, and negotiability of the public debt, the development of the joint-stock form of business organization, and the financial press and other literature. Recent research has emphasized the role of banks in capital formation.[2] But the success of banks as financial intermediaries was contingent upon the development of a market for securities. Banks could not easily satisfy the need for long-term capital out of their own funds; though some banks did extend long-term capital for industrialization, it was often at the price of eventual insolvency to themselves. The role played by banks would have been impossible without the parallel development of the mechanisms for marketing securities, joint-stock companies, and the opening up of new sources of funds.

The expansion of the market for government securities was the first step in the creation of a national capital market. It anticipated the development of a national market for private securities and helped educate and encourage the saving and investing public in holding securities, rather than maintaining unproductive hoards. A national capital market for *rentes* gradually appeared between 1815 and 1848, and was greatly expanded during the Second Empire.

The debt on January 1, 1815, amounted to 63.3 million francs in five percent *rentes*,[3] held almost entirely in Paris. By 1830 the debt had more than tripled—202.4 million francs in *rentes* on August 1, 1830 [4]—and approximately ten percent of it was held in the provinces. The rise in provincial holdings was aided by the establishment of a *grand-livre auxiliaire* in each department in 1819, which facilitated the marketing and transferability of *rentes*

[2] Especially the work of Rondo Cameron, David Landes, Bertrand Gille, and Maurice Lévy-Leboyer.

[3] A. Vührer, *Histoire de la dette publique en France* (2 vols.; Paris, 1886), II, 541. A five percent *rente* entitles its holder to an annual revenue of five francs. The issue price and the subsequent market value are dependent upon the going rate of interest. In 1815 the five percent *rente* fluctuated between a high of 81 francs 65 centimes and a low of 52 francs 30 centimes. To capitalize the public debt of 63.3 million francs of five percent *rentes* on January 1, 1815, one would have to multiply by approximately 15.

[4] *Ibid.*, p. 540. Almost 38 million francs of the *rentes* in 1830 were in the hands of the *Caisse d'amortissement*.

for those living outside of Paris. This innovation was the work of the minister of finance, Baron Louis, who consciously aimed at tapping the unproductive wealth of the provinces.[5] The base of potential purchasers was broadened in 1822, when the minimum *rente* which could be inscribed on the *grand-livre* was reduced from 50 to 10 francs,[6] thus reducing the minimum cost of a *rente* (in 1822) from approximately 800 francs to 160 francs.

The total debt increased only by about 20 percent during the July Monarchy (from 202.4 million francs of *rentes* to 244.3 million by March 1, 1848),[7] but the amount of it held in the provinces increased to about a third of the total. Clearly, Paris investors were divesting themselves of *rentes* for other holdings and these *rentes* were being absorbed in the provinces. This migration of the debt to the provinces during the July Monarchy freed Parisian capital for investment in private securities.

Following 1848 the number of holders of the debt greatly increased with a proportionately larger number of *rentiers* residing in the provinces. In 1847 there were 207,000 *rentiers,* of which three quarters resided in Paris. By 1854 the number had risen to 664,000, of which half lived in the departments. Many small holders were represented; 94,000 had *rentes* of 20 francs or less.[8] The public subscription, an important innovation of the Second Empire, further broadened the market for *rentes.* In 1854 the first public subscription for a loan of 250 million francs drew 98,000 subscribers, of which 72,000 were from the provinces and 26,000 from Paris.[9] This method of government borrowing was used with increasing success during the Second Empire. A loan of 450 million francs in 1868 drew 781,291 subscribers for 660,-184,270 francs of *rentes*, or 34 times greater than the amount of the loan.[10]

An important institution which helped broaden the base of in-

[5] *Ibid.,* pp. 142–43; Marcel Marion, *Histoire financière de la France depuis 1715* (6 vols.; Paris, 1914–31), V, 4–5. Of course the purchase of existing securities does not mobilize capital but merely transfers funds from one person to another.

[6] Eugene Bayard, *La Caisse d'épargne et de prévoyance de Paris* (2d ed.; Paris, 1900), p. 44. The banker, Benjamin Delessert, had proposed a reduction to five francs in 1821.

[7] Vührer, *Histoire de la dette,* II, 540.   [8] *Ibid.,* pp. 283–84.

[9] *Ibid.,* p. 284.

[10] *Ibid.,* p. 306. Anticipating a reduction of their subscriptions, it was a common practice for speculators to oversubscribe.

vestment in government securities—or "democratize the *rente*,"
to use a favorite expression of contemporaries—was the savings
bank (*caisse d'épargne*). The first *caisse d'épargne* was founded
in Paris in 1818 under the patronage of members of the *haute
banque* led by Benjamin Delessert.[11] It was founded from philan-
thropic motives and aimed at encouraging thrift in the working
class. The deposits were to be invested only in *rentes* and inscribed
in the name of the depositor, once a sum had accumulated sufficient
to purchase a 50 franc *rente* (reduced to 10 in 1822). The *rente*
could be left at the *caisse* and the interest on it credited to the
depositor's account. This initiative found many imitators in the
departments where the lead was taken by prefects, chambers of
commerce, and municipal councils in founding *caisses d'épargne*.[12]
The most active period of foundation occurred between 1834 and
1837 when 244 new *caisses* were organized.[13] By the end of 1847,
there were 354 *caisses* in operation with 175 branch offices.[14] There
were on this date 553,502 depositors with total deposits of 278,259,-
501.21 francs or an average deposit of 502.72 francs.[15] The categories of depositors[16] were:

	Percent of total depositors	*Percent of total deposits*
Workers	26	25
Professional	26	33
Domestic Servants	21	19
Minors	18	12
Soldiers and Sailors	4	6
Other	5	5
	100	100

Although the large number of depositors was impressive, and
their number continued to grow in the second half of the nine-

[11] *Bulletin des lois*, series 7 (1818), pp. 278–84, for the authorizing ordinance,
charter, and list of founders.

[12] Fernand Lepelletier, *Les caisses d'épargnes* (Paris, 1911), p. 22.

[13] Robert Bigo, *Les banques françaises au cours du XIXe siècle* (Paris, 1947),
pp. 203–4.

[14] Ministère de l'agriculture et du commerce, *Rapport au Président de la
République sur les caisses d'épargne, Année 1847* (Paris, 1851), pp. vii–viii.

[15] *Ibid.*, pp. viii–ix. These figures are for 344 *caisses*. As a result of the depression, 1847 was the first year in which total deposits declined in the course
of the year—by almost 11 million francs.

[16] *Ibid.*, p. xi.

teenth century, the *caisses* were incapable of alleviating the poverty of the poorer classes. Only the aristocracy of labor was able to make use of the service provided by them. The *caisses* failed to become the bulwark of social stability that their more sanguine promoters had hoped. Although the proportion of the debt held by the *caisses* was small (about five or six percent), they helped stabilize the market for government securities and they familiarized a large number of people, broadly dispersed throughout the country, with this form of holding.[17] The *caisses* also deserve considerable credit for preparing the success of the public subscriptions of the Second Empire.

No historian of the growth of the capital market can afford to neglect the role of newspapers, which devoted some or all of their space to matters of interest to investors. The financial press stimulated the growth of the capital market, and is a crude barometer of that growth. It is difficult to conceive of the growth and broadening of the securities market without the ready availability of current information on the state of the market and new issues.

The *Journal du Commerce,* a daily founded in 1819, was the first paper to devote much of its space to economic matters. Its focus was political as well as commercial, and it was concerned more with trade and the commodity market than with the Bourse. Not until the boom of the mid-1830s did a specialized press appear which concerned itself with the shares of joint-stock companies. Between 1835 and 1839 at least ten journals appeared, mostly weeklies, devoted to the stock market. They contained advertisements offering the shares of companies in process of formation, annual reports from management to stockholders, and current information on the state of the market. Some offered critical evaluation of various stocks. Two of them, *L'Europe Industrielle* and *La Bourse, Revue Générale des Sociétés par Actions,* served their readers as intermediaries in the buying and selling of shares, thus anticipating what became standard practice during the Second Empire. A few, such as the *Moniteur Industriel,* which was closely allied to Jacques Laffitte's Caisse Générale du Commerce et de l'Industrie, had substantial financial backing; some were organized

---

[17] The Paris *caisse* had in 1847 one third of the total depositors and slightly less than a third of total deposits.

as joint-stock companies; others were the creation of enterprisers without much substance. None of them appear to have been very profitable and only two, the *Moniteur Industriel* and the *Office de Publicité*, survived the collapse of the boom of the 1830s.[18]

The boom of the 1840s, largely dominated by the creation of companies to construct and operate railroads, saw the appearance of at least five new financial journals. The most important and successful of these was the *Journal des Chemins de Fer*, founded by an Englishman, F. E. Whitelock, in 1842. It soon extended its coverage to all important industrial companies. It became the model for other successful journals of this type founded during the Second Empire. Less successful, but still important, was the *Journal des Travaux Public*, founded in 1842 and also primarily concerned with railroads.[19]

The chief financial journals of the Second Empire were all the instrumentalities of banks interested in the negotiation of securities. They were addressed primarily to those interested in the buying and selling of securities and greatly expanded their readership in the provinces. The *Journal des Chemins de Fer*, acquired by Jules Mirès in 1848 with borrowed money, served its readers as brokers first through Mirès' Caisse des Actions Réunis, and later through the Caisse Générale des Chemins de Fer, which Mirès created in 1853. The *Journal du Crédit Public*, the *Journal des Actionnaires, l'Industrie*, and the *Journal des Travaux Publics* also possessed their *caisses*. These journals recommended shares in which their *caisse* was interested and were not above attempting to depress the price of certain shares if it served their purpose. Another important financial journal of the Second Empire, *La Semaine Financière*, served the interests of James de Rothschild.[20]

The circulation of financial journals increased greatly during the Second Empire as the number of stockholders increased. In 1850 the circulation of the *Journal des Chemins de Fer* was 2,700 and that of its rival *l'Industrie* about 1,000. By 1857 the circulation of the *Journal des Chemins de Fer* was estimated at 4,500, that of

[18] Bertrand Gille, "Etat de la presse économique et financière en France," *Histoire des entreprises*, No. 4 (1959), pp. 61–65; "A propos de l'état de la presse économique et financière en France," *Histoire des entreprises*, No. 6 (1960), pp. 78–79.
[19] Gille, "Etat de la presse économique," pp. 65–66.
[20] *Ibid.*, pp. 67–71; Rondo Cameron, *France and the Economic Development of Europe* (Princeton, 1961), pp. 131–32.

the *Journal du Crédit Public* at 6,700, and that of the *Semaine Financière* at 3,300.[21]

In addition all the large daily newspapers now possessed a financial columnist. Attested instances of their receiving some form of "payola" are numerous enough to make one conclude that the practice was general. In other newspapers the ties were more direct. Jules Mirès, the editor of the *Journal des Chemins de Fer,* controlled the financial columns not only of the progovernment newspapers the *Pays* and the *Constitutionnel,* but of the antigovernment *La Presse* and the *Courrier du Dimanche* as well. Thus, Mirès was able to reach investors of diverse political beliefs.[22] Many newspapers simply sold their financial column. The financial column of the *Gazette de France* was leased to a banker, M. Serres, for 13 years at a minimum price of 24,000 francs annually. The financial column of *l'Ami de la Religion* was sold for 24,000 francs annually for five years, and the *Journal des Villes et des Campagnes* agreed to rent its financial column for 10,000 francs annually for ten years.[23] Thus, paid advertising and editorial comment on financial matters became almost indistinguishable in most newspapers.

Along with the growth of the financial press, investment manuals designed to acquaint the prospective investor with the mechanics of speculation and the various share-issuing enterprises made their appearance. Possibly the first investment manual was L. C. Bizet-DeFrayne's *Précis des diverses manières de spéculer sur les fonds publics, et usage à la Bourse de Paris,* published in the early years of the Restoration. The third edition, which appeared in 1818 and ran to 74 pages, dealt with three types of French government securities and the shares of four private enterprises—the Bank of France and three newly formed insurance companies. Most of the volume was concerned with the usages of the Paris Bourse. It ran to at least four editions by 1821, the fourth edition being expanded to 199 pages.

Another investment manual appearing during the Restoration was by Jacques Bresson, who picked up where Bizet-DeFrayne left off. By 1830 six editions had appeared; the first edition, in 1820, contained 94 pages and the sixth edition of 1830 had grown to

[21] Louis Girard, *La politique des travaux publics du Second Empire* (Paris, 1952), p. 114n; Gille, "Etat de la presse économique, p. 68.

[22] Georges Duchêne, *La spéculation devant les tribunaux* (Paris, 1867), p. 306.

[23] *Ibid.*, pp. 103–4.

249 pages, keeping pace with the expansion of the Bourse. The seventh edition of Bresson's *Des Fonds publics français et étrangers et des opérations de la Bourse* (1834) discussed all the securities negotiated on the Paris Bourse and devoted about 70 pages (out of 276) to the techniques of the Bourse. A ninth edition of this manual appeared in 1849. From investment manuals, Bresson expanded his services to investors and launched a periodical in 1833, the *Cours Général des Actions,* which appeared twice a month. This was succeeded in 1842 by the *Cours Général de la Bourse de Paris,* which continued at least until 1861. A supplement to these periodicals on the shares of industrial enterprises was issued; it became a separate publication in the 1850s under the title of *Cours Général des Actions des Entreprises Industrielles et Commerciales.* In 1839 and 1840 Bresson also edited an *Annuaire* on joint-stock companies, but this was discontinued. In 1842 he engaged in yet another enterprise, the editing of a weekly financial journal, the *Moniteur des Chemins de Fer et de la Navigation à Vapeur,* which lasted only six months.[24] Although Bresson had many able collaborators, this journal failed, while Whitelock's *Journal des Chemins de Fer,* founded the same year, was eminently successful.

Bresson, possibly the first Frenchman to make a career as a financial publicist, appears to have done fairly well; he is listed among the stockholders of the Compagnies des Mines de la Loire in 1854 for 47 shares.

The first investment manual to give attention to shares of companies not quoted on the Paris Bourse was A. E. Sala's *Manuel des Placemens Industriels* (1836). Sala gave information on 73 companies, including 38 *sociétés anonymes* and 33 *sociétés en commandite,*[25] of which only half were quoted on the Paris Bourse. The shares of the other companies were negotiated by the Coulisse, a counterpart to the Bourse, which, although tolerated by the authorities, was not legally recognized. Sala advised investors to seek security of their capital and a return higher than that of government *rentes.* He also advised investors not to invest all their funds in a single enterprise and to give constant attention to their investments.

[24] Gille, "Etat de la presse économique," p. 65.
[25] Two were *sociétés civiles.*

A more comprehensive manual, Emile Bères *Manuel de l'action-naire*, appeared in 1839. It contained information on more than 200 companies, including 109 *sociétés anonymes* and 103 *sociétés en commandite*, of which less than half were quoted on the Paris Bourse. Bères devoted considerable space to delineating the advantages and disadvantages of the two types of joint-stock companies. He also warned investors to take account of the price of shares and the revenue of the enterprise and avoid those with a low yield.

Investment manuals enjoyed an even greater vogue during the Second Empire, as the number of securities and the number of investors increased enormously. The most popular manual was that of Alphonse Courtois, the financial columnist of the *Journal des Economistes*. Courtois' *Manuel des fonds publics et des sociétés par actions* went through five editions between 1856 and 1863, each edition growing longer. The success enjoyed by this manual continued into the early years of the Third Republic. The shares of foreign companies were included, mirroring the wider ranging interests of French investors. Courtois was also the author of a popular *Traité élémentaire des opérations de bourse*, which went through eleven editions from 1867 to 1892.

Unique among nineteenth-century French investment manuals was the *Manuel du Spéculateur à la Bourse* by the prominent socialist thinker, Pierre J. Proudhon, which appeared anonymously in 1854. For this work Proudhon received a large advance of 1,500 francs from the publisher, Charles Garnier.[26] The *Manuel*, which Proudhon initially regarded as unpleasant hack work, enjoyed considerable success, achieving five editions by 1857. The enlarged third edition (1856) was the first on which the author's name appeared, thus reflecting a change in Proudhon's attitude toward the work.

The prospective investor undoubtedly found more in this manual than he was seeking. Over 200 of the 511 pages of the fifth edition are devoted to an explanation, analysis, and condemnation of the *féodalité industrielle* of the Second Empire. Unlike the writers of other investment manuals, Proudhon treated his reader to a comprehensive discussion of speculation and its institutional framework. Pitfalls for the investor are fully treated; techniques of short

[26] George Woodcock, *Pierre-Joseph Proudhon* (New York, 1956), p. 190.

selling and the use of margin are explained, accompanied by arithmetic examples. The role of the entrepreneur and risk taking are discussed in terms reminiscent of Joseph Schumpeter. Proudhon denied that piecemeal reforms could cure the ills of the system; what was needed was a drastic reshaping of French society. This must have struck a discordant note with the investing bourgeoisie.

The role of this genre of literature in the growth of the capital market is difficult to assess. Certainly it reflected the growth of the capital market and contributed to that growth, though perhaps only in a minor way, by helping familiarize the investing public, both in Paris and in the departments, with the nature of the securities market. Investment manuals, with the aid of the financial press, helped prepare many sheep for the shearing.

In 1815 the Bourse of Paris quoted only four securities: 5 percent *rentes,* the shares of the Bank of France, the Midi Canal, and Trois Vieux Ponts sur la Seine. The total nominal capital of these four securities totaled only about 1.5 billion francs.[27] By 1820 the shares of six recently created insurance companies had been added, plus *rentes* and bonds (*obligations*) of the City of Paris, and the bonds of the City of Bordeaux. One foreign security had also appeared—Neapolitan *rentes.* During the following decade the number of French securities grew to 30 and the number of foreign securities increased to seven. The most important domestic additions were securities of canal companies formed in the 1820s, including capital shares with a fixed return guaranteed by the state and participation shares (*actions de jouissance*), which provided for participating in the net revenues of the canals above a certain level. Although approximately 100 *sociétés anonymes* were organized in the 1820s,[28] except for canals and some insurance companies, only the shares of the Caisse Hypothécaire and the Compagnie des Salines et Mines de Sel de l'Est were quoted on the Bourse. The Paris Bourse did not list the shares of any *sociétés en commandite* in 1830.

The boom of the mid-1830s marked the beginning of a significant expansion of the Paris Bourse. By 1840 the list of shares

---

[27] Edmond Théry, "Les valeurs mobilièrs en France," *Congrès International des Valeurs Mobilières, Documents* (4 vols.; Paris, 1900), II, 2.

[28] Charles E. Freedeman, "Joint Stock Business Organization in France 1807–1867," *Business History Review,* XXXIX (1965), 201.

quoted saw the addition of banks (other than the Bank of France), the first railroads, and mining and metallurgical companies. Approximately 40 banks and insurance companies, 13 railroads, and 23 mining and metallurgical companies were listed, which together comprised about half the total number of securities quoted in 1840. The shares of some *sociétés en commandite* had also appeared.

Although the depression of 1846–47 and the Revolution of 1848 caused a temporary setback, the growth of the Paris Bourse was resumed during the Second Empire. The number of domestic securities quoted on the Paris Bourse increased from 90 in 1850 to 298 by the end of 1869, and the nominal capital represented by these securities increased from 8,980 million francs to 25,612 million francs.[29] In addition, French investors spent perhaps 10 billion francs for foreign securities during the Second Empire.[30]

Other institutions also channeled savings into the securities of joint-stock companies. Since only a minority of all issues were admitted to quotation on the Paris Bourse, a large number of issues were floated through the intermediary of banks and traded by *coulissiers* and other unofficial brokers. Provincial stock exchanges —Lyons, Marseilles, Bordeaux, Toulouse, and Lille—were also important. Lyons was the largest of the provincial bourses, having been an important money market since the Middle Ages. In 1845, 77 securities were quoted on the Lyons Bourse. By 1860 the number had increased to 136, including 44 gas companies, 17 foundries, seven steamship companies, and eight bridge companies, in addition to government securities and railroad issues, both domestic and foreign.[31] Many of these issues were for local industries whose capital was entirely supplied from the Lyons area.

New investors were undoubtedly attracted to the market by the declining denomination of shares. Before 1830 the par value of most shares was 1,000 to 5,000 francs; after 1830 an increasing number of companies emitted shares of 500 francs or less. Almost all railroads issued 500-franc shares. Rarely did the par value of

[29] Pierre Dupont-Ferrier, *Le marché financier de Paris sous le Second Empire* (Paris, 1926), p. 241.

[30] This is a rough estimate. Rondo Cameron has estimated the total capital export in the period 1850–70 at approximately twelve billion francs. Not all of it went into securities. "The Credit Mobilier and the Economic Development of Europe," *Journal of Political Economy*, LXI (1953), 461.

[31] Jean Bouvier, *Le Crédit Lyonnais de 1863 à 1882* (2 vols.; Paris, 1961), I, 121.

the shares of *sociétés anonymes,* whose charters had to meet standards established by the Conseil d'Etat, fall below this figure. By contrast, the promoters of *sociétés en commandite par actions* were free to set any par value they chose. Some *commandites* issued shares with a par value of 100 francs or less to attract less affluent speculators.

Two innovations involving security differentiation were especially noteworthy: one was the issue of *actions au porteur,* or bearer shares, the second the use of *obligations,* or bonds, to raise additional funds for existing enterprises. After 1815 a growing number of companies issued *actions au porteur,* either in part or entirely. Some companies left it to the option of the shareholder whether or not his shares would be *nominative* or *au porteur.* On *nominative* shares the name of the owner appeared on the share certificate and the share was inscribed in his name on the books of the company. Bearer shares, which were not issued by British or American companies, were popular because they satisfied the predilection of many French businessmen for secrecy. The major disadvantage of bearer shares was the possibility of their being lost or stolen. Even the French government instituted *rentes au porteur* to satisfy the desire for anonymity of some investors.

The other innovation was the issue of *obligations,* which are the French equivalent of American bonds and English debentures. They were not important before the 1840s, although some were issued.[32] They became significant only when railroad companies began to issue them in large amounts in the 1840s to complete construction of their lines. These railroads resorted to *obligations* to avoid depressing the market for shares already issued, or for fear that new equities could not find ready takers. At first they were issued in denominations of 1,000 francs or more. Not until 1847 was the "democratic" obligation of 300 francs issued, pioneered by Paulin Talabot and Emile Péreire.[33] These offered more security than capital shares and they competed with government *rentes* because of their slightly higher rate of return. The Second Empire was the great age of low-priced *obligations.* Without them the completion of the French railway network would have been

---

[32] Bertrand Gille, *La banque et le crédit en France de 1815 à 1848* (Paris, 1959), pp. 159–60.

[33] Jean Bouvier, *Les Rothschild* (Paris, 1960), pp. 143–44; Louis Girard, *La politique des travaux publics du Second Empire* (Paris, 1952), p. 47.

more difficult. They fulfilled the same need in France as preference shares in Britain. The additional fund requirements of railroads were huge because initial construction costs had been greatly and habitually underestimated; *obligations* were also issued in large amounts during the Second Empire to construct connecting and feeder lines. The companies, after 1852, preferred to issue *obligations,* rather than equities, to maintain high dividends on their capital shares.[34] By the end of 1856, the railroads had raised 1,324 million francs by *obligations* as compared with 1,181 million francs raised through equities.[35] The six main lines issued over 1.8 billion francs of *obligations* during the period 1862–67.[36] Their successful use by the railroads found many imitators among other companies. Certainly they attracted the funds of small savers, many of whom would have declined to risk buying equities. Among the 4,100 holders of *obligations* in the small railroad line from Graissessac to Béziers in 1862 were 596 domestics, 212 concierges, 325 workers, 646 salaried employees (*employés*), 475 widowed or single women, and 313 cultivators.[37] Not all of those listed above were small savers, but most of them undoubtedly were. Few foreign investors were attracted by the *obligations* of French companies.

The 1830s and the succeeding decades also saw a great increase in the number of individuals, many of whom were from the provinces, purchasing the shares of private companies. The number of shares available greatly increased with railroad companies alone adding a billion francs' worth of shares in the 1840s. The *haute banque,* which acted as an intermediary in company formation and the placement of shares, found it necessary to seek new sources of funds by the 1840s; their clientele was too limited to absorb the shares of railroads for which a wider range of investors was necessary. New investors, responding to the publicity of the financial press, acted independently. During the Second Empire, joint-stock investment banks, relying heavily on the new techniques of publicity, played an increasingly important role in company formation and placing shares.

[34] Girard, *La politique des travaux publics,* p. 149.
[35] *Ibid.,* p. 181.
[36] *Ibid.,* p. 293. Many railway bonds carried government guarantees.
[37] *Ibid.,* p. 207n.

Railroad companies led the way in attracting new shareholders. The list of original shareholders in the Bordeaux to Cette line, authorized in 1846, contained about 10,800 names, for an average of 26 shares per stockholder. Only 477 held more than 100 shares.[38] Since many of the original subscribers were only speculating on an immediate rise, the shares had a tendency to be spread more widely after a brief period. A report of the Board of Directors of the Nord Railroad in 1846 stated that in a period of little more than three months (from October 28, 1845, to January 31, 1846), 571,741 shares had been transferred: 8,884 persons had sold shares and they had been purchased by 17,496 persons. On the latter date the line's 400,000 shares were held by about 18,000 stockholders, an average of 22 shares per stockholder.[39] Of the 16,365 shareholders of the Paris-Lyon, only 1,123 possessed more than 50 shares in 1848.[40] In the same year the *Journal des Chemins de Fer* estimated that 200,000 persons held railroad shares,[41] a number only slightly less than those holding government *rentes*.

In most other companies shareholding tended to be more concentrated, but nevertheless a tendency toward the dispersion of shareholders, both in size of holding and geographically, can be discerned. The Compagnie des Mines de la Loire, which comprised most of the mines of the Loire area, was organized in 1845, but attacks on it as a dangerous monopoly and government pressure forced its division into four separate companies in 1854. At that time stockholders in the old company received equivalent shares in each of the four new companies. Each of the new companies had 80,000 shares, divided according to size of holding and geographically as in Tables 1 and 2.[42]

The average number of shares per shareholder was 41.5. Among the small holders, those with less than ten shares, 350 out of a total of 752, resided in the Paris area. The geographical distribu-

[38] *Bulletin des lois, Partie supplémentaire* (9th series), XXX (1846), 247–362.

[39] P. J. Proudhon, *Manuel du Spéculateur à la Bourse* (5th ed.; Paris, 1857), pp. 155–56.

[40] A.-J. Tudesq, "La crise de 1847, vue par les mileux d'affaires parisiens," *Bibliothèque de la Révolution de 1848*, Vol. XIX, *Aspects de la crise et la depression, 1848–1851* (La Roche-sur-Yon, 1956), p. 9.

[41] *Ibid.*

[42] Compiled from the shareholder list: *Bulletin des lois, Partie supplémentaire* (11th series), V (1855), 186–248.

tion shows stockholders residing in 64 departments in France, largely concentrated in the Paris and Lyons areas. The Loire Department, where the mines were located, was a distant third. Of foreign holdings, Swiss investment was appreciable. The geo-

Table 1. Share Distribution

Shares	Number of Shareholders	Percent of Total Shareholders	Percent of Total Shares
1–9	752	39.0	3.5
10–49	783	41.0	20.6
50–99	207	11.0	15.9
100–499	154	8.0	35.6
500–999	11	.5	8.9
1,000 or more	9	.5	15.4
Total	1,916	100.0	99.9

graphical concentration of shareholding partly reflects areas where the output of the mines was marketed, namely the area around

Table 2. Geographical Distribution

	Number of Shareholders	Percent of Shareholders	Percent of Total Shares
Seine Department (Paris)	734	38.3	28.9
Rhône Department (Lyons)	557	29.0	42.8
Loire Department	87	4.5	8.9
61 Other Departments	312	16.3	9.2
Switzerland	209	10.9	9.8
Other Foreign	6	.3	.1
Unknown	11	.6	.2
Total	1,916	99.9	99.9

the upper Rhône and Loire valleys and in Paris. The dispersion in 61 other departments reflects the growing disposition of provincial capitalists to invest in the shares of private companies, other than railroads and local enterprise.

The Société Générale Algérienne, a bank, was authorized as a *société anonyme* in 1866, with a capital of 100 million francs divided into 200,000 shares, of which only 50,000 shares of 500 francs each were emitted.[43]

Table 3. Share Distribution

Shares	Number of Shareholders	Percent of Total Shareholders	Percent of Total Shares
1–9	1,715	67.6	8.9
10–49	631	24.9	21.8
50–99	89	3.5	9.9
100–499	90	3.5	28.4
500–999	6	.2	6.0
1,000 or more	6	.2	25.0
Total	2,537	99.9	100.0

Of the 2,537 shareholders in the company, slightly over two thirds were small shareholders, holding less than ten shares. The

Table 4. Geographical Distribution

	Number of Shareholders	Percent of Shareholders	Percent of Total Shares
86 Metropolitan Departments	1,616	63.7	41.7
Seine Department	721	28.4	55.1
Algeria	176	6.9	1.7
Foreign	8	.3	1.2
Unknown	16	.6	.3
Total	2,537	99.9	100.0

average holding was 19.7 shares. If one subtracts the 6,500 shares held by large institutional holders in Paris (Société Générale, 5,000; Bischoffsheim, Goldschmidt et Cie., 1,000; and Hentsch-Lutscher et Cie., 500), the shares held in metropolitan France were almost equally divided between Paris and 86 other departments, with investors in the departments outnumbering those in

[43] *Bulletin des lois, Partie supplémentaire* (11th series), XXVIII (1866), 1037–89. The Société Générale played a prominent role in the founding of this enterprise and three of its directors became directors of the Société Générale Algérienne. Three other directors were directors of the Crédit Foncier, two were directors of the PLM, and two of the Messageries Impériales.

Paris by more than two to one. Only one department, the Lozère, had no shareholders.

By 1870 the French securities market had come to play a central role in capital formation. Negotiable securities had become, along with landed property, an acceptable and desirable form of wealth. From the limited Paris market in 1815, the securities market by 1870 had become a national market capable of mobilizing a substantial portion of the savings of the whole nation.

Many writers have emphasized the *rentier* mentality of the French saver, and certainly a large portion of French savings went for the purchase of French and foreign government securities, both state and local, and the bonds of railroads and other enterprises. But large amounts of risk capital were also raised for the shares of enterprise, especially from the transportation, mining, metallurgical, and financial sectors of the economy. It seems probable that at least one third of the total amount absorbed by negotiable securities was risk capital. The booms of 1835–39, 1842–46, and 1852–56 do not indicate any reluctance on the part of French investors to run risks. During these booms large amounts of capital were raised by enterprises organized as *sociétés en commandite par actions*, which, unlike the *société anonyme*, did not require government authorization.

Also, the picture of the French investor that one receives from jurists, government officials and parliamentary debates during the booms of the 1830s, and again during the 1850s, is exactly the reverse of the cautious *rentier*. In official eyes, the French investor was a reckless plunger, who required regulatory legislation to protect him from his own enthusiasm. Legislation was actually passed in 1856, which virtually destroyed the *commandite par actions* as a form of organization for large enterprise.[44]

Certainly the *"rentier* mentality" was present, but it should not be assumed that this attitude was all-pervading in France. That about two thirds of French savings went into securities with a fixed return may indicate something about the availability of this type of security. Enough risk capital was forthcoming to show that the

[44] Charles E. Freedeman, "The Coming of Free Incorporation in France, 1850–1867," *Explorations in Entrepreneurial History* (2d series), IV, no. 3 (1967), pp. 213–17.

French investor was not adverse to this type of investment. Perhaps the scope of entrepreneurial *opportunity* was as important in determining the proportion of *rentier* and risk capital as the attitude of the French saver.

Negotiable securities were issued by two types of joint-stock enterprise: the *société anonyme* and the *société en commandite par actions*. The first required the authorization of the government; the second could be freely formed. *Sociétés anonymes,* although not numerous, served for large enterprise in transport, mining, metallurgy, and the financial sector. About 616 *sociétés anonymes* appeared between 1817 and 1867, an average of twelve per year, with an initial nominal capitalization exceeding four billion francs.[45] They remained the preserve of a small group or groups, who alone were able to get the necessary government authorization. But the *commandite par actions* was open to anyone. Moreover, this type of enterprise favored the entrepreneur by legally prohibiting stockholder control over the enterprise. They provided opportunities for new men and new enterprise. They were formed in large numbers from the 1830s until the restrictive law of 1856. During the period 1840–59, an average of 218 *commandites par actions* were formed annually.[46] Although adequate statistical data on their capitalization is lacking, enough information is available to attest to their importance. When their role in the economy has been further explored, the claims of some regarding the lack of risk capital and the unenterprising character of the French entrepreneur may be still further attenuated.

[45] Freedeman, "Joint Stock Business Organization in France, 1807–1867," *Business History Review*, XXXIX, 198, 201.
[46] *Ibid.*, p. 202.

The Journal d'agriculture pratique and the Peasant Question during the July Monarchy and the Second Republic

CHARLES K. WARNER

UNIVERSITY OF KANSAS

AROUND 1750 there had begun, in France, that continuing debate, with all its social, political, and economic overtones, on the merits of large agricultural properties versus small ones[1] or, to put it in its eighteenth-century context, the advantages of the large-scale agriculture then emerging in England as opposed to peasant small holding. Although there were some dissenting opinions, the majority of *agronomes*—the physiocratic influence was strong here—favored larger enclosed farms and greater investment of capital in agricultural enterprise on the English model.[2] This was a bias that left little room for the peasant small holder, and we can easily agree with Marc Bloch's verdict that the "boldest" of the *agronomes* "did not draw back from the eternal tragedy of the betterment of humanity. They wanted progress and accepted the fact that it would create victims."[3] There is also Lefebvre's conclusion that the French Revolution ignored both the aspirations and the condition of the "immense majority" of peasants.[4]

[1] The most pertinent summary is still Michel Augé-Laribé, *Grande ou petite propriété?* (Montpellier, 1902).

[2] On this point, see André J. Bourde, *The Influence of England on the French Agronomes 1750–1789* (Cambridge, 1953), pp. 95–106.

[3] Marc Bloch, *Les caractères originaux de l'histoire rurale française,* I (new edition; Paris, 1964), 234.

[4] Georges Lefebvre, "La Révolution française et les paysans," *Annales historiques de la Révolution française,* 1933, pp. 97–128.

By contrast, the period covered in this essay showed an unprecedented concern for the peasantry. It was expressed on a broad front—social, political, and literary—ranging, to give a few examples, from the sociological investigations of J.-A. Blanqui and the rustic novels of George Sand to Hippolyte Carnot's exhortation to "gallant peasants" to stand for election to the National Assembly in 1848.[5] What interests us here, however, is the manner in which this concern was shared by an elite made up of agronomists, enlightened proprietors, government officials, rural economists, and others whose primary interest was in an improved agriculture—a group that, except for its defense of small holding, closely resembled the *agronomes* of the eighteenth century.[6]

This group finds its collective voice in the *Journal d'agriculture pratique*, which, from its founding in 1837, was one of the principal organs of agricultural progress in France and, until the Second Empire, a forthright and independent commentator on the political, social, and economic aspects of the agrarian scene.[7] As one turns the pages of the *Journal* for the first two decades of its

[5] Jérome-Adolphe Blanqui, "Tableau des populations rurales de la France en 1850," *Séances des travaux de l'Académie des sciences morales et politiques* (2d series), VIII (1850), 313–34, IX (1851), 145–71, X (1851), 125–43; George Sand, *La mare au diable* (1846), *La petite Fadette* (1848), *François le champi* (1850); Hippolyte Carnot, *Le Ministère de l'instruction publique et des cultes depuis le 24 Février jusqu'au 5 Juillet 1848* (Paris, 1848), pp. 24, 31.

[6] By the middle of the nineteenth century the word *agronome* had a more scientific connotation. This is why I have resisted the temptation to call this group "latter-day" or "nineteenth-century" *agronomes*. For the changing meaning of the word, compare the entry "Agronome" in Abbé Rozier, *Cours complet d'Agriculture . . . ou dictionnaire universel d'Agriculture* (Paris, 1785), I, 288, with A. de Gasparin, "L'Agronome, le Cultivateur et l'Agriculteur" in "Variétés," *Journal d'agriculture pratique* (hereafter referred to as *JAP*), 1850, p. 256.

[7] Discussion of these topics was much curtailed by the Empire's censorship. After 1867 the *Journal* became closely associated with the *Société d'Agriculteurs de France*, a conservative large-landowner's group, and lost its earlier liberal orientation.

Contributors of articles on the nontechnical aspects of agriculture during the period covered by this essay included J.-A. Blanqui, Michel Chevalier, the statistician Moreau de Jonnès, Cavour, Royer-Collard, and the economists Leonce de Lavergne and Lullin de Chateauvieux. Writing on more purely agricultural topics were Mathieu de Dombasle and the Count Adrien de Gasparin, two of the foremost agricultural personalities of the time, although, like many lesser agricultural figures, they also submitted articles on rural and political economy. The Count de Gasparin, for example, was one of the staunchest defenders of small property from a social as well as an economic point of view, and it is significant that Dombasle on his famous model farm at Roville experimented with methods best suited for small or medium-sized properties with little capital at their disposal. A study of the *Journal*'s early contributors and their definition as a group form the subject-matter of a work in progress by the present writer.

existence, one cannot fail to be struck by the insistence, even vehemence, with which peasant small ownership was defended—this at a time when excessive subdivision (*morcellement*) of the soil was being increasingly criticized in France[8] and comparisons, damaging for France, were being made between the productivity of French and British agriculture, some of these in the pages of the *Journal* itself.[9]

The *Journal d'agriculture pratique,* it should be explained, did not press its support of small holding to the exclusion of larger properties. Large and medium-sized farms with sufficient capital at their disposal had, in fact, an indispensable role to play as pace-setters for an improved agriculture, but agricultural progress could, indeed would have to operate through small peasant proprietors.[10] Also, were not "14 million *cotes foncières* paid by 6 million heads of families . . . representing 24 million French a guarantee of order and stability?"[11] According to the *Journal,* however, the miracles of agricultural progress and social stability were not to be achieved by the simple accession of peasants to property. The peasant also needed education and financial credit, and he needed to play a larger role in the economic and social life of the nation.

The peasantry's expanded role was to be effected, in part, through participation in the election and deliberations of chambers of agriculture where it was hoped the peasant's horizons would be broadened, at least to the point where he would realize that his real interests were those of all agriculture. Easy credit would make it possible for peasants to raise the level of their productivity, which, in turn, would help free them from various forms of tenantry. Finally, the need of schooling for a largely illiterate class was obvious, but a system of agricultural education, particularly at a basic practical level, was considered equally necessary. As in the defense

[8] Augé-Laribé, *Grande ou petite propriété?,* pp. 51–89.

[9] Especially Michel Chevalier, "Revue bibliographique," *JAP,* 1845–46, pp. 258–62. The *Journal* gives the somewhat paradoxical impression of appearing to admire the techniques of English agriculture at the same time that it criticized the English agrarian structure.

[10] The following are not untypical: "The whole future of agricultural production lies in *morcellement* and small rural property." Lefour, "Des votes des conseils généraux dans les questions agricoles," *JAP,* 1837–38, p. 195; "But small holding should grow even more. . . . We repeat . . . in our time the small proprietor is the big producer." "Chronique agricole . . . ," *JAP,* 1841–42, p. 285.

[11] D'Angeville, "Inconvénients du morcellement de la propriété," *JAP,* 1843–44, p. 541. This title is misleading. As the quotation suggests, the writer is in favor of *morcellement.*

of small holding, one cannot fail to be impressed by the space devoted to these three topics in the *Journal* during the 1840s and early 1850s.

At the same time, similar proposals figured to an extraordinary degree in the deliberations of the societies of agriculture and the various agricultural congresses.[12] But here where agriculture's pleas for "equal treatment" with commerce and industry were most often heard, the *Journal*'s more exclusively social concern for the peasantry was confounded with considerations of prestige and advantage for the agricultural establishment. Thus, for example, the question of rural credit was most often broached by attacking the difference in rates between mortgage notes and the less expensive commercial loans (generally unavailable to the agriculturist). This approach overlooked the fact that, in any case, bank credit was seldom applied for or extended to the peasantry, whose chief source of borrowing remained the village usurer. Likewise, to give another example, demand in the 1840s for an institute of higher learning in agriculture only remotely concerned the peasantry, but it was intimately connected with agriculture's desire to imitate commerce's and industry's prestigious schools.[13] But the problem of mixed motives and its attendant difficulties for the *Journal*'s position is, perhaps, best illustrated in the campaign for the chambers of agriculture.

For all that it was criticized for favoring industry and commerce, the July Monarchy offered at least one notable encouragement to agriculture. Building on foundations laid in the previous regime, it stimulated, through increased and more regular subsidies, a rapid expansion of societies of agriculture on the departmental and

[12] Such topics as tariffs, taxes, land-clearing, and rural roads may have been of more immediate concern to the congress delegates, but these involved questions of priorities and conflicting regional interests, and the conditions of their formulation varied from year to year. Chambers of agriculture, rural credit, and agricultural education, on the other hand, occupied an unvaryingly central position on the annual lists of resolutions and provoked the liveliest of discussions.

My conclusions in this portion of the essay have been based on summaries of the annual meetings of the Central Congress of Agriculture at Paris, the *comptes rendus in extenso* of several regional congresses, and an examination of the proceedings of various local societies of agriculture.

[13] Particularly the following: *Conservatoire des arts at métiers* (1819), *L'Ecole centrale des arts et manufactures* (1825), *Ecole spéciale de commerce* (1820).

arrondissement level and committees of agriculture or *comices agricoles* in the cantons.[14] A rough estimate for the whole Restoration period notes the existence of 100 societies of agriculture and only 10 *comices*.[15] An 1844 estimate puts the number of *comices* at 800 and the number of societies at 200 to 300.[16] In addition, out of these groups grew important regional associations—the oldest dates from 1832. These were also eligible for subsidies and held annual congresses to which the societies and *comices* sent delegates. An outgrowth of the regional congresses was the Central Congress of French Agriculture which first met at Paris in 1844.

At about the same time that this expansion began, the government reorganized the general councils of commerce, manufactures, and agriculture.[17] Although the reorganization brought some improvements in its wake—agriculture, for example, was promoted from a desk in the Ministry of the Interior to twin billing with commerce in a new ministry—it otherwise could not have been better designed to feed agriculture's inferiority complex, to remind it, in Michelet's words, that it was the "forgotten older sister of industry." [18] A brief look at the composition of the councils will show why this was so and why the great majority of congresses, societies, and *comices* should have constantly demanded the formation of chambers of agriculture.

The General Council of Commerce had thirty-five members en-

[14] Some of the societies traced their origins to the ancien régime. Twenty of them along with thirty affiliated *bureaux* were chartered between 1757 and 1789. They were suppressed in 1793. In 1798, the former *Société Royale* at Paris was reconstituted as the *Société libre* of the Department of The Seine and chartered as the *Société Imperiale d'agriculture* in 1804. By the end of the empire there were 51 societies of agriculture in existence. However, it was the Decazes ministry (1819–20), under the Restoration, which gave the societies a new lease on life and instituted the *comices*.

For the societies during the ancien régime, see Douglas Dakin, *Turgot and the Ancien Régime in France* (London, 1939, New York, 1965), pp. 79–91; Emile Justin, *Les sociétés royales d'agriculture au XVIIIe siècle* (Saint-Lô, 1935); E. Labiche, *Les sociétés d'agriculture au XVIIIe siècle* (Paris, 1908); Henri Sée, *La vie économique et les classes sociales en France au XVIIIe siècle* (Paris, 1924), pp. 5–24.

[15] Anacharsis Combes, "Des sociétés agricoles et de la nécessité de les réorganiser," *JAP*, 1839–40, p. 339.

[16] Lefour, "Session du Congrès central de l'agriculture française," *JAP*, 1843–44, p. 385.

[17] *Ordonnance* of 29 April 1831. *Ordonnances* of 2 March and 19 September 1836.

[18] Jules Michelet, *Le peuple* (centennial ed.; Paris, 1946), p. 45.

tirely elected from their own membership by each of the chambers of commerce in the kingdom. The General Council of Manufactures had twenty members elected from their own membership by each of twenty consultative chambers of arts and manufactures in different cities and forty members chosen by the Minister of Agriculture and Commerce. The General Council of Agriculture was composed of only "thirty proprietors or members of societies of agriculture" entirely chosen by the minister. The councils deliberated separately on matters within their own competence or jointly on matters of common concern, but decisions had to be examined by the three councils meeting as one and were voted by simple majority. By this arrangement agriculture saw itself perpetually doomed to the position of an inferior estate. But worse, from the general councils decisions were submitted for final recommendations to a Superior Council of Commerce, whose name, as the society of agriculture of Clermont pointed out, "indicates well enough . . . whose interests are preferred." [19]

To help correct this situation, a bill was presented to the Chamber of Deputies in 1840 calling for consultative chambers of agriculture in every Department. These were to be composed of one member from each canton elected by an assembly composed of "notable agriculturalists" designated by the municipal councils of each commune. The chambers in every two adjoining departments were to combine to elect two candidates, one of whom would be chosen by the Minister of Agriculture and Commerce for the General Council of Agriculture. In addition the minister was to appoint 12 members of his own selection for a council totalling 54.

This was, of course, a very moderate bid falling quite short of equal representation for agriculture in the councils. More advanced proposals supported by the *Journal d'agriculture pratique* called for direct and democratic election of chambers in every Department each of which would send one of their members to a Superior Council of Agriculture reporting directly to a separate Ministry of Agriculture.[20] Nevertheless, an only slightly improved

[19] *La Société d'Agriculture de Clermont (Oise) à M. le Ministre de l'Agriculture et Commerce,* reprinted in "Des chambres consultatives d'agriculture," JAP, 1839–40, pp. 304–7.
[20] "Des chambres consultatives d'agriculture," JAP, 1839–40, pp. 304–7; Combes, "Des sociétés agricoles," JAP, 1839–40, pp. 337–44; "Chronique agricole . . . ," JAP, 1840–41, pp. 184–85.

version of the 1840 bill was discussed and reported in and out of committee, but it remained a dead letter on the eve of 1848.[21]

This we can believe was deliberate. There is evidence including a circular letter to the prefects which indicates that the July Monarchy was concerned as to how "purely agricultural" the proposed chambers would be.[22] Given the temper of the times, there were grounds for such suspicions, but it may be noted that after 1848 and the establishment of universal suffrage demand for the chambers was as insistent as ever.

More interesting from our point of view is another question raised in the circular letter just mentioned. The prefects were directed to ask why the aspirations of agriculture were not already satisfied by the *comices*, the societies, the congresses, the General Council of Agriculture, and the Superior Council of Commerce, which had, according to the circular, "representatives of agriculture" sitting on it.[23] Also, why didn't agriculture feel it was represented in the departmental and *arrondissement* councils and in the chambers of peers and deputies? This enumeration, copied from the letter, is almost plaintive. It is as though the government, having helped create hundreds of agricultural assemblies, was now afraid of being overwhelmed like the sorcerer's apprentice by hundreds more. But the question is a good one.

One answer was that the societies and *comices* were primarily committed to the promotion of good agriculture. Why not have a division of labor and leave matters of agricultural policy to the chambers of agriculture? This makes apparent sense, but it must be remembered that the main business of the congresses, which were composed of representatives from the societies and *comices*, was the filing of resolutions on agricultural policy. Also, the existence of the congresses did not inhibit the societies and even the

[21] The government, however, raised the membership of the General Council of Agriculture to 54 (*Ordonnance* of 20 October 1841).

[22] *Circulaire* of 1 August 1840. Gouin, Minister of Agriculture and Commerce, to the Prefects. Quoted in "Chronique agricole . . . ," *JAP*, 1840–41, pp. 184–85.

[23] The president of the General Council of Agriculture was *ex officio* a member of the Superior Council of Commerce. The attributions of the 30 members of the Superior Council are listed in the *Almanach Royal*. Only one attribution, that of the president of the General Council of Agriculture, was specifically agricultural, although most of the peers, deputies, and *conseillers d'état* who constituted a majority in the Superior Council were undoubtedly landowners. None of them, however, was what might be called an "agricultural personality."

comices from firing off letters to the Minister of Agriculture and Commerce when they felt like it. From all accounts, they had both the inclination and the time to deliberate agricultural policy. Of course, there is a difference between gratuitous advice and the quasi-official advice planned for the chambers. But this does not mean that the societies could not have been reorganized to do the job.

This was proposed by one society as early as 1839,[24] and again in 1845 by the government,[25] but received little or no support from the congresses. The societies, it seems, valued their independence and exclusiveness and feared both the entanglement with the government and the broadening of their membership involved in making them into representative bodies. The *Journal d'agriculture pratique*, by the same token, seemed to favor the chambers precisely because it believed the societies, *comices*, and congresses could not or would not widen their membership to include the peasant.

The societies were, in effect, provincial academies. Their membership, recruited from the local elite, was fixed by their charters, with vacancies filled by election as they occurred. In the *Journal's* least complimentary view they were "bourgeois et parfois litteraire,"[26] a place where the "poets of the prefecture" gathered.[27] This is undoubtedly severe. The *Journal's* attitude toward the societies might best be described as ambivalent. They were important agents in the diffusion of new agricultural techniques and, in company with the *comice*, propagandists for good farming. Enlightened proprietors and others interested in the welfare of the peasantry did not stand outside them, and the *Journal* was hopeful in its praise of their good work.[28]

[24] "Adresse de la Société d'agriculture de Compiegne au ministre du Commerce," quoted in "Chronique agricole . . . ," *JAP*, 1839–40, pp. 33–34.
[25] "Chronique agricole . . . ," *JAP*, 1845–46, p. 73.
[26] *Ibid.*   [27] "Chronique agricole . . . ," *JAP*, 1839–40, p. 180.
[28] Not to be included in the category of good works were long papers on local antiquities, the natural history of exotic flora and fauna, and other nonagricultural subjects, not to mention the occasional poem. These were balanced, however, by an impressive volume of papers on new fertilizers, rotations, and crops, and by what appears to be a very lively correspondence with other societies on useful topics. Some societies offered noteworthy encouragements to local farmers to improve their methods, underwrote model farms, and even offered low-cost loans and medical assistance to peasants.
There is a great need for a special study of the societies in this period on the scale of that done for the ancien régime (see above n. 14). For an interest-

But the criticism of the composition of their membership appears justified. In 1839, for example, the Society of Seine-Inférieure had 45 members including two honorary ones, the prefect and the mayor of Rouen.[29] Of the 45, only 21 listed themselves as proprietors, and of these seven listed additional vocations such as deputy, pharmacist, or municipal councilor. Among those not listing themselves as proprietors were six lawyers, an abbé, a merchant, and an architect. About half the members lived in Rouen. It should be added there were seven nobles, a rather low number; the Society of Cher, for example, with a smaller membership, had thirteen.[30] Clearly there was not much room for a peasant in these organizations.

In principle the *comice* was more accessible to the peasant. Membership was open to anyone who could pay dues, usually of from five to ten francs a year. But even if the ordinary peasant could afford to sacrifice this sum—ten francs was the price of a fat pig— he was, from contemporary accounts, hardly more likely to sit down with "ceux du bourg" than they were to welcome him. The *comice*, however, at least came into contact with the peasant once a year. The occasion was the annual agricultural show, where prizes of money and medals were given for the best farm animals, the best managed farms, plowing contests, and, in what was usually the emotional high point of the day, awards were made to farm servants for long service on a particular farm. There is a faithful and entertaining description of one of these events, during the July Monarchy, in Flaubert's *Madame Bovary*. It also gives a clue to the weaknesses of the *comice*.

Often the agricultural show was the *comice*'s only function and often it degenerated into a political and social field day where "the leading people gave themselves a party at the expense of the state." [31] Also, in at least one case, the political speeches went on for so long that the prizes were never distributed.[32] The *Journal*

---

ing but tantalizingly brief look at the possibilities of this subject and a favorable verdict on the work of some societies, see Philippe Vigier, *La Second République dans la région alpine. Etude politique et sociale,* I (Paris, 1963), 32–35.

[29] *Extrait des travaux de la société centrale d'agriculture du département de la Seine-Inférieure,* LXXV (Trimestre d'octobre 1839), 407 ff.

[30] *Bulletin de la Société d'agriculture du départment du Cher* (1846), p. 329.

[31] "Chronique agricole . . . ," *JAP,* 1841–42, p. 182.

[32] *Ibid.*

d'agriculture pratique deplored the intrusion at these occasions of "drawing-room farmers professing agriculture to peasants who could teach them the first notions," and concluded that the dues requirement of the *comices* incorporated them into an "agricultural aristocracy . . . which represents after all only the interests of a minority." [33]

There remain the congresses. Without the peculiarly local and sociable aspects of the societies and *comices,* they might have been expected to be more representative. But the Congress of Brittany, for example, was "another of those Estates-General of Agriculture where the third estate is missing." The third estate was the peasant, and the time had come, according to the *Journal,* to submit a new version of Sieyès' famous question.[34] Also, while the *Journal* had some kind words to say about the first Central Congress at Paris in 1844, it wanted to know whether this "meeting of 300 men, proprietors, professors, scientists, lawyers, journalists, fertilizer and grain merchants, where the real farmer is a tiny minority . . . can be considered as truly representing our 6 to 8 million agricultural families." [35]

When the revolution broke out in 1848, the Central Congress was in annual session discussing, as it had every year since 1844, the mode of election and composition of the proposed departmental chambers of agriculture. In the euphoric mood of the first days of the Republic, the Congress defeated election of the chambers by intermediate bodies and blocked a move to have the electorate limited to proprietors, *fermiers,* and *métayers* owning or cultivating five or more hectares, recommending instead that regularly employed farm laborers also be included along with tenants or owners of properties of any size.

Of course the new Republic had more pressing problems on its hands in February and March than the chambers of agriculture, but the way to action on them seemed open when, in July of 1848, the Cavaignac government appointed as Minister of Agriculture and Commerce Tourret, a deputy from the Allier with a reputation

---

[33] "Chronique agricole . . . ," *JAP*, 1839–40, p. 82.
[34] "Chronique agricole . . . ," *JAP*, 1844–45, pp. 223–24.
[35] Lefour, "Session du Congrès central de l'agriculture française," *JAP*, 1843–44, p. 385.

as an enlightened agriculturalist.[36] Using the Congress' proposals as a base, Tourret elaborated his own *projet de loi* which, while it dropped laborers from the chambers' electorate, also excluded proprietors who leased their lands strictly for cash. This last was in accord with the *Journal*'s often repeated view that the only man of value to the soil was the man who was actively interested or engaged in its cultivation, and it was supposed to help keep absentee proprietors from dominating or influencing the chambers. Tourret's bill unfortunately had to await the drafting of the new Republic's constitution, as the organization of the departments and *arrondissements* was in question. Meanwhile, however, Tourret initiated proposals for rural credit [37] and a separate Ministry of Agriculture, and he earned a secure niche in the *Journal*'s pantheon by drawing up a comprehensive system of agricultural education and pushing it through the Assembly against great odds. An Institut National Agronomique for higher agricultural learning was founded at Versailles. A maximum of 20 regional schools of agriculture was to provide training at an intermediate level and provisions were made for the establishment of farm schools in every canton or *arrondissement*.[38] These last would, it was hoped, attract the sons of peasants, although the requirement of a primary education proved to be something of an obstacle. In any case, it was also planned that the farm schools would educate by example for their

[36] A graduate of the *Ecole polytechnique*, he had also been a *rapporteur* for the 1840 bill on the chambers of agriculture and a member of the General Council of Agriculture. He was described as an "agronome practicien fort habile" on his properties in the Bourbonnais (Allier). M. Mauguin, *Etudes historiques sur l'administration de l'agriculture en France*, II (Paris, 1877), 500.

[37] This credit would have been financed by successive issues of up to 2 billion francs worth of negotiable notes backed by revenues from the *contribution foncière*. Loans would have been made by the state at 3 percent with an additional 2.32 percent for amortization of the principal. The combined rate was well below the prevailing interest rates of from 9 to 12 percent for agricultural loans.

The *Journal d'agriculture pratique*, although it had had reservations in the past about government-financed credit, was enthusiastic over the project. Initially the plan was well received by the Assembly but was defeated in an attack led by Godchaux, banker and Minister of Finance. The notes were described by the project's opponents as "assignats," and government-financed credit was branded as "socialism."

[38] It is only fair to note that three of the four regional schools in operation by 1849 had, as private institutions, received subsidies from the July Monarchy. The July Monarchy also intermittently subsidized about 20 to 30 farm schools and administered such specialized institutions as the veterinary school at Alfort.

surrounding area,[39] and by 1849 70 of them were in operation.

With the election of Louis-Napoleon as president in December of 1848, Tourret left the ministry. After his departure, his projects for rural credit at low interest and a separate Ministry of Agriculture were dropped and action on the chambers of agriculture lagged badly. The Conseil d'Etat was of the opinion that the latter could be established by decree; the ministry preferred that they have the sanction of a law. Finally, after nearly three years of shifting responsibility and a half-hearted attempt at setting up provisional chambers, the National Assembly took the matter in hand. A law of March 20, 1851, called for chambers of agriculture in each department which would elect one of their members to a new General Council of Agriculture. The chambers were to be composed of one representative from each canton elected by the *comices*. There was to be at least one *comice* in each *arrondissement* and membership was open to *all* proprietors, *fermiers*, and *métayers* domiciled or *having their property* in the *comice's* circumscription. Although this law nearly realized some of the more advanced proposals of the 1830s and '40s, the *Journal d'agriculture pratique* was furious at the abandonment of Tourret's attempted exclusion of absentee proprietors. Forgetting its earlier criticism of the *comices,* the *Journal* predicted that these "spontaneously organized groups of agriculturalists" would be invaded by "the eternal enemies of agriculture . . . townspeople, idlers . . . lawyers looking for opportunities to speak." [40]

There was not much opportunity for this invasion to take place. After the coup d'état a law of March 25, 1852, drastically amended the earlier legislation. Chambers were to be set up in each *arrondissement,* whose members, one from each canton, would be picked by the departmental prefect. The meetings of the chambers were to be presided over by subprefects and, in the *arrondissement* of the *chef-lieu,* by the prefect. The General Council of Agriculture was to be composed of members of the chambers, one from each department picked by the Minister of the Interior, Agriculture, and Commerce. Also, in March of 1852 the Central Congress was for-

[39] There is an interesting description of one of these schools and its influence on the local peasantry in R. Thabault, *Mon village, 1848–1914* (Paris, 1945), pp. 92–102.

[40] "Chronique agricole . . . ," *JAP*, 1851(2), pp. 388–89.

bidden to meet on the presumed grounds that it was now a re-
dundant organization. The *comices,* it may be added, returned to
their old way of life. It was not without irony that a preamble to
the new legislation should have announced that one of the law's
purposes was to safeguard their autonomy.

Over a year later, in May of 1853, the first meeting of the new
General Council was called for the following December. A little
more than a week before it was to meet, when some members were
already on their way to Paris, the session was prorogued. The excuse
given was that the chambers had failed to provide enough resolutions or reports for discussion. After that date, the pages of the
Journal, once so full of the subject, became totally bare of news
about the General Council and the chambers. The council continued to exist only on paper. When vacancies occurred in its membership, replacements were often not appointed. In 1860 there were
eight vacancies; by 1870, 26. The fate of the chambers was similar.
They appear to have engaged in some desultory activity at the
beginning of the Empire, but by 1860 there were 54 *arrondissements* without a chamber; in 1870, 82. Special agricultural representation, for all intents and purposes, ended in 1853.

A somewhat similar situation developed with Tourret's crowning
achievement. In May of 1852, amidst rumors of a budget cut for
agriculture, a high official of the Ministry of the Interior, Agriculture, and Commerce made a speech that was generally regarded
as critical of agricultural education. In June the *Journal* noted with
alarm that poultry had been removed from their rearing pens at
the Institut Agronomique in Versailles to be replaced by pheasants
and orders given to cut only half the grain harvest so as to leave
food and cover for game. In September, at the beginning of the
shooting season, the Institut was dissolved by decree on grounds of
economy, the director, Count de Gasparin, learning this only from
the pages of the *Moniteur.* By October one of the four regional
schools had been closed and twelve farm schools had gone out of
business. The latter were managed by private individuals, and
there were in some cases extenuating circumstances for which
the government cannot be blamed. But the *Journal* spoke ominously
of the shock effect produced by the closing of Versailles,[41] and it

---

[41] "Chronique agricole . . . ," *JAP,* 1852(2), p. 352.

is a matter of record that agricultural education went into a pronounced decline during the Second Empire.[42]

It is not to be supposed from the preceding that Louis-Napoleon was an enemy of agriculture. The contrary would appear to be the case. Land clearing, drainage, and irrigation were notable achievements of his regime. The Crédit Foncier (1852) and the Société Général du Crédit Agricole (1861) did not fulfill the *Journal's* dream of easy credit for the peasant, but they were guideposts in an area where little had been done before. Typically the government was generous in its assistance to an improved network of regional prize shows for livestock and produce, and the Legion of Honor even began to appear on some peasant blouses.

In contrasting the *Journal d'agriculture pratique's* program of the 1830s and '40s with what may be called the agricultural policy of the Second Empire, we seem to be confronted with two different approaches which appear, each in its way, equally prescient. It is as though the *Journal* realized that the French Revolution, by bringing land, agricultural production, and rural labor into a free capitalist economy, had also begun the dissociation of the peasant community. Yet the latter, still clinging to an older social and economic system, did not appear to have, during the larger part of the nineteenth century, the means or the abilities to bring itself successfully and painlessly into the new order. Thus the *Journal* advocated reaching out to the peasant, broadening his horizons, educating him, supplying him with credit—in short, transforming him into an entrepreneur.

Louis-Napoleon by comparison seems to have preferred letting events take their course. It is as though he realized that outside forces rather than programs would bring the results desired by the *Journal*. Of far greater consequence to the peasantry than any specific encouragements to agriculture were the social and economic revolutions brought to the countryside in Louis-Napoleon's time by the railways, road building, and foreign competition. These developments also speeded technological change. It is only with the coming of the railway age that the full impact of the agricultural

---

[42] The budget for agricultural education which had stood at 2,700,000 francs in 1852 declined to 1,300,000 francs by 1870.

revolution in progress since the middle of the eighteenth century finally hit the French peasant.

Was Louis-Napoleon right? The Second Empire has been called the most prosperous period in the history of French agriculture.[43] As Labrousse tells us, production and prices rose together at an "accelerated speed," while for the first time in the modern era the agricultural population declined markedly.[44] Difficult periods began with the long depression (1875–96), but the progress of social and economic change begun under the Second Empire continued during the Third Republic.

As the bulk of the peasantry were pushed from a semiclosed economy into producing for extended markets, more and more peasants, with the help of the Republic, found their way to the village school and became active in a new proliferation of agricultural organizations more suited to their needs than the societies or *comices*. Rural credit on relatively easy terms began to be available in the 1890s. Agricultural education was reorganized and extended. The Institut National Agronomique reopened its doors in 1877. A separate Ministry of Agriculture was established in 1881, and the departmental chambers of agriculture were revived in 1924 as essentially peasant organizations.

These measures did not, of course, resolve all the problems of the peasantry. Developments in our own time have emphasized how many of these problems the Third Republic left unsolved,[45] but it can at least be said of the Third Republic that it realized the *Journal d'agriculture pratique*'s program of the 1840s.

Are the mid-nineteenth century agrarian reformers who wrote for or supported the *Journal*'s program of interest, then, only as precursors or visionaries out of touch with their time? They prided themselves on understanding the peasant, but if one looks at the so-called peasant cahiers resulting from the Second Republic's investigations of labor conditions, one is struck by how little, with the very obvious exception of rural credit, the *Journal*'s program

[43] Michel Augé-Laribé, *La révolution agricole* (Paris, 1956), p. 103.

[44] C.-E. Labrousse, *Le paysan français des physiocrates à nos jours* (Paris, 1963), p. 9.

[45] On this topic and the development of peasant organizations, see Gordon Wright, *Rural Revolution in France: The Peasantry in the Twentieth Century* (Stanford, 1964).

figured in them.[46] On the other hand, an extended study of agriculturalists, proprietors, and others who wished to help the peasantry into the new agrarian order would have to take account of
what a terribly closed community the peasant world still was at
the middle of the nineteenth century.

In this respect, one story comes to mind. Among the many accomplishments of the celebrated agronomist Mathieu de Dombasle
was the perfection of a plow incontestably superior to other models
generally available in France at the time. Proprietors in the neigh-
borhood of Dombasle's famous experimental farm at Roville gave
some to their tenants but they remained unused in the barn. Peasants were shown how the plow required something like half the
exertion and time wasted on their own plowing, but it was fifteen
years before a local peasant bought one. Their earlier comment
on the demonstrations at Roville was "C'est un monsieur qui
s'amuse." [47] How much less patience they may have had with an
agrarian bourgeois preaching such "abstractions" as agricultural
education or representation of the agricultural interest we can only
guess at.

It would not be fair, of course, to put all the blame on the
peasants for the failure of a program to improve their condition.
Emile Guillaumin in *La vie d'un simple: memoires d'un métayer*
gives us a wonderful typology of proprietors. This interesting book
presumably recounts the life of Guillaumin's father from his boyhood in the 1820s to his old age in the 1890s, during which time
he worked or share tenanted for five owners. Only one of these was
interested in progressive agriculture and the welfare of his peasants,
but as Guillaumin's father tells us, "his ideas were so contrary to

---

[46] "They were worked up over the lack of capital and the usury which de-
voured them; they demanded agricultural banks and the organization of rural
credit; they denounced the growing cost of labor resulting from the emigration
of day workers to the cities. They complained of the expensiveness of fertilizers,
of the direct tax which weighed on real property while transferable securities es-
caped it, of the right of the creditor to seize the house of the peasant while
government bonds were untouchable, of the law which made the proprietor the
beneficiary of any increment created by the work of a tenant; they demanded
the amelioration of rural roads, reductions in the cost of the transport of goods,
the creation of public granaries, and a rural police code. They also desired that
a decoration be reserved for them and that agricultural shows and prize money
for the encouragement of agriculture be increased." Gerard Walter, *Histoire des
paysans* (Paris, 1963), pp. 415–16.

[47] Moll, "Des fermes-écoles," *JAP*, 1848, p. 6.

our usual ways that . . . we laughed in his face." [48] The rest of the proprietors, however, were a pretty grim lot.

One announced to his *métayers*: "To obey and to work, that is your business. I don't ask anything else. For instance, don't bother me about repairs. It is a principle of mine not to make any." [49] On his farm there was "only one end to attain: to continue to give the proprietor a sum equal to that which he had been given the previous year." [50]

Another proprietor is called M. Noris.

M. Noris was an agriculturalist, that is to say he spent his life doing nothing, for one could not call the management of two farms "work." . . . At Moulins he belonged to a Society for the Promotion of Agricultural Interests which was composed entirely of bourgeois like himself who called themselves farmers. . . .

M. Noris was niggardly; I was not long finding that out. He haggled about expenses, preferred to sell livestock in bad condition rather than buy oil cake or meal to improve them; and we never dared to speak to him of buying fertilizer.

"No, no," he would say, "no phosphates! The farm manure ought to be enough."

And he would shake his old birdlike head with terror. For a member of the Society for the Promotion of Agricultural Interests, that was not very good reasoning.[51]

Routine then was not an exclusive attribute of the peasant but extended into the ranks of all agricultural classes. A study of the persistence during the nineteenth century of the view of agriculture as a source of dependable or ordinary income rather than an enterprise would have to be included in a fuller explanation of the failure of the *Journal d'agriculture pratique*'s program. From what has been offered here, the chief significance of this program would seem to be the early and special formulation it gave to what is still called in France "la question paysanne."

[48] Guillaumin, *La vie d'un simple* (Paris, 1904), p. 73.
[49] *Ibid.*, p. 151.　　[50] *Ibid.*, p. 178.　　[51] *Ibid.*, pp. 243–44.

The Alsace-Lorraine Question
in France, 1871–1914

FREDERIC H. SEAGER

UNIVERSITY OF MONTREAL

THE QUESTION OF Alsace-Lorraine in France was raised by the cession of that territory to Germany following the Franco-Prussian War in 1871. It was settled, in so far as France was concerned, by the peace treaties that formally ended the First World War. When the so-called revisionist historians began searching for the true origins of the 1914–18 conflict, they inevitably mentioned Alsace-Lorraine. "The story of Franco-German relations since 1871," writes G. P. Gooch, "is the record of France's endeavour to regain her lost territories and of Germany's attempt to retain them." In time, he concludes, all of European diplomacy became entwined about the question. "Each of the protagonists sought and found allies, until almost the whole of Europe was involved in their implacable vendetta." [1] Although other historians of the "revisionist" school refuse to ascribe the creation of two power blocs to this single cause, they agree that French irredentism contributed to tension between France and Germany.

Nowadays it is generally accepted that Bismarck based his entire foreign policy on the assumption that France would try to recover its lost provinces. [2] What is less clear is the role played by Alsace-Lorraine in the molding of French public opinion and in the formation of French foreign policy. On one hand, the

---

[1] George Peabody Gooch, *Franco-German Relations, 1871–1914* (London, 1923), p. 5.

[2] Pierre Renouvin, *Histoire des relations internationales*, VI (Paris, 1955), 17.

French government did encourage the formation of the Triple Entente, which by 1914 constituted an effective counterweight to the Bismarckian system. It fostered patriotic education for French schoolchildren, in which the ties between France and Alsace-Lorraine were emphasized.[3] On the other hand, militant nationalism was actively discouraged in France between 1871 and 1914. The Ligue des Patriotes was broken up and its leader imprisoned. No irredentist movement was formed by exiles from Alsace-Lorraine, whose influence in foreign affairs was, in any case, negligible. Among the French public at large, the attitude toward the lost provinces appears to have been one of general indifference, broken only by isolated eruptions of anti-German feeling. Indeed, public interest in Alsace-Lorraine was largely the result of Franco-German tension rather than its cause.

Part of the difficulty in studying the importance of the Alsace-Lorraine question in France is defining the term *revanche*. Probably the best definition is the one given by Gambetta when he first used the word in the context of French recovery following the defeat of 1870. In a speech at Saint-Quentin on November 16, 1871, he first emphasized the need for "a little order, a little calm . . . a government adapted to [France's] present needs and above all to the necessity for our country to regain its true role in the world." To this end, he added, Frenchmen must avoid rash words or deeds: "Let us never speak of the foreigner, but let it be understood that we are always thinking of him. Then you will be on the true road to *revanche,* because you will have acquired self-government and self-discipline."[4] These are the words not of a *fou furieux,* but of a serious republican dedicated to the rebuilding of his country. From this speech it is obvious that the *revanche* proposed by Gambetta excluded militant, tub-thumping nationalism.

On the specific question of Alsace-Lorraine, Gambetta was equally categoric. As long as the northeastern departments were still French, he had steadfastly opposed their cession to Germany. At the meeting of the National Assembly convened in Bordeaux in February, 1871, to discuss the peace terms, it was Gambetta who had drafted the protests read by the deputies from Alsace-

---

[3] Cf. Raoul Girardet, ed. *Le nationalisme français, 1871–1914* (Paris, 1966), pp. 70–84.

[4] Joseph Reinach, ed., *Discours et plaidoyers politiques de M. Gambetta,* II (Paris, 1881), 172; hereafter cited as Gambetta, *Discours.*

Lorraine.[5] In this declaration they argued against cession on three grounds: national self-determination of the Alsatians and Lorrainers; the peace of Europe, which was based on this principle; and the national integrity of France.[6] These arguments have deep roots in the French republican tradition.

Once Alsace-Lorraine was under German rule, however, the former organizer of National Defense accepted the *fait accompli* as a matter of practical politics. On May 9, 1872, he received a gift from a group of Alsatians whose spokesman expressed the conviction that their homeland would eventually return to France. Acknowledging the honor, Gambetta recalled the loyalty of Alsace to the French nation. He then added this warning: "But these are trying times, Gentlemen, and I fear that if we heeded only our patriotic yearnings and the bitter memories that would lead us back to hopeless struggles . . . we would compromise a cause which we could better serve otherwise." The cause of France, he continued, could be served only by public acceptance of the Republic, which in turn required a display of moderation by the republicans. He therefore urged the Alsatians to accept their new status "in a spirit of sacrifice and resignation." [7]

If Gambetta was ready in 1872 to subordinate the cause of Alsace-Lorraine to that of France, this holds true a fortiori of the conservative republicans. For Thiers, the recovery of France took the form of paying the war indemnity and of reorganizing the country's military establishment.[8] Inasmuch as this policy necessitated undisturbed relations with Germany, any hint of irredentism was deliberately muted. When certain Parisian newspapers announced the formation, shortly after the Treatly of Frankfurt, of a so-called League for the deliverance of Alsace-Lorraine, Bismarck demanded its immediate dissolution. The French government hastened to comply; it did not want to give Germany any provocation.[9]

In the legislative branch of government the same moderation

[5] Henri Galli [Gallichet], *Gambetta et l'Alsace-Lorraine* (Paris, 1911), p. 21.
[6] Alfred Villefort, ed., *Recueil des traités, conventions, lois, décrets, et autres actes relatifs à la paix avec l'Allemagne*, II (Paris, 1873), 3–4.
[7] Gambetta, *Discours*, II, 268–70.
[8] Adolphe Thiers, *Memoirs*, trans. F. M. Atkinson (New York, 1916), pp. 266–67.
[9] E. Malcolm Carroll, *French Public Opinion and Foreign Affairs, 1870–1914* (New York, 1931), p. 48.

prevailed. Jules Grévy, who in 1871 was President of the National Assembly, sternly advised a young deputy of Alsatian birth to accept the cession. "France must renounce Alsace," warned Grévy. "Do not believe the madmen who tell you otherwise and who have aggravated our misfortunes by espousing a hopeless cause." [10] French diplomatists reflected similar caution. In 1874, for example, the French ambassador in Berlin asked his foreign minister to keep the French press from exulting over the recent victory in the Reichstag elections of *protestataires,* candidates from Alsace-Lorraine who protested the annexation.[11]

This expression of loyalty to France by the inhabitants of the annexed territory illustrates the difficulty of the French position on Alsace-Lorraine. Although the French government carefully avoided any suspicion of irredentism, the election results did have the effect of reinforcing France's claims to the region. At the beginning of the election campaign most Alsatians and Lorrainers under German rule had preferred not to vote at all. Gambetta himself encouraged voting, and it was largely as a result of this initiative that an entire slate of *protestataires* was elected.[12] Here was ample proof that the annexation of Alsace-Lorraine by Germany violated the principle of national self-determination. Yet Gambetta himself knew that France was in no position to enforce this principle in the lost provinces, henceforth called a *Reichsland*—literally, a colony of the German Empire. By the end of the nineteenth century the people of Alsace-Lorraine realized that their return to France was at best a remote possibility. They then ceased to elect *protestataires,* preferring candidates who favored autonomy within the Empire.

In the meantime, Frenchmen apparently enjoyed being reminded that Alsace was still loyal to France. Popular literature of the early postwar period sought to emphasize the French character of the annexed provinces. One example is a song written for the *café-concert* and entitled "Le maître d'école alsacien." Its refrain enjoyed a great vogue around 1873:

---

[10] Auguste Scheurer-Kestner, *Souvenirs de jeunesse* (Paris, 1905), p. 263.

[11] France, Ministère des Affaires Étrangères, *Documents diplomatiques français, 1871–1914,* I (1st series; Paris, 1929), 310; hereafter referred to as D.D.F.

[12] Auguste Lalance, *Mes souvenirs, 1830–1914* (Paris, 1914), pp. 50–51. The author was himself a *protestataire.*

La patrouille allemande passe,
Baissez la voix, mes chers petits,
Parler français n'est plus permis,
Aux petits enfants de l'Alsace! [13]

In a similar vein is Alphonse Daudet's short story, "La dernière classe," published the same year. Here is told the heart-rending tale of the last class given in French in an Alsatian school. When the lesson ends, the old schoolmaster, too moved by sorrow to speak, writes "VIVE LA FRANCE" in large letters on the blackboard. Although some French intellectuals referred to the cultural ties between France and Alsace, this was a tenuous argument at best, since the native tongue of nearly all Alsatians was—and still is—a dialect of German. Most French claims to the region were based not on language, but on nationality.

By 1873, in any case, many of the inhabitants of Alsace-Lorraine most loyal to France were already living on French soil. Under article II of the Treaty of Frankfurt, any resident of the *Reichsland* who wished to retain his French citizenship could do so by making a declaration of this intent to a competent authority and by transferring domicile to France by October 1, 1872.[14] Nearly 100,000 were able to meet this deadline, and 150,000 more emigrated to France later.[15] Finding work and lodging for these exiles was the primary task of their service organizations. The largest and wealthiest of these, called the Société de Protection des Alsaciens et Lorrains Demeurés Français, was founded in January, 1872, with the initial aim of settling as many as possible in Algeria. Of royalist leanings, this body made no attempt whatsoever to influence French policy toward Germany.[16] Next in size was the Association Générale d'Alsace-Lorraine, a strongly republican group, founded in August, 1871. Unlike its royalist counterpart, it made no secret of its desire to see the lost provinces return to France, and it did try to keep the Alsace-Lorraine question before the public. In the early 1870s, however, it devoted most of its energies to resettling

[13] Galli, *Gambetta et l'Alsace-Lorraine*, p. 88.
[14] Villefort, *Recueil des traités,* I, 66.
[15] Frédéric Eccard, *L'Alsace sous la domination allemande* (Paris, 1919), p. 154.
[16] L. Louis-Lande, "Les Alsaciens-Lorrains en Algérie," *Revue des Deux Mondes,* XI (September 1, 1875), 91.

the exiles in France, mainly in Paris, and finding jobs for them.[17]

Not until these practical questions were dealt with did any of the exiles begin to publish journals devoted to their homeland. The first of these, which appeared from 1877 to 1890, was a monthly called *La Revue Alsacienne*. Its maiden issue gave notice that it would not serve as a platform for irredentism. "Questions involving politics will in no case be treated in the *Revue*," it announced on the first page. "Our readers will understand the reasons which oblige us to limit our scope to literature, science, etc.; we shall not insist on this point." [18] Later issues of the journal gave ample proof that the editors, who described themselves simply as a group of young Alsatians, remained faithful to this statement of intent. Articles on current affairs in Alsace carefully avoided controversy; the *Revue* brought France and its lost province closer only in cultural terms.

In political terms the moderation advocated by Gambetta in 1872 helped the republicans win a majority of seats in the Chamber in 1876. By 1880 they were firmly in control of all state institutions; the Republic was now thoroughly republican. It was not, however, *une République pure et dure*, radical in domestic matters and aggressive in foreign affairs. A Jacobin republic would have fulfilled Bismarck's wish to keep France in diplomatic isolation, but a moderate republic could become as respectable as any monarchy. "Once we take control of the Republic," Gambetta confided to a friend in 1873, "it will find allies just as well as a monarchy, no matter what Bismarck may think." [19] With allies, France could resume its rôle as a world power. This, as Gambetta had proclaimed publicly in 1871, was the true road to *revanche*.

It was a difficult road to follow. Although the French government encouraged moderation in foreign affairs, it did not wish to discourage patriotism at home. In the public image, the Alsace-Lorraine question was somehow bound up with the greater issue of patriotism. Under the aegis of Jules Ferry, a moderate republican, French public education was reorganized to instill a greater sense of national pride in young schoolchildren. In 1880 Ferry had a

[17] Association générale d'Alsace-Lorraine, *Statuts, rapport général* (Paris, 1916), p. 5.

[18] *La Revue Alsacienne*, I (February, 1877), 1.

[19] Juliette Adam, *Nos amitiés politiques avant l'abandon de la revanche* (Paris, 1908), pp. 15–16.

new standard map of Europe lithographed for classroom use. It showed France, Germany, and Alsace-Lorraine in three different colors so that pupils were given to understand that the annexed territory was not really German.[20] This reminder came none too soon, since interest in Alsace-Lorraine among their elders had declined in direct proportion to interest in the late war.[21] The following year appeared a plea for military training along Prussian lines as a means of encouraging greater patriotism among French youth. To illustrate his argument that this quality was declining in France, the author simply alluded to the general lack of interest in Alsace-Lorraine.[22]

An organization to foster Prussian-type nationalism among young Frenchmen was indeed founded in 1882 under the name of Ligue des Patriotes. Initially it had the official support of leading republican politicians, who seemed to feel that military drill and patriotic lectures would exert a salutary influence on *lycée* students. The Ligue's president, Paul Déroulède, was not satisfied with mere patriotic education, however. He tried to influence French foreign policy, which in the early 1880s was directed toward colonial acquisitions and an informal accommodation with Bismarck. Failing this, he turned against Jules Ferry and, in 1888, joined the Boulangists, who were preparing an assault against the bourgeois republic.[23] As *Le Temps* was quick to note, "For revision of the Treaty of Frankfurt, the new Ligue is substituting revision of the constitution." [24] The defeat of Boulangism and the subsequent destruction of the Ligue gave added weight to Gambetta's earlier contention that extreme nationalism had no place in *revanche*.

This lesson was not lost on the exiles from Alsace-Lorraine. Having chosen to live in France, they were in no position to contest the validity of a regime acceptable to the vast majority of Frenchmen. In 1880 a weekly entitled *L'Alsacien-Lorrain* began publishing the political views of leading exiles. Its first issue openly expressed the hope that their homeland would eventually be re-

---

[20] Adrien Dansette, *Le Boulangisme* (Paris, 1946), p. 12.

[21] Claude Digeon, *La crise allemande de la pensée française, 1870–1914* (Paris, 1959), p. 385.

[22] Raoul Frary, *Le péril national* (Paris, 1881), p. 4.

[23] Raoul Girardet, "La Ligue des patriotes dans l'histoire du nationalisme français (1882–1888)," *Bulletin de la Société d'histoire moderne*, 12th series, no. 6 (1958), pp. 3–6.

[24] *Le Temps*, May 4, 1888.

joined to France.[25] When the Ligue des Patriotes was founded, the journal gave it a warm welcome and singled out Déroulède for special praise.[26] From 1882 through 1886 the various exile organizations accepted the presence and support of the Ligue in their annual July 14 ceremony in front of the statue of Strasbourg on the Place de la Concorde.[27] As the Ligue moved further away from orthodox republicanism, however, it lost the favor of the exiles. The Association Générale d'Alsace-Lorraine sent a telegram of sympathy to Jules Ferry immediately after an attempt on his life in December, 1887.[28] This was long after Déroulède had publicly accused Ferry of being antipatriotic. By June of 1888 there was a growing disaffection among the exiles toward Déroulède following his attacks on the regime.[29]

These attacks were now led by General Boulanger, who had entered politics a few months previously as the champion of a Jacobin, militantly nationalist republic.[30] At this point the *Alsacien-Lorrain* underwent a brief crisis: some members of its editorial staff favored the general in the hope that he would hasten the reunion of their homeland with France, while others opposed him as a potential dictator.[31] Although the paper remained officially neutral during the general elections of 1889,[32] it was apparent by then that the bulk of the exiles preferred the opportunist republic of Gambetta and Ferry.

The opportunist republic, representing moderation in both domestic and foreign affairs, did indeed triumph in the 1889 elections. Within a few years after this victory, Gambetta's prediction that a republican regime would be respectable enough to win allies as well as a monarchy was to be fulfilled. Now that the Third Republic was no longer associated with the aggressive policies of 1793, the Russian government was willing to conclude an alliance with France. While strengthening France's position on world affairs, the alliance with Russia did not bring reunification with Alsace-Lorraine one step closer. On the contrary, French statesmen "could not help but see that Russia had no interest in securing Alsace-

[25] *L'Alsacien-Lorrain,* August 3, 1880.   [26] *Ibid.,* May 21, 1882.
[27] *Ibid.,* August 11, 1886.   [28] *Ibid.,* December 8, 1887.
[29] *Ibid.,* June 17, 1888.
[30] See Frederic H. Seager, *The Boulanger Affair: Political Crossroad of France, 1886–1889* (Ithaca, 1968).
[31] *L'Alsacien-Lorrain,* April 22, 1888.   [32] *Ibid.,* November 1, 1889.

Lorraine for France. . . ." [33] In order to keep Russia as an ally, France virtually had to renounce irredentism. The tsar went out of his way to explain to the French ambassador that, as far as the lost provinces were concerned, "You will have to wait with dignity." [34]

Not only the ambassador, but the French public at large seemed content to wait during the 1890s. Now that France was once again a world power, the defeat of 1870 receded still further into the background of public consciousness—and with it the question of Alsace-Lorraine. By 1897 an Alsatian journalist in France ruefully admitted that irredentism was a dead letter because "the pain of defeat has lost its acuity. . . ." [35] His verdict was confirmed by a survey taken late that year by the literary monthly *Mercure de France*. Of the 130 people questioned as to whether the Franco-Prussian War and the Alsace-Lorraine question—the two were linked in the poll—were still important issues, nearly all replied in the negative. Only the historian Charles Seignobos attempted to discuss Alsace-Lorraine without reference to the war but rather as a question of national self-determination. Everyone else accepted the connection as natural, and only a few intellectuals admitted having given any real thought to the lost territory. [36]

If the French were no longer thinking about Alsace-Lorraine, they nonetheless liked to feel that the Alsatians and Lorrainers were still loyal to France. But by the end of the century, as we have seen, no more *protestataires* were being elected from Alsace-Lorraine to the Reichstag. Noting this, a French political weekly admitted that, although the inhabitants of the annexed provinces would have liked to remain French, they were being won over to German rule by economic gains, such as improved rail service. [37] When many readers expressed shock at such an idea, the review had to modify its earlier position and assure them that the Alsatians and Lorrainers were still French at heart. [38]

[33] Wiliam L. Langer, *The Franco-Russian Alliance* (Cambridge, Mass., 1929), p. 89.

[34] Renouvin, *Histoire des relations internationales*, p. 128.

[35] *L'Alsacien-Lorrain*, September 12, 1897.

[36] "L'Alsace-Lorraine et l'état actuel des esprits," *Mercure de France*, XXIV (December, 1897), 641–815.

[37] "La Question d'Alsace-Lorraine," *Revue Bleue*, XLVII (July 15, 1899), 65–69.

[38] "En Alsace-Lorraine," *Revue Bleue*, XLVII (December 30, 1899), 833.

To the extent that the Alsace-Lorraine question was associated with France's defeat in the War of 1870, it faded from public awareness after the Boulanger affair. There was, however, a small group of writers and pamphleteers—many of them Alsatians—who insisted on keeping the question alive on its own merits. Their writings were especially abundant in the last decade of the nineteenth century and had one theme in common: the Alsace-Lorraine question should be settled peacefully—for the sake not of France or Germany, but of the Alsatians and Lorrainers. During the heat of the Boulangist crisis, Auguste Lalance, an Alsatian engineer who had been elected to the Reichstag as a *protestataire* in 1874, argued that the true wishes of the Alsatian people had been distorted by both French and German polemicists. It was time that Alsace returned to the rôle to which her geographical position had assigned her: "that of mediator between two great peoples." [39] Shortly after the crisis had abated, Ernest Lavisse warned that the greatest loser in a war between France and Germany would be Alsace-Lorraine itself. For one thing, most of the fighting would be done in the annexed provinces, laying waste much of the land; secondly, such a conflict would set Alsatian against Alsatian and Lorrainer against Lorrainer, since there were many of each in both the French and the German armies. [40]

Those who did argue for the return of Alsace-Lorraine to France during this period invariably proposed peaceful means. One of the most prolific writers on the subject was an Alsatian exile named Fernand de Dartein, who in 1894 placed his hopes in the growth of socialism in Germany. Once in control of the government, the German socialists would presumably be willing to return Alsace-Lorraine to France on the grounds of national self-determination. [41] The territory should then be demilitarized, so that the Germans would not feel threatened by France. [42] The author's later works, which were written in an effort to remind Frenchmen of Alsace-Lorraine, all emphasized the need for peaceful relations

[39] Carroll, *French Public Opinion*, p. 146.

[40] Ernest Lavisse, *La question d'Alsace dans une âme d'Alsacien* (Paris, 1891), pp. 21–23.

[41] Jean Heimweh [Fernand de Dartein], *L'Alsace-Lorraine et la paix* (Paris, 1894), pp. 73–74.

[42] *Ibid.*, pp. 15–16.

with Germany.[43] In a similar vein, Jaurès argued that Alsace-Lorraine would attain its rights only in a democratic Europe, free from militarism, where such rights could be respected.[44]

Proposals for a settlement took account of the current international situation. When the Fashoda incident brought France momentarily closer to Germany, the question of Alsace-Lorraine was discussed with an eye to a possible Franco-German entente. Lalance proposed late in 1898 that a French colony be exchanged for the *Reichsland*. Once the only real obstacle to Franco-German reconciliation were thus removed, an alliance could be formed between France, Russia, and Germany.[45] A similar suggestion was advanced a month later by Emile Keller, who in 1871 had led the delegation from Alsace-Lorraine at the National Assembly. Like other Alsatian exiles in France, Keller was not opposed to the principle of an entente between France and Germany; he merely did not wish to see it consecrate the annexation of his homeland.[46]

The much-heralded reconciliation between France and Germany failed to materialize. Indeed, after 1905 relations between the two countries grew steadily worse—not because of Alsace-Lorraine but out of conflicting colonial claims in North Africa. The ensuing wave of anti-German feeling in France helped revive interest in Alsace-Lorraine, primarily as a reaction to German moves elsewhere.[47] This new interest in the lost provinces was largely literary. In *Les Oberlé*, a novel written in 1901 and later dramatized, René Bazin presents the tension within an Alsatian family torn between loyalties to France and to Germany. Two novels by Maurice Barrès reveal divided loyalties within the individual conscience. *Au service de l'Allemagne*, which appeared in 1906, tells of the difficulties facing a young Alsatian doctor who, though loyal to France, must serve in the German army. In *Colette Baudoche*, a young girl from

[43] Jean Heimweh, *Droit de conquête et plébiscite* (Paris, 1896); *La parole soit à l'Alsace-Lorraine* (Paris, 1897; *Allemagne, France, Alsace-Lorraine* (Paris, 1899).

[44] France, *Journal Officiel, Chambre des Députés, Débats parlementaires* (1895), p. 769; hereafter cited as *J.O.C.*

[45] Auguste Lalance, "La Nouvelle Triplice," *Grande Revue*, IV (December 1, 1898), 266–27.

[46] Emile Keller, "L'Alliance allemande," *Le Correspondant*, CLVIII (January, 1899), 433.

[47] Eugen Weber *The Nationalist Revival in France, 1905–1914* (Berkeley, 1959), pp. 87–89.

Metz rejects her German suitor after attending a mass in honor of the soldiers from her native city who fell for France in the War of 1870. In all three novels, Alsace-Lorraine is clearly the battleground for French and German influences.

The battleground theme was taken up by a monthly review entitled *Les Marches de l'Est,* which was published from 1909 until the outbreak of the First World War. In this case the battleground was extended to include all areas where Gallic and Germanic cultures met: Alsace-Lorraine, Belgium, Luxembourg, and Switzerland. As Barrès explained in an introductory article, "For these eastern regions politically separated from France, French culture is the civilizing element. . . . Yet they are also of great help to France. They are our forward bastions!" [48] In addition to presenting literary articles on Alsace-Lorraine, the journal alluded frequently to resistance to German culture along Germany's borders, as in Poland, Bohemia, and Schleswig-Holstein. Opposition to Pan-Germanism had driven Barrès and his friends into a sort of pan-French movement, which seems to have had little following either among the French or among exiles from Alsace-Lorraine.

By this time the exiles had ample opportunity to express their views. In addition to the periodicals already mentioned, a review named *Le Messager d'Alsace-Lorraine* was published from 1904 to 1914. Vaguely royalist in tone, this journal confined itself largely to vaunting the distinctions, such as the Legion of Honor, won by leading Alsatians and Lorrainers in France. In foreign affairs, it demanded "the greatest possible autonomy" for the annexed territory. "Only then will Alsace-Lorraine be able to resume its rôle as a link between France and Germany and to prepare an entente. . . ." [49] A new constitution for the *Reichsland* in 1911 did allow somewhat more autonomy, but this alone could not reconcile France and Germany. Rather, certain French nationalists, fearful lest autonomy for Alsace-Lorraine rob them of an issue, fought to reaffirm the importance of the lost provinces in the light of strained relations with Germany.[50] This was apparently the position of the Ligue des Jeunes Amis d'Alsace-Lorraine, a group founded in 1912

---

[48] *Les Marches de l'Est,* I (February, 1909), iii.
[49] *Le Messager d'Alsace-Lorraine,* II (October 21, 1905), 1.
[50] Gilbert Ziebura, *Die Deutsche Frage in der Öffentlichen Meinung Frankreichs von 1911–1914* (Berlin, 1955), pp. 24–25.

by right-wing Catholics with the aim of reminding French students of the cultural ties that bound France to her lost provinces.[51]

Just as these nationalists tried to use the Alsace-Lorraine question as a propaganda weapon against Germany, French pacifists tried either to minimize the issue or to bury it altogether. In 1913 the socialist leader Marcel Sembat argued that only if France recognized the territorial settlement of the Frankfurt treaty as final could there be lasting peace with Germany.[52] That same year a series of interviews with leading Alsatian political figures appeared in *L'Humanité*. All but one favored autonomy within the Reich as a solution to the Alsace-Lorraine problem.[53] The socialist journal then concluded that France could form an entente with Germany without offending the Alsatians.[54] In a similar vein, a group of young intellectuals, including the historian Albert Mathiez, published a manifesto early in 1914 calling for an end to the arms race and acceptance by the French government of the status quo as to Alsace-Lorraine.[55]

If French public opinion was occasionally concerned about Alsace-Lorraine between 1871 and 1914, French diplomacy largely ignored the issue. The principal task of the Quai d'Orsay was not to recover the lost provinces but to improve France's diplomatic position. The only instance on record of positive action taken by France on the question of Alsace-Lorraine is in 1878, when the French ambassador to Germany held private talks with *protestataire* candidates with a view to encouraging their election to the Reichstag.[56] Apparently the French foreign ministry believed that the presence of recalcitrant Alsatians in the German lower house would weaken Germany's stance in world affairs.[57] As fewer and fewer *protestataires* were returned, however, this policy—if it ever was a policy—was abandoned. By 1908 André Tardieu admit-

[51] Agathon [Henri Massis and Alfred de Tarde], *Les jeunes gens d'aujourd'hui* (Paris, 1913), p. 39.

[52] Marcel Sembat, *Faites un roi: sinon, faites la paix* (Paris, 1913), pp. 171–73.

[53] *L'Humanité*, March 23–April 10, 1913.

[54] *Ibid.*, April 3, 1913.

[55] Michel Laurent, et al., *La paix armée et le problème d'Alsace* (Paris, 1914), pp. i–v.

[56] D.D.F. (1st series), II, 309–11.

[57] See "L'Alsace-Lorraine et l'Empire germanique," *Revue des Deux Mondes*, L (July 15, 1880), 281.

ted in a series of lectures delivered at Harvard that irredentism played no rôle in the formulation of French foreign policy. Tardieu, who was then honorary first secretary to the French diplomatic service, explained that the Alsace-Lorraine question was subordinated to the general aim of French diplomacy: finding allies. "Instead of seeking for her revenge on the field of battle," he remarked, "France has taken it in the Chancelleries. . . ." [58]

In Tardieu's American lectures, which constitute perhaps the most authoritative public statement of French diplomatic aims in this period, it is apparent that Gambetta's definition of *revanche* was accepted in the highest official circles. If France was ever to achieve the recovery Gambetta wished, irredentism was not only useless; it was positively harmful. No foreign power would ever want to sign an alliance with a country that was ready to go to war for lost territory. To win allies, the French had to prove their peaceful intentions. That they succeeded is shown by the diplomatic gains won by France after 1890. The measure of this success can be seen in a conversation of 1910 between Sir Edward Grey, the British foreign secretary, and Count Metternich, the German ambassador to Britain. In an obvious attempt to draw Britain away from her partner in the *Entente cordiale,* Metternich raised the spectre of French irredentism. The French, he claimed, had never renounced a war of *revanche* for Alsace-Lorraine; they were dissuaded only by the superior might of Germany. Grey then writes:

> I said France could hardly be expected formally to renounce the lost provinces, but as a matter of fact I was not conscious that an attack upon Germany to recover them played any part in her relations with other Powers. I did not know the terms of the Franco-Russian alliance, but I did not suppose it embraced this point.
> Count Metternich said it certainly did not. [59]

In view of the French government's overriding desire to win allies even at the expense of Alsace-Lorraine, one may reasonably ask what plans, if any, republican politicians of the 1871–1914 period had for the lost territory. Inasmuch as the conservative republicans never mentioned the subject publicly, it may be assumed

[58] André Tardieu, *France and the Alliances* (New York, 1908), pp. 305–6.

[59] George Peabody Gooch and Harold Temperly, eds., *British Documents on the Origins of the War, 1898–1914,* VI (London, 1930), 576; hereafter cited as *B.D.*

that Grévy's privately expressed views that France must renounce Alsace represented their attitude. More liberal politicians occasionally spoke of justice for Alsace-Lorraine, but it was plain that they were prepared to wait. In a speech at Lille on February 6, 1876, Gambetta was careful to remind his audience that "justice for our separated brethren" depended on the adoption by France of a peaceful republican regime.[60] Jaurès referred to this speech during the Chamber debate on ratification of the *Entente cordiale*. The Anglo-French treaty, he cautioned, should not be considered as a weapon against Germany, but rather as an instrument of general reconciliation in Europe. Only in such a framework of international cooperation could nationality problems, such as the status of Alsace-Lorraine, ever be settled.[61]

After the First World War Joseph Caillaux used similar arguments to justify his policy of conciliation with Germany in 1911. The French alliance system, he maintained, had given France increased influence in world affairs, whereas Germany's allies were only handicaps. Once revolution ripped apart the tottering Ottoman and Austrian empires, Germany would have to come to terms with France. These terms would naturally include Alsace-Lorraine, which France would be perfectly justified in demanding as compensation for German annexations in Central Europe.[62] Such a possibility was in fact taken quite seriously prior to the First World War. The British ambassador in Saint Petersburg reported in a dispatch dated March 19, 1914, that plans to partition the Hapsburg monarchy were then being discussed among Russian diplomatists and other members of Europe's ruling circles. In these conversations it was assumed that the imminent death of the Austrian emperor would lead to the disintegration of the Dual Monarchy. In the resulting partition Germany would annex Austria proper, while Galicia would fall to Russia. France would then receive compensation in the form of Alsace-Lorraine.[63]

The French public was not, of course, a party to these diplomatic conversations. Yet its over-all attitude toward Alsace-Lorraine during the 1871–1914 period was in most respects similar to that of the French foreign ministry. In rejecting militant nationalism,

[60] Gambetta, *Discours*, V, 81.   [61] J.O.C. (1904), pp. 2377–78.
[62] Joseph Caillaux, *Mes audaces—Agadir* . . . , *1909–1912*, Vol. II of *Mes mémoires* (Paris, 1947), pp. 113–16.
[63] B.D., X, 769–70.

in defeating the Jacobin republic proposed by Boulanger and his followers, and in rallying repeatedly to the bourgeois republic, the French electorate manifested its confidence in leaders who opposed irredentism. From 1871 to about 1890 the loss of Alsace-Lorraine was associated in the public mind with the defeat of 1870, but France was too weak to take any action on this score. In the 1890 –1905 period both the defeat and the question of Alsace-Lorraine were largely forgotten. By 1913, however, a new confidence in France was noted among French youth. *"La revanche* has taken on a new form, entirely intellectual and moral." [64] A new generation of Frenchmen, which had not known the humiliation of military defeat, in effect accepted the definition of *revanche* originally proposed by Gambetta in 1871 and reaffirmed by Tardieu in 1908. On the eve of the First World War the French could look with pride on their country's place in the world. They could afford to be patient on the question of Alsace-Lorraine.

[64] Agathon, *Les jeunes gens,* p. 38.

The French Colonial Frontier

RAYMOND F. BETTS

GRINNELL COLLEGE

IF THE French overseas empire of the late nineteenth and early twentieth centuries evoked no great popular enthusiasm from the citizenry of the Third Republic, it did become the source of inspiration, reflection, and purpose for a small group of Frenchmen who were attracted by what might be called its "frontier qualities." Although the French colonial frontier was never graced with a bold and unifying theory, such as the one Frederick Jackson Turner provided for the American West, it did afford the space, the atmosphere, and the isolation in which self-styled men of action and energy could exercise their ambitions and fulfill their desires, could renew their lives, and could dedicate themselves to national causes.

It is with the attitudes and purposes of these men that this essay is concerned. More particularly, it will concentrate on that small articulate element among them who left behind memoirs, letters, and fictional accounts of this new world as they saw and assessed it. The bulk of this material appeared before the First World War when colonial conquest was still fresh and the imperial idea was yet untarnished. Although it is evident that such writings appeared sporadically well after the war and even as late as the end of the Second World War, the major themes and opinions had by then already been stated and elaborated. After 1914 one generally finds only echoes and reverberations.

It is rather tempting to bring these colonialists together as a "group," for most of them were either acquainted with one another's writings or knew one another personally. More than this, they shared, with but minor variations, the same sentiments about the colonial experience. Even further, their literary efforts, following upon the "exotic" school of French colonial literature—last successfully instructed by Pierre Loti—were serious attempts to understand and describe this new colonial world: whether technically, from the point of view of conquest and administration; whether culturally, from the point of view of the psychology of cultural contact and collision; or whether personally, from the point of view of self-revelation.[1] In both fiction and nonfiction local color gave way to hard analysis and sincere introspection; the tourist's glance to the expert's stare. Indeed, most of this literature was not designed to amuse and distract but rather to reveal and inform. The didactic purpose which was behind its publication was the awakening of an indifferent people to the value of colonial empire. Here was an attempt to create a colonial consciousness.[2]

Yet for this group of colonial authors the real interest in empire lay not in the now stock economic and political arguments but rather in the possibility of forming overseas personal and social qualities which were thought either to be lacking or atrophied in metropolitan France. As in the history of the American frontier, one finds an imagined opposition existing between two divergent social environments: one which confines and restrains, the other which liberates and inspires. Perhaps the two adjectives most frequently used to describe the condition of France were "sickly" and "anemic." By contrast, the adjectives "energetic" and "manly" appear regularly to describe the condition of colonial life.[3]

---

[1] On this subject see Marius-Ary Leblond, *Après l'exoticisme: Le roman colonial* (Paris, 1926), pp. 7–8; A. Roland Lebel, *Histoire de la littérature coloniale* (Paris, 1931), pp. 86–87; and Jean Rodes, "L'Exoticisme nouveau," *La Grande France,* June, 1903, pp. 352–53.

[2] The thought is that of Lebel, *Histoire de la littérature coloniale,* pp. 87–88.

[3] The following are offered as examples of this sentiment:

"A sick person is not bothered by the fetid odor of his room. But when a healthy person comes in from outside, he will heave with disgust and vomit. This is what happens to us, men of the desert, when we return to civilization."—Ernest Psichari, *L'Appel des armes* (Paris, 1945), pp. 322–23. The volume was first published in 1908.

"I am entering into the huge palace of nature by the main door. . . . I . . . feel myself a male in the midst of our sickly generations."—Letter of Abel Jeandet dated September 15, 1886, in B. H. Gausseron, *Un Français au Sénégal: Abel Jeandet* (Paris, 1913).

Almost all the conditions and qualities which are seen as accompanying modern urban-technological existence were condemned by the colonialists. In a sense they were Arcadians seeking to return to an older way of life, to a world unspoiled and unpampered. And if they were Arcadians, they were also Spartans. Like Rousseau they upheld that civic virtue which was expressed in the words "duty" and "devotion." Their concept of the good life was not at variance with that of other nineteenth-century thinkers who searched nostalgically for the disappearing yeomen, frontiersman, or even the knight in shining armor.

How unlike their ideal, therefore, seemed the world of the Third Republic. Complacency, materialism, and intellectualism were deemed national afflictions. Bourgeois objectives and positivist thought processes were believed to engender only a desire for comfort and an unhealthy fascination with the efficacy of ideas. With such a negative assessment went the additional belief that the factionalism of national politics and the do-nothingness of bureaucracy made France a nation without direction and devoid of will. As a result of their attitudes, the colonialists became socially disaffected and, in large measure, anti-intellectual. Conversely, they were idealistic and romantic, if by that term the notions of chivalrous action and dedication will be allowed. To characterize them, one might say they were "marginal men," uncomfortable in the social environment which nurtured them and yet, because of their sense of loyalty or duty, unwilling to revolt openly against it. Instead, they found in the colonial empire the means not only to escape from, but also to escape to. Overseas they became aware of the national unity and personal purpose which had eluded them at home

As might be imagined, the literature which these colonialists produced tended to have one dominant theme which might best be summed up in terms of a simple dialectic: decadence and renewal. Contemporary metropolitan France was the thesis; the colonial empire, the antithesis; and the synthesis was to be a rejuvenated France blessed with national purpose and the will to carry it out.

Hubert Lyautey, who was both the outstanding exponent of the new colonial idea and its living paradigm, expressed himself more frequently and more forcefully than any of his contemporaries on the notion of French decadence. His prolific and revealing correspondence is interlaced with personal appreciations of this problem. In an early letter from Indochina he insisted upon the existence of a social obligation for men like himself to save France from decomposition and ruin.[4] In another letter, written about the same time, he denounced France's institutional vice: "this omnipotent, incompetent, unstable, and irresponsible parliamentarianism." [5] As for the bureaucracy, he spoke of it later in similar words: its "formalism, slowness, obstruction to all practical schemes" was berated.[6] Of the ivory-towered intellectual, he warned, "Beware of mandarins." [7] And, finally, he bemoaned the existence of the army officer at home, whose chief functions were to lead cotillions and to engage in amorous manoeuvres.[8]

At the very least, Lyautey had gone far beyond Lamartine's much earlier belief that France was suffering from ennui.

It would be erroneous to assume, however, that the concern with decay in metropolitan France was exclusively a preoccupation of late-nineteenth-century colonialists. Throughout the history of the Third Republic a minor note of disagreement with the institutions and values of the regime is sounded. The attempted philosophy of Vichy is but the last and official expression of such concern. In the first three decades of life under the new Republic, when memories of 1870 were still painfully fresh and domestic scandals were all too frequent, the theme of contemporary social degeneration enjoyed a certain notoriety. Not unusual was the dismal assumption of "Latin decadence," an assumption that was freighted by the end of the century with heavy thoughts about the vigorous activity and abounding successes of the Anglo-Saxon and Germanic worlds.[9] France, by national comparison, seemed to be

[4] Letter dated February 20, 1897, in Lyautey, *Lettres du Tonkin et de Madagascar* (2d ed.; Paris, 1921), p. 489.

[5] Letter dated February 26, 1897, *ibid.*, p. 496.

[6] Speech given at Fez on October 30, 1921, in Lyautey, *Paroles d'action* (Paris, 1927), p. 352.

[7] Letter dated June 26, 1895, in *Lettres du Tonkin et de Madagascar*, pp. 221–22.

[8] Letter dated December 23, 1894, *ibid.*, p. 86.

[9] On this subject see Raymond F. Betts, *Assimilation and Association in French Colonial Theory, 1890–1914* (New York, 1961), pp. 38–42. As an example of expressions of "Latin decadence" see Edmond Demolins, *A quoi tient la supériorité des Anglo-Saxons?* (Paris, 1899).

proving the significance of the Social Darwinian metaphor of organic social growth: she was an old nation.

Where the French colonialists parted company with other critics of the contemporary situation was in their belief that colonialism was the way to rejuvenation. Joseph Chailley-Bert, one of the most ardent and persistent advocates of colonialism, argued that "new blood is infused by youth into the elderly, by the young colonies into the old *métropole*." [10] Gabriel Hanotaux, who denied the idea of "decay," was none the less given to write of the colonial empire in *L'Energie française*: "What a rich and wonderful field! Don't repeat the notion that France is only a second-rate nation and that she must bow before her destiny: discover the role which is hers, thanks to this recent and commendable effort. . . ." [11] A great admirer of Lyautey, André Tarde, put it this way: "Flux and reflux: the colonies return reinvigorated the strength we have lent them." [12] And one of the heroes in a novel written by Eugène Melchoir de Vogüé, literary critic and friend of Lyautey, seriously contemplated France's colonial role as he returned from a brief trip to Senegal. "At length during the days on the sea his careful thought worked over the antithesis on which it was fixed: the germs of recomposition which he had left in Africa; the ferment of decomposition which he was going to find in Paris." [13]

All these statements were variations on the theme of the new world redressing the wrongs of the old. They were, therefore, a reaffirmation of the possibilities of French greatness, of the nation's ability, thanks to her colonial empire, to enjoy dignified status with the other great nations of the world, and particularly with a Germany which was threatening her militarily and a United States which was awing her industrially. In this respect, the colonial mood was complementary to the nationalist one.

As frequently happens in themes of national revitalization, great emphasis was placed on the role to be fulfilled by youth, by a new generation in healthy opposition to the old and dominating one. Again it was Hubert Lyautey who turned most frequently to youth and who, indeed, became something of its hero. In his controversial

[10] Chailley-Bert, *La vie intime: Les discours du President Roosevelt* (Bordeaux, 1903), p. 32.

[11] Hanotaux, *L'Energie française* (Paris, 1911), pp. 364–65.

[12] Tarde, *Maroc: Ecole d'énergie* (Paris, 1923), p. 37.

[13] Vogüé, *Les morts qui parlent* (Paris, 1899), pp. 231–32.

Rôle social de l'officier, first appearing in the *Revue des Deux Mondes* of 1891, he commented with satisfaction that the youth of his day were inclining more to rugged and purposeful action than to quiet speculation.[14] For Maurice Barrès, this characteristic was not unique to this generation, however pronounced it might then be: "To achieve great tasks in face of a very clear ideal, whether this be the deliverance of Christ's tomb or the establishment of France in Algeria . . . has been the constant dream of young Frenchmen across the centuries. . . ."[15] With this Chailley-Bert would concur. For him the Frenchman exhibited two sides: the comfort loving, thoughtful one; the dynamic, adventuresome one. The prevalence of the former, he hoped, was now giving way to the latter, as it had done on occasions in the past.[16] The spirit these men were describing is caught up in the words of a young colonial administrator writing from Senegal shortly before his death: "Here we live and here we act; everyone does his bit: *gesta Dei per Francos.*"[17]

The combination of action and idealism, this crusading spirit which Lyautey and his contemporaries in France attributed to the new generation was, if anything, not singularly French. It was clearly discernible elsewhere in the Western world, and it occupied the thoughts of men in countries other than France. The young gallants who ran up San Juan Hill with Teddy Roosevelt, the *Jugend* who wended their way through the Black Forest with a song on their lips, and the *ardenti* who were soon to follow D'Annunzio wholeheartedly into the city of Fiume also believed in the primacy of rude action over studied speculation.

In France this generational change was most seriously considered by André Tarde and Henri Massis—writing under the pseudonym "Agathon"—in their influential volume, *Les jeunes gens d'aujourd'hui,* published in 1913. On the basis of a selective sampling of opinions and attitudes of the educated youth of the day, they concluded that love of action had become the dominant contemporary theme. They also concluded that the pivotal date for this change in attitude was 1890, the year in which Paul Le

---

[14] Lyautey, *Le rôle social de l'officier* (Paris, 1935), p. 2.
[15] Barrès, preface to *L'Ame de colonial: Lettres du Lt. Colonel Moll* (Paris, 1912), p. i.
[16] *Ibid.,* p. 9 *et passim.*
[17] Letter dated November 14, 1887, cited in Gausseron, *Un Français au Sénégal.*

Bourget published his *Disciple,* a work that "Agathon" evaluated as a manifesto against the "vanity of pure reason. . . ." [18] The preceding generation had been hopelessly turned in on itself, as it were, inescapably confined within the circles of its thought. An imagined antithesis between thought and action plagued that generation, with the result that all its intellectual energy had been spent in the search for reasons to justify action. Here, with less irony, is Kierkegaard's intellectual who decides to decide—and gets no farther. In contrast with that earlier generation "Agathon" happily found the youth of 1890 breaking from the vicious circle by tending toward "a belief, a synthesis, a dogmatism which is precursor to action." The new generation was basically anti-intellectual; it "hardly considers life as an intellectual debate. . . ." [19] Or, put otherwise and in a fashion which would be agreeable to most of the colonialists, it placed thought in the service of action.

For this animated youth the obvious field in which to deploy its talents was the empire. "You young people who do not know what to do . . . go people our colonies," one writer exhorted, "where you will become transformed men, men of energy and of will. . . ." [20] Lyautey had already anticipated such a metamorphosis and had even provided it with a descriptive figure of speech which was soon popularized: "school of energy." "I have found in our colonies in Asia, in Africa and here [Algeria] the most glorious school of energy in which our race is being retempered and recast as if in a crucible." [21] The school was, of course, one of environment, a Toynbeean world of challenge and response. Daily colonial life, whatever its scale, necessitated complete personal engagement. The young colonial officers in Indochina were, for instance, described by Lyautey as "simple, diligent and modest workers [who] at 35 years of age had already lived a full life dedicated to action, to the *immediate.* . . ." [22]

Removed from the comfortable and closeted existence which the *métropole* too easily afforded, or so at least the colonialists generally thought, the young military administrator would be forced

[18] Agathon, pseud., *Les jeunes gens d'anjourd'hui* (Paris, 1913), p. 13.
[19] *Ibid.,* pp. 8–9 and 19.
[20] J. B. Piollet, *La France hors de France* (Paris, 1900), p. 85.
[21] Speech given in Oran, July 12, 1907, cited in *Paroles d'action,* p. 53. This particular speech is one of the best summaries of Lyautey's ideas.
[22] Letter dated December 23, 1894, in *Lettres du Tonkin et de Madagascar,* p. 86.

to employ hitherto unused faculties and develop new skills in order to cope with the rudimentary existence which was, of necessity, to be his. He was not to be the fractionalized man, the bureaucrat of single function, or the worker of single tasks, but the man of many talents and occupations, a whole man, an individual relying solely on himself and his own abilities. "He soon acquires a taste for this existence, for he is aware that he is not simply one of the many gears in an administrative machine; he feels that he *is accomplishing something,* that he has been, in a restricted area, a creator." [23] This was the description of an ideal type of *broussard* provided by Maurice Delafosse, one of France's great colonial teachers. The real heroic counterpart of *broussard* was no doubt Colonel Henry Moll, a colonial officer killed in the line of duty, and a man Barrès described as the "eternal French cavalier." [24] Of his life in Mauretania, Moll wrote: "Here one finds action in a setting of vast horizons. Here is the out-of-doors life under the sun." [25] And it was, in his estimation, a life that was never monotonous, however tedious it might be: military operations one day, peaceful persuasion another, administrative organization still another. It was a full life: "Ah! If I were not able to try to be useful and to live by strong, virile action, how unfortunate I would be!" [26]

When asked what the colonies were producing, one of Vögué's heroes forcefully replied: "Men . . . we are forming the cadres of our national awakening." [27] None of the colonialists would have disagreed with him.

While all the colonies were considered reserves of national energy, most authors saw Africa in particular as the real "school of energy." This last continent to be opened to the curiosity and the ambitions of Western man appeared to stand forth as a New World: vast and empty, untracked and primitive, a site of new frontiers and large horizons. The appeal of Africa was that of the

[23] Delafosse, *Les états d'ame d'un colonial* (Paris, 1909), pp. 38–39. For a similar expression of thought see Robert Delavignette, *Les vrais chefs de l'empire* (Paris, 1939), p. 27.

[24] Barrès, preface to *L'Ame de colonial,* p. vi.

[25] Cited by Auguste Terrier in an introductory note, "Le lieutenant-colonel Moll en Afrique," in Barrès, *L'Ame de colonial.*

[26] *Ibid.,* p. 29.   [27] Vögué, *Les morts qui parlent,* p. 224.

elemental, a world still seemingly primordial and unspoiled, a world uncontained when compared with complacent, composed, and cramped Europe.

As has already been asserted, the French attraction fastened on the effects of environmental influences. Speaking of Algeria, one author wrote: "The energetic and voluptuous men who inhabit such a country conceive of life quite differently from the septentrional peoples with pink skin." [28] So also thought the colonial administrator-militarist whether in North Africa, the Sahara, or the bush of West Africa.

That crossing of the Mediterranean or the slow descent of the Atlantic was, in effect, the passage from one world to another. For the French, as for Joseph Conrad in *Heart of Darkness*, or E. M. Forster in *A Passage to India*, transportation was transformation, from the Mediterranean and European world with its emphasis on calculated measure and fixed dimension to an alien world in which space and light combined in such a way as to upset the traditional European vision. If ever the phrase "non-Western world" had meaning, it was then and to these writers.

It is true that distinctions in the literature appear according to what part of Africa the author is treating. The division of Africa into two parts widely separated by the endless Sahara, was frequently made, as it still is today. Indeed, North Africa has a place in French literature, colonial and otherwise, which is older and more distinguished than that of other regions. Furthermore, there is something in the argument that North Africa is part of the Mediterranean world with its own link to the Latin past. Certainly French writers of the period here under consideration had that past in mind when they spoke of a new race of "Africans" emerging in North Africa. Wrote one: "The Latin of Africa has come out of the necropolises of history and archeology to live once again. The word 'African' is taking on the significance it had in the times of Apuleius and Saint Augustine. . . ." [29] It was appealing to the French to imagine themselves as Neo-Latins, as colonial settlers remaking the old land and linking it again with the West. And just such an image also allowed Lyautey to see North Africa as being

---

[28] Robert Randau, *Les colons* (Paris, 1926), p. 51.
[29] Louis Bertrand, preface to *Notre Afrique* (Paris, 1925), pp. 1–2.

"for our race what the Far West was for America: the land, par excellence, of energy, of rejuvenation, and of fertility." [30] Certainly sub-Saharan Africa was not considered at this time as being capable of lending itself to such development.[31]

None the less, all of French-held Africa gained its own unity through the setting that it provided and the atmosphere that it created, a land in which the Frenchman would be whole, return to his self: emotional and sensual, violent and voluptuous, thoughtful and idealistic.

Discussing the new French African writers, Louis Bertrand, a novelist himself, commented: "They present us with types of whole humanity—vices and virtues—brimming over with life, with will, with intelligence, and naturally heroic." [32] These writers almost seem to be Camuses before their time; their attitude was rather paleo-existentialist: they felt life as well as reasoned about it. But they also struggled for a purpose. Unwilling to deny all metaphysics, they were often given to seeking a higher cause, an ideal: that of France, if not that of God.

Two writers in particular stand out as examples of this spirit and attitude. The first was Robert Randau, an Algerian-born novelist whose several novels occupy an important position in French colonial literature. The second was Ernest Psichari, grandson of Renan, friend of Péguy, mystic and nationalist.

Randau, who was born Robert Arnaud, was hailed in his time as the first serious author of a colonial school of literature, one of those men who lived in the colonies and therefore wrote with the authority and sensitivity of the insider. He was born in 1873 at Mustapha in Algeria and spent his early life in the colony. Later he entered and was graduated from the Ecole Coloniale in Paris; subsequently he served as a colonial administrator in Algeria, Upper Volta, and Senegal. From this varied experience he drew materials for his novels which were, in his estimation, but a single work: "*Les colons*," he wrote of an early volume, "is the first episode of the *Geste africaine*, I have only written one novel; each of my volumes describes the doings of a man of action." [33]

[30] Speech of July 12, 1907, in *Paroles d'action,* p. 52. See Tarde on this same subject, *Maroc,* p. 28.

[31] Pierre Fontaine, writing under the pseudonym, "Pierre Navarre," saw sub-Saharan Africa as an American Far West immediately after the Second World War. See his *Visions impériales* (Grenoble, 1946), p. 229.

[32] Bertrand, *Notre Afrique,* p. 22.

[33] Dedication page, *Les colons* (Paris, 1926). First published in 1907.

Whether colonial-settlers in Algeria, colonial-militarists in Mauretania, or colonial-administrators in Senegal, Randau's heroes are
rough and violent men who work, love, and hate with consummate
passion. His Algerians, for instance, have been described as a
"brutal race, greedy, practical, frank, and naturally detesting European sentimentalities and the classical ideal which has made
France anemic." [34] All his strong characters are men who were re-
formed by an unrelenting sun. "Light and will, such are the bases
of our African art, imperiously solar," comments one of his minor
characters.[35] Randau says of another one: "He renewed his energy
in the rays of the tropical light which modifies in its own way the
character of men." [36] This is hardly *douce France* with its subtle
nuances. Rather this is a violent world, sharp, brutal, unrelenting,
and inescapable. "The exercise of the will is imposed on the individual who desires to survive. Under the immense energy of the
tropics . . . the energy of the white man must be up to things." [37]

The most attractive of Randau's heroes, Jean Cassard, knows this.
He has faced the primordial struggle and has succeeded. Like
Randau, he was Algerian-born, Parisian-educated, and called upon
to serve in West Africa—at least in the novel, *Les explorateurs*.
After a hardy and dramatic excursion of pacification in Mauritania,
Cassard prepares to return to Algeria and reflects on the fierce
nature he has endured:

The wind pitilessly infests love and kills it. The prolific forces of the
sun, the ocean, the sands, and the marshes cradle nature between their
giant arms. The fertile cruelty is beautiful with a beauty of ecstasy.
The man of action has the confused desire to embrace these forces of
sensual excitement and extermination so that he himself, indifferent
to petty social matters, might die from this same embrace.[38]

Cassard thus found the beauty of force and violence in a foreign
environment. And he survived because he knew how to dominate
himself as well as the people and the setting around him. Randau
stated that his intention in this novel had been "to sketch the
psychic history of a European gripped by African nature. . . ." [39]
Psichari's personal history suggests much of the same thing.

[34] Marius-Ary Leblond, preface *ibid.*, p. 9. Hanotaux, too, spoke of the French
Algerians as proud and violent men. See *L'Enérgie française*, p. 310.
[35] *Les colons*, p. 109.
[36] *Les explorateurs* (Paris, 1929), p. 89. First published in 1909.
[37] *Ibid.*, p. 30.
[38] *Ibid.*, pp. 338–39.
[39] Preface, *ibid.*, p. 9.

Superficially, Psichari's life seems to be representative of the generational change which Lyautey mentioned and which "Agathon" analyzed. Somewhat like Martin du Gard's hero, Jean Barois, Psichari left an anticlerical, positivist atmosphere to return to the traditional and the absolute, but for Psichari the search took place at a very youthful age and in the army—more particularly, in the army in Africa. Because he was Renan's grandson and because he was raised in a highly refined intellectual milieu, his conversion was all the more dramatic.

After obtaining a brilliant *licence en philosophie,* Psichari decided to enlist in the army. He served in the infantry for one year and then reenlisted in the regular army in 1904. Desirous of action, he asked to be transferred to the colonial artillery and was soon off on an expedition to the Congo under the command of Colonel Lenfant. He returned to France in 1908, but the attraction of Africa was very strong, and so he left in 1909 for what became a three-year tour of duty in Mauretania. His African experience yielded several books, all frankly revealing of the author's personal odyssey through mind and soul as well as across the jungles of Sangha and the barren wastes of Mauretania.

Most critics have seen Psichari's writings as expressions of the phases leading to his conversion, or his submission—for it was that, too.[40] Psichari was one of those persons who find freedom under authority, who long for an immutable order in which to take their places and to serve. Of all the manly virtues he praised, fidelity enjoyed the highest position.[41] The discipline of the army first and the order of the Church later were to fulfill his needs, not only because both institutions clearly defined duty and inspired fidelity, but also because, for him, they stood forth firmly against a world of change, materialism, sophistry: the bourgeois order that all the colonialists berated. Captain Nangès, the hero of Psichari's highly personalized novel, *L'Appel des armes,* "sensed that it [the army] represents a great force of the past, the only one—along with the Church—which has remained virginal, not sullied or dis-

---

[40] See particularly Henry Daniel-Rops, *Psichari* (Paris, 1942), pp. 36–39; and Eugen Weber, "Psichari and God," *Yale French Studies,* No. 12, pp. 19–33.

[41] Speaking through Maxence, one of his fictional heroes, he said: "Nothing appeared more noble to this soldier than fidelity. It alone is peace and consolation. . . . It alone is the highest." *Le voyage du centurion* (Paris, 1947), p. 75. First published in 1915.

colored by the new impurity." [42] That impurity was essentially material progress.

Like Moll, Psichari was a man out of joint with his times; he, too, was a crusader of yore. Also like Moll, he found in Africa his proper domain, there where spirit and action combined and were almost elevated to the ethereal:

The action which was there stimulated is so pure, so heroic, that it already enters completely into the category of dreams. . . . In a forest of Sangha I heard, rustling in the verdant passes, the far-off call of Parsifal. . . . Read the accounts of the travelers in Africa. These men are the new mystics, full of the faith which moves mountains. . . .[43]

When Psichari wrote these lines his style and thought were still quite romantic and his faith had not yet transcended the army and the France it served. But the questioning and restless mind which was his, and the mysticism which hurried it on, soon led him to Catholicism and to a more Pascalian style.[44]

Like his contemporaries Psichari found this personally reformative experience in part the result of a return to the primordial, to something approaching the threshold of man's existence on earth. His sojourns in Africa were, in a way, what had been Joseph Conrad's: a journey into the heart of darkness, into those recesses of the soul long hidden by the overlaying of civilization. But Psichari, unlike Conrad, drew no profoundly frightening or nihilistic conclusions. Granted he was aware of the tug of Africa on the soul as it aroused personal vanity along with humility, the primordial was for him essentially simple and pure: it tended to dignify the man who entered it.

Oh, exile, taste the joy of being true to yourself. The Western world is no longer. The lies, the vain speeches, the sophisms are for you as if they never existed. You are alone here in the sweet thought of night, and, tomorrow, in the frugal morning, you will be a man at grips with the land, a primitive man on a primitive planet, a free man in open space.[45]

Such an existence had awakened in Psichari, as it had in Randau —or Lyautey, for that matter—the love of action, of physical en-

[42] *L'Appel des armes,* pp. 32–33.
[43] *Terres de soleil et de sommeil* (Paris, 1947), p. 244. First published in 1908.
[44] See Daniel-Rops, *Psichari,* p. 39.
[45] *Le voyage du centurion,* pp. 127–28.

gagement. He saw Africa as one of the last refuges of "national energy." "Here in the land of barbarians," he wrote, "I reacquired hope; I again believe in the goodness of action, and I believe that it will succeed in dominating the laziness of the weak." [46] And, he concluded, the time might soon come when violence would no longer be equated with injustice. On the contrary, it might be seen as:

the natural play of a soul strong and tempered as if of steel. The hour will come when goodness will cease to be fruitful and will become unmanly and cowardly. Then war will be an inexpressible poem of blood and beauty. Then we will find the most normal and the most noble of these infinite sources of energy . . . which circulate in us incessantly. . . . This is the vision which I have taken from the conquered land . . . the last word of Africa before I was to regain the bright threshold of France.[47]

Psichari's Africa was both a new and a last frontier where meditation and action might be harmonized, and where France could again be found and, along with her, noble, dutiful Frenchmen. Maxence, hero in Psichari's last novel, appropriately named *Le voyage du centurion*, speaks for the author when he says of Mauretania:

This desert is full of France; it is found at every turn. But it isn't the France that is seen in France; it is not the France of sophists and false savants, nor of reasoners devoid of reason. Here is virtuous France, pure and simple; the France helmeted with reason, armed with fidelity.[48]

Psichari then adds that "No one can understand it fully who is not Christian," a thought with which some of his contemporaries might differ. But with Lyautey, Moll, and Vögué, Psichari found away from France the eternal France he wished to see: unified and charged with a historic mission

For these same people Africa in particular was the place in which they found their manhood, their whole personality. Here man and earth met directly; nothing divided them.[49] The confrontation was

---

[46] *Terres de soleil et de sommeil,* pp. 228–29.
[47] *Ibid.,* pp. 232–33.
[48] *Le voyage du centurion,* pp. 7–8.
[49] Wrote Psichari: "One is in direct relationship with the earth; nothing is interposed between men and it. Sensation of an absolute primitivism, unknown elsewhere except in Africa." *Terres de soleil et de sommeil,* p. 134.

one with space and with silence; there were no means of escape and no objects of diversion. Unlike the existence which might be found in the French colonies in the Far East, there was nothing of the exotic in Africa. The setting was variously monotonous and barren, as in the desert, or humid and primitive, as in the bush and the jungle. What the French colonial learned to live with was solitude; what he learned to live by was will. "Whites of weak character or lazy intellect were never able to console themselves over the loss of European horizons." [50]

Much as André Malraux and Albert Camus were to do after the First World War, the articulate and thoughtful colonialists in Africa were grappling with the human condition. And they tended to anticipate Malraux's and Camus's conclusions about it: existence preceded thought; the deed, the word. Man found himself by plunging into his environment, not by observing it with detachment. Could not Psichari have written of Western civilization and his African world the following: "The first wants to bring the universe to man; the second offers up man to the universe . . ."? [51] Yet this was Malraux describing the differences between West and East.

It would appear that many of the Frenchmen who were fired with enthusiasm for empire in the two decades before the First World War were both nationalists and budding existentialists: men looking for a cause, men revolting against the rational, positivist tradition of their day. They were doers, not thinkers, although most of them were thoughtful men.

I am decidedly an "animal of action"; I have always known it and the facts have finally confirmed it; after twenty years of wasteful fiddling I finally believe I have grasped "action." . . . More than ever I sense that without productive, imperative, and immediate action, I would waste, rot. [52]

This is the way Lyautey put it, he who found the colonial life at forty years of age and then urged it on the youth of his day so that their experience would not be so long delayed as his had been.

Few of the colonialists were as sensitive, perceptive, or revealing

[50] Randau, *Les explorateurs,* p. 79.

[51] Malraux, *Temptation of the West,* trans. Robert Hollander (New York, 1961), p. 86. First published in 1926.

[52] Lyautey, letter dated August 15, 1895, in *Lettres du Tonkin et de Madagascar,* p. 382.

as Lyautey or Psichari, but all of them felt that their removal from France was something of a "magnificent exile" [53] from a narrow and limited existence. "This is the great and independent life," wrote Moll, a life in which love of country, of action, and of the out-of-doors were combined in an exhilarating way.[54]

When the First World War broke out, men like Psichari met their death nobly and dutifully acting for the eternal France in which they believed. With pride Lyautey could say in 1919 that the *poilu* who had defended France in her critical days had been formed on the colonial frontier.[55]

After the war the spirit and the purpose which had animated the prewar colonialists either declined or was often channeled into perverse forms, such as fascism. The heroic days of empire were now over. For better and for worse the process of "pacification," of conquering and dominating with blood and sword was completed. Everywhere administrators were replacing the older path-finders and soldiers. Delafosse sensed the change even before the war: The *ronds-de-cuir* were edging the *broussards* out.[56] The age of Sarraut's *mise en valeur* was at hand.

The French colonial frontier thus closed but a few years after the American one. It had well served the purpose for which the colonialists claimed it. They conceived of and exaggerated a way of life which fascinated and inspired the youth at home.[57] They had managed to awaken a sense of colonial consciousness, at least among one segment of the population.

The personal ideals of these men may seem somewhat naïve or misplaced to us today, but such ideals became fashionable in France in the few years before the war. A new nationalism, more sentiment than doctrine, floated above parties and factions, and seemed to unify, however momentarily and tenuously, France faced by a renewed German menace.[58] Bergson's *élan vital* and the army's

---

[53] Psichari in a prefatory note to *L'Appel des armes*.

[54] Letter dated August 18, 1910, in *L'Ame de colonial*.

[55] Speech at Casablanca, July 29, 1919, in *Paroles d'action*, pp. 292–93.

[56] Delafosse, *L'Etats d'âme*, pp. 73–74.

[57] "How can one ignore the success which the accounts of our colonials achieved, most particularly perhaps on this intellectual youth that we are studying here?" Agathon, *Les jeunes gens*, p. 33.

[58] On this subject see Eugen Weber, *The Nationalist Revival in France, 1905–1914* (Berkeley, 1959).

famous pronouncement, *offensif à outrance,* were most compatible
with Lyautey's philosophy and, obviously, with Psichari's!

Long ago, indeed at the very time the men considered in this
essay were alive and doing their adventuresome deeds, J. A. Hob-
son recognized in his classic *Imperialism: A Study* that, while the
taproot of imperialism was economic, the initiators of particular
imperialist acts were often men of lofty purpose and sincere dis-
interestedness. The frontiers they found newly opened to them,
or still waiting to be opened, often allowed for heroism and even
some form of sainthood.[59] Perhaps there was a psychological type,
the "imperialist personality," who was driven by aggression, by
loneliness, or by social discomfort, to seek solace and self overseas.
Whatever their motives and drives, the prewar colonialist group
that provided France with much of her best colonial literature and
some of her best colonial administrators all agreed with General
Gallieni's simple and sincere statement about the overseas experience: "I love this life."

[59] The Sahara was particularly singled out as the land of the heroic and the
saintly colonialist. For the fullest treatment of this subject, see Joseph Peyre,
Sahara éternel (Paris, 1944). See also Tarde, *Maroc,* particularly pp. 29–30.

Edouard Herriot in Lyons: Some Aspects of His Role as Mayor

SABINE JESSNER

PURDUE UNIVERSITY
(INDIANAPOLIS CAMPUS)

"Beaucoup de radicaux se pourraient définir
les bonapartistes de la République."
—Edouard Herriot, *Notes et maximes*

In 1932 Albert Thibaudet, one of the foremost French literary critics, wrote a book on politics, *Les idées politiques de la France*. In it he asserted that all radicals belonged in the Jacobin tradition, but went on to distinguish between the *radical de proconsulat* and the *radical de comité*. The former, he said, derived from the centralized and authoritarian or "proconsular" trend in Jacobinism, while the latter followed the revolutionary cell and club, or *comité* tradition.[1] In Thibaudet's opinion, Edouard Herriot, the Radical Socialist leader, premier, and mayor of Lyons, belonged to the committee tradition.

With due respect to the eminent French critic, this author believes that the case of Edouard Herriot may not be quite so simple. It is the object of this essay to examine the "proconsular"

---

[1] Albert Thibaudet, *Les idées politiques de la France* (Paris, 1932), pp. 147–48.

aspects of Edouard Herriot. Being one of the most eloquent spokesmen for Radical Socialism during the second half of the Third Republic, he contributed to the formulation of the party creed in numerous books, articles, and speeches delivered both in and out of parliament. While Herriot was not elected president of the party until 1919, he had been active in its inner councils since 1907, collaborating in drawing up party platforms.

The Parti Républicain Radical et Radical-Socialiste was formally established in 1901. Basing their political creed on nineteenth-century radical tradition, the Radical Socialists stressed their adherence to the "glorious principles" of the French Revolution, to the support of the Republic based on popular sovereignty and on opposition to the influence of the Catholic Church. They cherished individualism and defended the right of private property as guaranteed in the Declaration of the Rights of Man. Herriot as a Radical Socialist always praised laissez-faire and, by insisting that policy should be established in response to the demands of the people rather than imposed from above, denigrated state intervention. There may not have been a narrowly defined Radical Socialist doctrine, but there did exist a flexible tradition incorporating most of these themes.

The loose organization of the party reflected this flexibility. Active party members, the *militants,* met at congresses and banquets to listen to their leaders who shaped the party platforms and represented the party in parliament. The strength of the party lay in the provinces and was greatest south of the Loire. It has, therefore, been called the most provincial of French parties. Thus, the decentralized structure of Radical Socialism belongs in the committee tradition and Herriot's pronouncements seemed to be a perfect expression of the *radical de comité* spirit of the party. But in sharp contrast to his words was the way in which he actually administered "his" city of Lyons for half a century.

Herriot had been a practicing politician for less than two years when, in 1905, he became the chief executive of France's second city.[2] Born in Troyes in 1872, he had trained for the teaching profession at the prestigious Ecole Normale Supérieure in Paris,

[2] The population of Lyons was 523,000 in 1911. Six years later it had risen to 723,000. Herriot stated that if the suburban areas had been included, the figure would have been close to a million. Edouard Herriot, *Lyon pendant la guerre* (Paris, 1925), p. xv.

coming to Lyons in 1896 as an instructor in the Lycée Ampère. Eight years later, in the midst of a promising academic career, he suddenly decided to run for the City Council.

Although Herriot did not seek office until 1904, his interest in politics had been awakened much earlier by the Dreyfus Affair, which stirred so many young intellectuals at the turn of the century. The "Dreyfus Revolution," as Georges Sorel called it,[3] resembled the July Revolution of 1830 in its effect on professors and intellectuals. Herriot had not, however, been an early "dreyfusard": descended on both sides from professional soldiers, he was reluctant at first to doubt the probity of the army leaders. But once he had made up his mind, he became publicly—and eloquently—committed to the cause of revision.

In Paris, in 1898, the League of the Rights of Man was founded to fight for a revision of the judgment against Captain Dreyfus. When a branch of the League was formed in Lyons, Herriot joined it, and met many prominent citizens, including the surgeon Victor Augagneur who was to become the mayor of the city. Herriot began to make speeches for the group.

The Radical groups were in the forefront of revision. It is true that even before the Dreyfus Affair Herriot, on his arrival in Lyons at the age of twenty-four, had joined the local Radical club in the sixth ward, which was primarily composed of young professors. Since many of them, like Herriot, had been educated on state scholarships, their adherence was, perhaps, not so much a political act as a gesture of gratitude to the Republic. Even earlier, however, Herriot had had a connection with radicalism; when he was still a student at the Ecole Normale, he had spent the summer of 1892 as tutor of the sons of Boissy d'Anglas.[4] He also acted as his secretary and helped him in his campaign against a conservative candidate by writing articles in two local papers. This brought him a severe reprimand from the director of the Ecole Normale.[5]

When, in 1904, his political mentor, the Socialist mayor Victor Augagneur, proposed his candidacy for the City Council, he naturally hoped that Herriot would run on the Socialist ticket.

---

[3] Georges Sorel, *La révolution dreyfusienne* (Paris, 1909).
[4] Edouard Herriot, *Jadis*, II (Paris, 1952), 646.
[5] Edouard Herriot, *Jadis*, I (Paris, 1948), 83.

But Herriot insisted on running as a Radical: he was already committed to the principles of the Radical Socialist party. Apart from his earlier Radical associations, the basis for his decision seems to have been his acceptance of the sanctity of private property which Marxist socialism was challenging. In spite of the difference in party labels, Augagneur continued to support his young protégé. Herriot's articles and speeches had already given him a wide reputation, and his name would add luster to Augagneur's administration.

Promising young intellectuals were in great political demand at that time. The political writer Hubert Bourgin remembered Jammy Schmidt telling him that Edouard Herriot had just joined the Radical Socialist party. As one of the leaders of the Radical party, Jammy Schmidt was elated, and Bourgin agreed that the acquisition of this brilliant young professor was a cause for rejoicing.[6]

The new member of the City Council was as yet only a part-time politician who still seemed bent on an academic career. He continued for a year and a half to teach at the Lycée Ampère and to pursue intellectual and academic advancement; in February, 1905, he defended his doctoral dissertations at the Sorbonne.

Then, in the fall of 1905, Mayor Augagneur resigned to become governor of Madagascar. Having himself broken with the recently unified Socialist party, Augagneur was not averse to helping a Radical Socialist candidate, that is to say, Herriot, become his successor. In the election, Herriot received thirty votes to twenty-two for Edouard Arnaud, his Socialist competitor,[7] and so became, on November 3, 1905, at the age of thirty-three, the new mayor of Lyons. He was the youngest mayor in France.

The election of 1905 marked the end of Herriot's teaching career. Coming as he did directly from the academic rostrum, trained only for intellectual exercise, and theoretically suspicious of power, Herriot might have been expected to approach his new duties with diffidence. But the contrary was true. In the first vol-

---

[6] Hubert Bourgin, *De Jaurès à Léon Blum: L'Ecole Normale et la politique* (Paris, 1938), p. 315. Bourgin was an acid critic of both Herriot and the Radicals. He goes on to say that the recruitment of Herriot, with his intellectual reputation, was a particular boon to a party which, though rich in material advantages, was poor in ideas (pauvre de pensée).

[7] Herriot, *Jadis*, I, 160. The popularly elected City Council elected the mayor.

ume of his autobiography, Herriot makes it quite clear that, from the start, he had relished the functions of the mayoralty. Boasting that Lyons had existed as an independent commune since 1340, he waxed lyrical about the classical beauty of the seventeenth-century city hall, which evoked for him the long and eventful history it had witnessed. He took pride not only in his city's age, but also in its size, pointing out that in 1905 Lyons had a budget of 20 million francs—a considerable sum for that period—and had employed 1,650 people.[8] Certainly bigness did not frighten him.

Nor did the demands of his office, which, rather, seemed to exhilarate him. He loved to work, expected those around him to work as hard as he did, and was always in a hurry to get things done. "M. Herriot does not like to wait," remarked one of his collaborators.[9] Herriot's trademark in office was an extraordinary vitality which he channeled into creative activity. He loved to build, whether schemes or buildings.

Immediately after his election, Mayor Herriot decided that his primary task was to increase the prosperity of Lyons, and he set out vigorously in pursuit of this objective. He formulated long-range plans for the development of Lyons as a river port, for the growth of local industries, for the expansion of education, including technical schools, and for the improvement of the conditions of the workers. To further these ends, he organized trade fairs, had permanent quarters built for the sample fair,[10] and began to plan, as early as 1910, an organization which would oversee the exploitation of the Rhône River. Ultimately he would set up, in 1921, the Compagnie Nationale du Rhône, whose board of directors included representatives of the French state, of the communes, and of the departments. This project was to be useful not only to the city of Lyons but was to revive the entire southeast of France. Actually the problem of the river was threefold: it had to be made navigable to improve the role of Lyons as a city port, it had to be used for purposes of irrigation to improve agriculture in the areas surrounding the city, and it had to provide for hydro-

[8] *Ibid.*, p. 172.
[9] Gustave Hirschfeld, *Tourvielle* (Lyons, 1917), p. 46.
[10] Herriot, *Lyon pendant la guerre*, p. 74. The first sample fair was held in 1916, a deliberate rival to the famous *Messe* in Leipzig.

electric works, in order to supply more power for the whole region.[11]

Since Herriot wanted to develop Lyons as a center of trade, he planned the construction of bridges and had a river port built at Rambaud on the Saône. The largest of the new bridges was to be inaugurated shortly after the First World War by a detachment of American troops. In order to encourage the cattle trade, a modern slaughterhouse was constructed in the La Mouche section of Lyons. This vast complex, including an indoor market hall, numerous stables, mechanized slaughtering facilities, a refrigerated storage area, and even its own railroad station, was completed in 1913.[12] Herriot also encouraged the traditional industries, for example, silk weaving, dying, food processing, metallurgy, leather, and chemical works. In the area of textiles, among other measures he created a new spinning school.

In a daring projection into the future, he arranged in 1910 for the construction of a municipal airport in the suburb of Bron. Three years later work was started on another major monument: a vast sports stadium. It was considered a landmark in twentieth-century building technique because it was constructed of unfaced concrete.[13] Herriot also streamlined government services, starting early in his administration by using electric trolleys for public transportation, purchasing trucks for use in both fire fighting and garbage removal, and renovating the water supply. Against the technological backwardness of France before the First World War, Herriot's vision shines boldly indeed.

In *Pourquoi je suis radical-socialiste*,[14] his most detailed examination of his political and economic ideas, Herriot continually emphasized the difference between his theories and those of the followers of Jean Jaurès and Léon Blum. Indeed, his title might more properly have been *Pourquoi je ne suis pas socialiste*. He disapproved of the amount of power which the Socialists demanded

---

[11] Henri Besseige, *Herriot parmi nous* (Paris, 1960), pp. 124–29. See also Herriot, *Jadis*, II, 96 ff.

[12] Herriot, *Jadis*, I, 172–73. It had been projected in 1906 and was built between 1909 and 1913.

[13] Dora Wiebenson, Tony Garnier's Cité Industrielle (unpublished M.A. essay, New York University School of Fine Arts, 1958), pp. 77–78. The stadium was completed in 1916.

[14] Edouard Herriot, *Pourquoi je suis radical-socialiste* (Paris, 1928).

for the state. More specifically, he opposed state ownership of the means of production, although he was ready enough to further free enterprise by state action.[15] If they agreed on anything, the Radical Socialists were united in their defense of the sanctity of private property. In presenting his plans for the progress of Lyons, Mayor Herriot always paid lip service to such tenets of Radical Socialist dogma as "free enterprise" or the "will of the people"; but the chapter of his autobiography covering the first years as mayor was entitled, significantly, "Municipal Action," and in it he expatiated —with a most unpolitical lack of reticence—on the joys of exercising power. Indeed, in imposing his will for progress on the people of Lyons, Herriot went counter to Radical Socialist democratic theory and in his passion for modernizing the city and its life, he went beyond party practice; that is, beyond the limits the party normally drew for state action in the economic sphere.

In order to effect his modernizations, Herriot had to struggle against the profound conservatism of his constituents, their habit of clinging to the old and the trusted. He succeeded by appealing to their civic pride as well as their desire for material improvement; and they endorsed his experiments by reelecting him for half a century. But certainly the voters did not initiate these ideas. It was Herriot who created policy, and exercised his full powers as chief executive to implement it.

While the mayor's primary goal was to increase the wealth of the city, an important secondary aim was the advancement of social welfare. Herriot believed it was the duty of the state to protect the poor against the rigors of an industrial age: "It is immoral for a Republic to leave the weak exposed defenselessly to the enterprises of the strong," he declared at the 1911 meeting of the party in Nîmes.[16] Such statements, it should be noted, were perfectly consistent with Radical Socialist theory as formulated at the party congresses during the first years of the twentieth century. At that time, the Radicals were still close to the conception of *solidarité* exponded by Léon Bourgeois, and their platforms endorsed social welfare measures. Nevertheless, in this sphere, too, Herriot diverged from the archetypical Radical Socialist, for though his party was

[15] See above, p. 150.
[16] Herriot, *Jadis,* I, 201.

rhetorically committed to state initiative on behalf of social welfare, its intentions were not often translated into governmental action— except in Lyons under Herriot's leadership.

Herriot turned his attention to social welfare early in his administration, and many measures were carried through before the outbreak of the First World War. Among these were fresh-air schools for tubercular children, a new orphanage for boys, and special schools for the deaf and dumb and for the blind. In 1910 he opened a restaurant for expectant and nursing mothers where they could get nourishing meals at little cost. And in 1919 he established the Maison des Mères, a home for unwed mothers in Gerland. In addition, he put through a law to increase old-age pensions, a cause for which he had fought at the 1905 congress of the Radical Socialist party in Paris.[17] He also at the beginning of his administration reopened the Bourse de Travail, which had been closed, and to help workers' organizations with their legal problems, he put at their disposal free consultations at the recently created Office Municipal du Travail.[18]

While most of Herriot's projects were executed exclusively by the municipal government, he initiated several successful experiments in social action through cooperation between private and public sectors. One example was his scheme for the construction of cheap housing for workers. Lyons was probably the first city in France where the local government intervened in the housing field. In the preface to a book on the subject of inexpensive housing, Herriot wrote as follows: "In most cities, the influx of rural population is usually in a larger proportion than the construction of new houses by private owners." [19] As early as 1907 the city had begun to buy up houses and lots which became the property of the municipality. The mayor favored direct city management for them but this was not possible. By 1912 the law allowed communes to construct housing as long as it was administered by private societies.[20] In this compromise solution the city used public funds to subsidize private building societies and the effort was coordinated by the newly created Office Public d'Habitations à Bon Marché.

[17] Armand Charpentier, *Le parti radical et radical-socialiste à travers ses congrès* (Paris, 1913), p. 396.
[18] Besseige, *Herriot parmi nous*, p. 110.
[19] A. Cénet, *Manuel des habitations à bon marché* (Paris, 1914), p. v.
[20] *Ibid.*, pp. vi–vii.

During the First World War patriotism, together with wartime scarcities, pressures, and needs, favored state intervention on behalf of the public welfare, and increased municipal action was evident throughout France. Nowhere was the effect so marked, however, as in Lyons, where the ground had already been prepared by Herriot. Here wartime tolerance permitted Herriot to implement activities which would not have been countenanced previously either by Radical theory or by the actual political situation.

One wartime scheme which Herriot pushed early was the establishment of a training school for disabled soldiers. In November, 1914, he raised this topic in *Le Journal*. The Municipal Council approved the idea on November 30, 1914, and the first pupils began to arrive at the still unfinished quarters on December 6. This was the first center for wounded veterans in France.[21] Later on a more elaborate school was established at Tourvielle with the mayor himself supervising everything closely, including the architecture.[22] This center offered a varied curriculum, including academic courses at night, but stressing technical training in such fields as shoe repair, toymaking, and wireless telegraphy. At first, these Ecoles Professionnelles de Blessés, as Herriot insisted on calling them, were supported by private charity,[23] but later they were taken over by the municipality. Herriot visualized these retraining schools as models for postwar technical schools where the children of workers would be able to "escape from the servitude of ignorance and from the brutality of the machine."[24] Thus the reeducation centers for the wounded in wartime which began as a necessity can be seen as the basis to future progress.

Herriot continued his active economic role after 1918, bolstered by the great need in France for postwar reconstruction. He redoubled his efforts on behalf of school programs and social welfare. Since it had also become possible to build again, he completed the construction of more bridges and of other public housing. Another first combined both his building program and his concern for education: he worried about housing facilities for students. In 1923 the oldest lodginghouse for students was finished and five years later even a dormitory for female university students was

---

[21] Herriot, *Jadis*, II, 77.　　[22] Hirschfeld, *Tourvielle*, p. 51.

[23] Edouard Herriot, *Agir* (Paris, 1917), p. 89. Herriot made several speeches on this subject during the war which are reprinted in *Agir*.

[24] Edouard Herriot in the preface to Hirschfeld, *Tourvielle*, p. 9.

inaugurated.[25] There was also the completion of the "ideal" hospital which was to Herriot perhaps the crowning achievement of his long administration.

He had broached the plans for the hospital long before, during his first term in office. As mayor of Lyons, he had inherited a city hospital so ancient that tradition attributed its founding to a son of Clovis.[26] Its inadequacy was particularly distressing to Herriot because of an experience he had had as a young soldier when, during a pneumonia epidemic, he was confined to the army hospital in Nancy.[27] He had been shocked by the conditions in the common ward, where infectious and surgical cases were mixed together, and convalescents and the dying lay in close proximity. The facilities at the Hôtel-Dieu hospital were hardly better, and Herriot was determined to replace them. Lyons should have more than a new hospital, it should have a model hospital—large, scientifically designed, with plenty of isolation wards, and located in spacious surroundings amid gardens, away from the center of town. This institution would be a source of pride to the inhabitants, and a monument to his administration.

The way in which Herriot handled the hospital project exemplifies his political tactics as well as his ideological approach. He began, typically, by calling in technical experts—in this case the architect Tony Garnier, and various doctors, engineers, and builders. When the initial plans had been formulated, Herriot presented them to the public in two articles printed by the newspaper *Le Progrès* in January, 1908. He then waited for the results of the municipal elections in May of that year.

As soon as the plans had been published, there blew up a storm of controversy so fierce that it passed beyond local boundaries. Even the Parisian newspaper *Le Journal des Débats* took Herriot to task. The opponents of the new hospital accused Herriot of anticlericalism—always a sensitive political issue—for wanting to abolish an institution with clerical antecedents; its replacement, they declared, would not only destroy tradition and profit local

---

[25] André Allix, "Edouard Herriot," *Annales de l'Université de Lyon* (Lyons, 1958), p. 76.

[26] Herriot in his capacity as a historian disputed these early origins. He concluded that the Hôtel-Dieu was founded in the twelfth century. Herriot, *Jadis,* I, 180.

[27] *Ibid.,* p. 107.

contractors, but also please the Freemasons! [28] The critics further denounced the grandiose planning which would ultimately burden local taxpayers. They even argued that the new hospital would oppress the poor: since it was to be located far from the center of town, visitors would have to use tramways instead of being able to walk. This last attack appears particularly unfair in view of Herriot's well-known concern for the "little man."

Evidently the "little man" himself did not feel betrayed, however, for in May, 1908, the Lyonnais returned Herriot to office by an overwhelming majority. Armed with this strong endorsement, he now went ahead confidently with the development of his plans, and in April, 1909, he submitted a resolution to the municipal council to secularize the old Hôtel-Dieu hospital. At the beginning of July the hospital administration voted to endorse the building plans in principle. The mayor then addressed a new report to the municipal council, and shortly thereafter set up a study commission. Headed by Herriot himself and including Tony Garnier, the group left in December of that year to visit major hospitals in Copenhagen, Hamburg, Frankfurt, Cologne, and Berlin, and ended up by inspecting the Pasteur Hospital in Paris. The commission produced a comparative study which was subsequently published.

Though local criticism continued unabated and the study trip was denounced as a junket, many distinguished scientists and physicians had come to the support of the hospital project, and in 1912 the plans were accepted by the Academy of Medicine. Construction began in the same year but, because of wartime and postwar delays in building, the new hospital was finished only in 1930. Located in the Grange-Blanche district, it was a model institution around which other medical activities were to cluster. In 1932 the Rockefeller Foundation provided the funds to move the Lyons Medical School to the new center. Humanitarianism, careful planning with the advice of experts, and exercise of the powers of the government had combined to produce an exemplary institution which was fittingly named the Edouard Herriot Hospital.

One French commentator has called this forward-looking, scientifically oriented attitude, with its emphasis on practical efficiency,

[28] As Benoît Faugier wrote in the *Salut Public* of February 18, 1910: "La politique aussi a mis là sa sale et vilaine main. Il y a trop de croix autour des pauvres malades et l'on voudrait remplacer le chapelet des soeurs par le triangle grotesque." Cited by Herriot in *Jadis*, I, 185.

the "American" aspect of Herriot's nature.[29] Although Herriot did not visit the United States until 1923, he had, in fact, studied American methods, some of which he applied to the administration of Lyons. While his government cannot be called exactly technocratic, Herriot did rely heavily on the advice of experts. It has often been pointed out that he could not have "rebuilt his city" if he had not found an extraordinarily able architect in Tony Garnier, a fine technician and a gifted artist whose excellence had been rewarded by a Prix de Rome. The mayor and his architect were both exponents of city planning and they shared basic ideas on the needs of a modern city.[30] Their approach was unusual in pre-1914 France, which lagged behind other European countries in city planning and in municipal support for modern architecture.

The scope of the building program which Herriot carried out under the guidance of his architect can be seen in a copiously illustrated book which Garnier published in 1921, *Les grands travaux de la Ville de Lyon*.[31] Interestingly enough, Tony Garnier had been on the verge of leaving for the United States when the new mayor discovered him.[32] Thus the architect, like his mayor, had American leanings.

On an ideological level, Herriot—the Radical Socialist, the man of the Third Republic—may never have made his peace with twentieth-century French technocrats. Yet, in his capacity as mayor of Lyons, Herriot constantly planned, with the aid of scientifically trained advisers, measures designed to modify the character and economy of Lyons; and he used all the powers of his office—augmented by his personal popularity and prestige—to bring them to fruition.

Herriot tried hard to reconcile his actions with the traditional principles of Radical Socialism, but his record as mayor of Lyons proves that theories were less important to him than facts. It was progress that mattered; and progress not as a philosophical ideal,

[29] Besseige, *Herriot parmi nous*, p. 118.

[30] Although his training had been classical, Tony Garnier (1869–1948) believed that buildings should be adapted to modern society. He was the author of *Une cité industrielle*.

[31] Tony Garnier, *Les grands travaux de la Ville de Lyon* (Paris, 1921). Herriot wrote a preface for this book.

[32] Edouard Herriot in a speech on October 30, 1955, reprinted in Ville de Lyon, *Jubilé municipal de M. le président Edouard Herriot, Maire, 1905–1955* (Lyons, 1955), p. 44.

but as a series of practical achievements which would improve the well-being of the people. He favored what he called a "politique de mouvement," and as he wrote in April, 1916: "It is up to the government to direct it; and up to us to serve it by our labor and our will!" [33] The same month, in a lecture, he exhorted his audience to "active meditation" in order to apply and extend this doctrine of energy, indispensable to the maintenance of "la grandeur française." [34]

Many of Herriot's writings and speeches reflect this emphasis on action at the expense of theory. Addressing a Radical Socialist banquet in 1912, for example, Herriot coined the slogan: "Progress through production," [35] and in *Agir* he wrote that it was important for Frenchmen to understand that the prosperity of the people was not dependent on a speech delivered in the Chamber of Deputies, but rather on the development of electricity or the opening of a new potassium mine.[36] In another book he mentioned that the construction of a large stadium or of a truly modern hospital could do more to further public health than any speech.[37] Indeed his books *Agir* and *Créer* are both, as their titles suggest, calls to action. In both works Herriot dealt with the reconstruction of France after the First World War—and sounded often as if he thought France were merely a larger Lyons. In *Créer* Herriot called for better organization in France to counteract German efficiency and appealed to the young to found the Fourth Republic.[38] *Agir,* incidentally, was dedicated to the memory of Colbert, the pioneer of economic organization in France, in the following words: "To Jean-Baptiste Colbert . . . Comptroller General of Finance who demonstrated the power of French order." [39]

Another authoritarian figure for whom Herriot showed a good deal of admiration was Napoleon I. A French journalist reports that everything concerning the emperor interested him passionately. One of his ideas for a book was to do a play in the style of George Bernard Shaw on Napoleon, whom he would show escaping from St. Helena and establishing himself in the United States.[40] "Napoleon teaches us energy," [41] Herriot said in a speech to the French

[33] Herriot, *Agir*, p. 77.   [34] *Ibid.*, p. 11.   [35] Herriot, *Jadis*, I, 202.
[36] *Agir*, p. 68.   [37] *Pourquoi je suis radical-socialiste*, p. 72.
[38] *Créer*, II (Paris, 1920), 372.   [39] *Agir*, p. 7.
[40] Geneviève Tabouis, *They Called Me Cassandra* (New York, 1942), p. 52.
[41] Herriot, *Etudes françaises* (Geneva, 1950), p. 257.

Academy, but he added that one is no more a Bonapartist for admiring Napoleon than one is a Royalist for cherishing Joan of Arc.[42]

The juxtaposition of these two opinions suggests that the difficulty in assessing Herriot's ideological position arises not only from the contradiction between his words and his acts, but also from a certain ambivalence in his attitude toward power. This ambivalence may, indeed, have characterized his party in general: an American historian has recently written that Herriot "was the chosen object of the Radicals' latent authoritarian urge to submit to an overwhelming personality." [43] Just as Radical Socialism, the most "republican" party of the Third Republic, had some underlying Bonapartist tendencies in theory, the Republic rested on some unacknowledged imperial institutions. Paul Deschanel, a moderate politician who was President of France in 1920, once said: "We have the Republic on top and the Empire underneath." [44]

Herriot intended no compliment when, in the quotation which heads this essay, he declared that many Radical Socialists could be labeled the "Bonapartists of the Republic." [45] Yet, he himself can surely be regarded as one of them. His "proconsular" side was not very evident either in his words or in the roles he played on the national and international political scene, but on the local level it was dominant. As mayor of Lyons, Herriot made maximum use of his creative intellect and executive powers to give the city fifty years of bold, methodical, and effective administration.

[42] *Ibid.,* p. 263.

[43] Peter J. Larmour, *The French Radical Party in the 1930's* (Stanford, 1964), p. 51.

[44] As quoted in Philip Williams, *Politics in Post-War France* (London, 1955), p. 2.

[45] *Notes et maximes inédits* (Paris, 1961), p. 28.

French Interwar Stagnation Revisited

MARTIN WOLFE

UNIVERSITY OF PENNSYLVANIA

AMERICAN ECONOMIC HISTORIANS are responsible for encouraging a good deal of confused thinking about recent changes in the French economy. Because we admire the French and wish them well we were dismayed by the poor showing of their economy in the years just after the Second World War. As historians must, we attempted to trace the roots of this problem back into France's past. Some of us expressed our concern and disappointment by constructing more or less elegant models demonstrating that economic stagnation characterizes France not only in recent times but also in the prewar era and the nineteenth century. We argued, informally and at conferences, whether the blame should be placed on France's resources or her attitudes. Three of our foremost practitioners carried on a famous and quite waspish controversy on the extent to which the presumed inferior quality of French entrepreneurs might be blamed.[1] Our impulses were good; we were responding to a need to use our position as interpreters of the past to urge the French forward in the present. Unfortunately this urge, spelled out so explicitly in Charles Morazé's *La France bourgeoise*

I acknowledge gratefully the generous help in preparing this essay given me by Richard Du Boff, Rondo E. Cameron, Joel Colton, Richard A. Easterlin, and Charles K. Warner. A caveat: while the historians seemed to like my general approach, two of the economists had more or less grave reservations.

[1] Davis S. Landes, Alexander Gerschenkron, and John E. Sawyer, in *Explorations in Entrepreneurial History*, vols. VI, no. 1 (1953); VI, no. 4 (1954); and VII, no. 2 (1955).

(from which many of us got our ideas), was not so openly displayed in our own publications.[2] Professor Clough himself was moved to write an often-quoted essay on "Retardative Factors in French Economic Development in the Nineteenth and Twentieth Centuries."[3] The dissertation on French interwar monetary policy which I wrote in 1950 for Professor Clough contains a number of facile references to stagnation.[4] And in 1958—by which time the rate of French economic growth had forged ahead of that in the United States—Warren C. Baum brought out his careful study *The French Economy and the State,* which claimed that, in addition to all the economy's other failures, government policy had done more harm than good and was part of the reason France was in the twentieth century "the sick man of Europe."[5]

New misunderstandings are sometimes as hard to dislodge as old myths, especially when they are structured on extensive research and brilliant reasoning. Most economists and economic historians who were studying France in the late 1940s and 1950s obviously realized that their observations were only preliminary and their models only partial—and that on certain occasions and in certain respects the French economy had performed splendidly. But consumers of their intellectual output (in particular, American students of general French history) understandably have come to characterize the French economy as "sick." Until very recently, essays on France seemed to be flawed by pessimistic attitudes and conclusions generated during 1946–56; and they displayed a rather patronizing tone that would have been infuriating to the French if they had ever bothered to read any French history written by Americans.[6]

[2] Charles Morazé, *La France bourgeoise, XVIIIè–XXè siècles* (Paris, 1946), esp. his introduction and conclusions. The enshrinement of the deterministic-stagnation error, of course, was the large number of brilliant articles in Edward Mead Earle, ed., *Modern France* (Princeton, 1951).

[3] *Journal of Economic History,* vol. VI, supplement (1946).

[4] *The French Franc between the Wars, 1919–1939* (New York, 1951). Except in a few cases I am omitting all specific references to this work or its sources.

[5] *The French Economy and the State* (Princeton, 1958), p. 1. But note that Baum really stopped his investigation in 1955. How difficult it was for some of us to relinquish our pessimism is shown in David S. Landes, "Observations on France: Economy, Society, and Polity," *World Politics,* IX, no. 3 (April, 1957).

[6] The watershed here seems to lie at some point in time between two fine texts: Gordon Wright, *France in Modern Times* (Chicago, 1960) (see pp. 490–91, 552–55); and Paul A. Gagnon, *France since 1789* (New York, 1964) (see pp. 466, 485, 524–27).

Today certain French leaders delight in thrusting under our noses, perhaps a bit too forcefully, the fact that the French economy is *not* "the sick man of Europe." Our irritation at such antics should not inhibit us from undertaking a reconsideration of our ideas on periods in the past when the French economy did perform disappointingly.

In the framework of this *Festschrift* it seemed appropriate that I return to the era I studied as Professor Clough's student twenty years ago, and that I attempt to use new tools and insights which have appeared since 1950. How should we view French interwar stagnation? Was it caused by events and trends generated specifically in those years or by basic, long-range weaknesses in French society and its value structure? To sloganize, did interwar stagnation come from France's character or from what the French call *conjoncture?*

Of course, one cannot hope, in the limits of a short essay, to comment on all the multitudinous events, policies, conditions, trends, and other factors that shaped France's economic history in this era. The causal lines are so complex, and our work of analyzing them at such an early stage, that we might as well employ a simple confrontation technique to summarize the main points that should be made. On the *conjoncture* side I shall group factors under the headings of government policy and "random" events; these, together with cyclical pressures, are the fortuitous events that seem to have been generated (to have come together or "conjoined") primarily during the period in question.[7] Then we shall be in a position to assess the importance of longer run considerations, which I shall group together under the headings of resources, values, and institutions.

If a French economist of the 1930s could have foreseen that in the 1950s we would be pointing to basic socioeconomic characteristics of his country for explanations of its economic distress, he might—quite understandably—have displayed some pained surprise. In 1933, beyond a doubt, he would have pointed in different directions: to the New York stock market crash and the devaluations of the pound and the dollar—all "outside" forces. He might

---

[7] The French, however, often use the word "conjoncture" to mean "a point in the business cycle." They have no exact equivalent of our "business cycle."

as an afterthought have mentioned the downswing of the business cycle, a factor common to all advanced industrial capitalist countries.[8] Unless he happened to be a communist, however, or one of the small group of economists who subscribed to the expansionist policies of Tardieu and Reynaud, the chances are he would not have listed his government's economic policies among the depressive factors. Today we can see that the length and seriousness of French stagnation cannot be understood without referring to the wrong economic decisions of the French government.

In turn, understanding the deflationary policies of the government requires that we recognize the power of the belief in France that there were special features of the economy and of the country's "safe and sane" economic management that would see her through the turmoil without the need for new and upsetting policies. There were three main reasons for this belief: the splendid achievements of the economy during the 1920s; the almost neurotic rejection of arguments for further devaluation of the franc; and the high and mighty fact that for about eighteen months after the New York crash France did not show many signs of economic distress.

A student who assumes that stagnation dominated all the French interwar years is ignoring half of them.[9] Viewed from any angle, France's economic performance during the 1920s was just as commendable as that of any Western power except perhaps the U.S.A. If we calculate growth not in aggregate terms but on a man-hour basis (given that France is a land of low birth rates) the ground

[8] "After all," said Sauvy (in 1965!), *"France was no longer an independent country economically speaking"* (his italics). Alfred Sauvy, *Histoire économique de la France entre les deux guerres.* Vol. 1: *De l'armistice à la dévaluation de la livre* (Paris, 1965). (As yet Sauvy's second and third volumes have not appeared.) Some non-French economists, of course, would agree: thus Ingvar Svennilson, *Growth and Stagnation in the European Economy* (Geneva, 1954), pp. 49–50 and *passim.* But the point is that Britain and Germany, who enjoyed higher growth or at least less stagnation in the 1930s, were also no longer independent countries, economically speaking—whatever that means.

[9] Cf. John B. Christopher, who sees that from 1905 onwards "the road . . . went downhill all the way to World War II" (in Earle, *Modern France,* p. 57). Even some Frenchmen repeat this error: see the introduction in Claude Fohlen, *La France de l'entre-deux-guerres* (Paris, 1966), where he says that public opinion and government policy from 1919 to 1939 condemned France to "stagnation and sterility." Perhaps the most damage here was done by Herbert Luethy, *France against Herself* (New York, 1955), e.g., p. 77. This last work, by a Swiss economic historian, exhibits the same motives for its highly pessimistic approach as those I ascribed to Americans in my introduction. The French pessimists, and particularly Marxists such as Charles Bettelheim (*Bilan de l'économie française, 1919–1946* [Paris, 1947]), may have had other motives.

that France lost in the 1930s, as severely as it cut into the gains of the 1920s, still left the country with an annual man-hour growth rate of 2.3 percent for the interwar decades, higher than any advanced country of Western Europe except Italy (2.6 percent) and Norway (2.7 percent).[10] And this was "development" (i.e., structural improvements) as well as "mere growth." [11] The older industries such as textiles, metals, and wines quickly regained their prewar stride. The elegant products of France's craft-conscious factories and shops were in higher demand abroad than ever during these boom years. But France also boasted several important new or essentially new industries, including automobiles, petroleum refining, canning, chemicals, tourism, and electrical goods. These new activities, plus the reconstruction effort in the war-devastated northeast (and the reacquisition of Alsace and Lorraine) gave France twelve years of prosperity with only one serious interval of recession (the first half of 1921) and two mild setbacks (the end of 1924 and mid-1927). It is true that until mid-1926 this expansion was made somewhat less joyful by an unnerving inflation and the sagging exchange value of the franc. But when in 1926 the franc became stable, the performance of the French economy became perhaps the most remarkable of all the great nations of the world—until 1931. Let us not forget that around 1930 France was able to provide employment for more than a million and a half foreign workers.[12]

We do not have to probe very deeply into French social psychology, therefore, to realize why the dominant attitude of business and political leaders regarding their economy was smugness. The first economic problem to attract national attention after the New York stock market crash was a slump in wheat and wine prices; but this was attributed to especially abundant crops. In May, 1930, the index of industrial production began to fall off; but it declined so slowly that at no time that year could an observer say for certain that the depression was making substantial inroads into French

[10] Angus Maddison, *Economic Growth in the West* (New York, 1964), p. 37, comparing 1938 with 1913. The average for the countries Maddison studied was 1.9 percent, and this includes Canada and the U.S.A. From 1913 to 1929 net national income at fixed prices rose about 33 percent in France; from 1929 to 1938 it declined about 11 percent (Sauvy, p. 277).

[11] For a contrary view see Christopher, in Earle, *Modern France*, p. 47.

[12] Val R. Lorwin, *The French Labor Movement* (Cambridge, Mass., 1954), p. 66.

manufacturing. Remarkably few manufacturing firms failed during this early stage of the depression. Iron and coal mining, it is true, did show signs of real distress by late 1930. A few score of the smaller regional banks and two or three of the larger Paris banks displayed some panic reactions to the enormous volume of financial failures abroad. But most of the French banks were saved by prompt support from the government and the Bank of France. Gold began to flow into the country in increasing amounts, fleeing currency insecurity elsewhere. Bank of France gold reserves jumped from 37 billion francs in mid-1929 to 44 billions in mid-1930 and to 56 billions in mid-1931.[13] During 1930 the cost of living remained high, the volume of commodity exports fell off slightly but remained eminently satisfactory, and there was no unemployment at all. In fact, 178,000 immigrant workers were granted work visas in 1930, and it was not until 1932 that the number of departing foreign workers exceeded the number of those coming in.[14]

Viewing the struggles of other countries caught in the onslaught of the Great Depression, the French—who knew as a matter of course that the French way is best—solidified their convictions. Parliamentary leaders did not have to respond with convincing arguments to the call by Tardieu and Reynaud for bold counter-depression measures; they had only to point to the record, a much less strenuous form of debate.[15] They fully expected that the devaluation of the franc in 1926–28 had provided definitive answers to all their economic problems.

Today we know that the parity of the franc established by the *de jure* and *de facto* devaluations put French exports in an enormously advantageous position, since the franc was substantially undervalued and French goods and services, as a consequence, were quite cheap for foreigners. Coming as it did well along during the world boom, the devaluation gave the French an especially favorable balance of payments.[16] This itself became a factor in

[13] *Bulletin de la statistique générale de la France.*

[14] *L'evolution de l'économie française* (Paris, 1937), table 7. Likewise, the peak year for additions to electrical power capacity before 1951 was 1932.

[15] Marguerite Perrot, *La monnaie et l'opinion publique en France et en Angleterre de 1924 à 1936* (Paris, 1955), pp. 199–238.

[16] This time—for once!—the decision was made for national growth rather than for "monetary honesty"—that is, a return to the full prewar gold value of the franc which the *rentiers* demanded.

the "golden afterglow," since the increased national income, operating through a process we call the foreign trade multiplier, worked its way through the economy with a time lag that extended its effects well past the first onslaught of the depression. But of course French leaders gave all the credit to themselves and to the superiority of French institutions.

Meanwhile the economic situation was worsening. Industrial production began to fall off more rapidly in the autumn of 1930. Foreign trade was hurt severely by the devaluation of the British pound in September, 1931. By fiscal 1931–32 the French budgetary situation, such a fine reason for self-congratulation until then, was showing highly worrisome deficits.[17] When the Great Depression finally became a matter of concern for French leaders, therefore, they saw it as a monetary and budgetary problem. This helps explain their infuriating obtuseness at the World Economic Conference in London in 1933 and their formation of the Gold Bloc.[18]

Looking backward, it is easy for us to see that the French government should have realized it had no choice after the devaluation of the pound but to respond with a devaluation of the franc. We also know that the economic situation called for massive intervention to help build up the purchasing power of the lower-income classes and to encourage the expansion of business; and it seems obvious that the French should have embarked on a great program of public works. Since arguments for such measures did not have to wait for the Keynesian revolution, let alone modern growth theory, and since other nations at the time were doing some of these things, the question as to why France did so little so late becomes a highly interesting problem for historians. I feel that part of the answer lies in the government's misinterpretation of the French economy's performance during the "golden afterglow" of 1929–30.

Another part of the answer, of course, lies in the fact that government policies reflected the class interests of *rentiers* and of the very rich. The grotesque tilting against the windmills of inflation we see in France—even as late as 1934 and 1935—therefore should be seen as part honest misinterpretation, part determination by the

[17] Germain-Martin, *Le problème financier, 1930–1936* (Paris, 1936), p. 96.
[18] Perrot, *La monnaie,* p. 229.

middle and upper classes not to pay the costs of a vigorous counter-depression campaign.[19] In the 1950s the government was at least somewhat responsive to the needs of the lower classes. But in the 1930s, that is, until the Popular Front, the government was concerned almost exclusively to restore the "confidence" of *rentiers* and business leaders.

One reason the selfish position of the rich and the *rentiers* went largely unchallenged was that the quality of the whole debate over depression policies was strikingly low. In other countries the best brains joined in public agonizing over how to end the depression. In France it is not too much to say that intellectuals not only were poor in economics but also that they were bored with it. It is only recently that the *élites* of France have learned how idealistic one can be in promoting the process of material advancement.[20] With a few notable exceptions, the journals and scholarly periodicals of the era (before the Popular Front election campaigns) give little attention to the fact that the grinding misery of the Great Depression was beginning to work its way into the lower strata of French society; national politics and international affairs crowd out all else.[21] Therefore the government was allowed to take its cue from leading bankers and other "experts" who, even had they wished, could not rise above the deplorably bad teaching in economics offered by France's law faculties, which at that time had a monopoly of university economics.[22] One can characterize the policy assumptions of such men by saying that they saw the rôle of government during the depression as limited to emergency repairs on an essentially automatic and self-regulating economic machine.[23]

[19] *Ibid.*, pp. 199–208, 213–20.

[20] An exception was Jean Fourastié's works in the late 1940s and especially his *Machinisme et bien-être* (Paris, 1951). But Fourastié did not enjoy a wide following until years later.

[21] Fohlen, *La France*, pp. 103–4.

[22] Sauvy, *Histoire économique*, pp. 431–32. Marguerite Perrot points out that men who were in the best position to be chosen as "experts" were well along in years and had formed their ideas before 1914 (*La monnaie*, p. 16). Even so, one can hardly believe one's eyes when a person as high in the academic world as Gaston Jèze is quoted as saying (in October, 1936!): "Devaluation constitutes for savers a deduction from capital or income which could reach 25 or 30 percent" (*La monnaie*, p. 223).

[23] This was the position of the Confédération générale de la Production Française (Henry W. Ehrmann, *Organized Business in France* [Princeton, 1957], pp. 29–32). See also Perrot, *La monnaie*, p. 198. Germain-Martin, Flandin's

The single most tragic consequence of such attitudes, perhaps, was parliament's rejection of Tardieu's "national retooling" (*outillage national*) project, a grand design to invest the budgetary surpluses of 1929–30 in better port facilities, canals, and other areas of what today we call social overhead capital. The amazingly small-minded argument used to defeat this proposal was that surpluses should be used to reduce the national debt.[24] As usual, we see here a mixture of causes: an institutional factor, that is, the ministerial instability built into the French political process, that made it easy for parliament to dump Tardieu; a chance factor, that is, Tardieu's irritatingly high self-regard, bordering on megalomania, which made it difficult for parliament to support his reform projects; and the cyclical and education factors already mentioned.

All the other great countries hurt by the depression reacted at first with misguided deflationary policies. The problem for us is not why France employed them but why she employed them so vigorously over such a long period of time. By the summer of 1933 it was all too evident that France and the rest of the world were, economically speaking, out of step.[25] In the spring of 1932 France had enjoyed a small but unmistakable upswing, a recovery of manufacturing and exports in line with the recovery of all industrial powers at that time (with the exception of Italy). But by 1933, while the rest of the world turned the corner toward recovery, in France all the economic indicators were becoming frighteningly worse. And this singular downward trend continued month after weary month; to judge by wholesale prices, for example, the lowest point of the Great Depression for the United States, Great Britain, and Germany was February–April, 1933; but France did not touch bottom until July, 1935.[26]

---

minister of finance, at one point responded to Reynaud's arguments for devaluation by insinuating that Reynaud was in league with those who sought for their own greedy purposes to touch off another inflation. (See Fohlen, *La France*, p. 100.)

[24] Rudolph Binion, *Defeated Leaders: The Political Fate of Caillaux, Jouvenel, and Tardieu* (New York, 1960), esp. pp. 294–304.

[25] J.-M. Jeanneny, *Forces et faiblesses de l'économie française, 1945–1956* (Paris, 1956), p. 71. For French economists this important work may signal the same sort of pessimistic/optimistic "watershed" I refer to above in n. 6.

[26] League of Nations, *Revue de la situation économique mondiale, 1934–1935* (Geneva, 1936), p. 48; and *Statistique générale de la France*, general index of wholesale prices of 126 articles (1913 = 100). The National Bureau of

Meanwhile, declining tax revenues, increasing outlays for unemployment, and rising budgetary deficits—factors we today would accept as built-in economic stabilizers—were regarded as steps toward "state bankruptcy." Even Herriot's moderate Left (Cartel des Gauches) regime in 1932 repeated the old saw about how "public morality" required that the gold parity of the franc be defended at all costs and how the "whole social fabric" of France was pivoted on the confidence of the small saver. Gaston Doumergue, the fatherly but bumbling ex-president called out of retirement after the February, 1934, riots, chose as his guideline "In a state budget as in a private budget, we must never have expenses higher than receipts. That is the rule." [27] He inaugurated a spectacular drive to cut down government expenses through firing (eventually) 30,000 government employees; and he ruled that for 1934 all state employees must be subject to a wages slash of between 10 and 20 percent. But his deflationary campaign was not enforced very vigorously; and the succeeding Flandin ministry mitigated its bad effects with a few feeble reflationary measures copied from the New Deal. It was the Laval regime in the second half of 1935 that demonstrated how strong was the government's commitment to budgetary and monetary stability.

Backed by powerful bankers, and armed with plenary powers for making laws by decree "to fight against speculation and to defend the franc," Laval between July and October promulgated literally hundreds of price- and wage-cutting decree laws. He was convinced that the chief cause of France's economic travail was that her prices were some 10 percent higher than those abroad; therefore, he came to the disastrous conclusion that what was needed was to force down the entire French price structure by a like amount—which accomplishment was supposed to spare France the need to devalue. The wage-price cutting spree was not limited to the government; price cuts were ordered in the products and services of "mixed" companies (subsidized concerns under partial government control) and in the colonial offices and public utilities. But of course an immeasurably greater effort would have been

---

Economic Relations places the trough for general business conditions in France (production, sales, and employment as well as prices) in April, 1935. See Arthur F. Burns and Wesley C. Mitchell, *Measuring Business Cycles* (New York, 1946), p. 78.

[27] *Le Temps*, March 26, 1934.

needed to have made French goods and services competitive again in world markets.

One can argue over the causes of such a frozen policy. But obviously it was, by 1935 if not earlier, much more than the "reflection, direct or distorted" of social interest to which Kindleberger limits government policy.[28] Because of its long life and wide acceptance it had become a sort of *mystique,* a force in its own right. Its harmful effects should not be traced back to structural features of French society alone.

Other nonstructural factors that made for stagnation can be seen that had little to do with government policy but appear to be quite accidental or "random," a matter of bad luck more than anything else. In addition to "outside" events such as the New York market crash, the personality defects of Tardieu, the devaluation of the pound and of the dollar, and the panic that followed the collapse of many Central European banks (1931) and the devaluation of Belgian currency (1935), we can place in this category the Stavisky scandal which, by leading to the February riots, acted to hurt the economy through a "values" factor, that of social hatred. It may also have been mainly a matter of bad luck that the leadership of French government from the end of 1932 to mid-1936 seems to have been monopolized by thoroughly uninspiring politicians; an electrifying leader on the order of a Roosevelt might have generated enough support to have crashed through all obstacles and jar his country out of its doldrums.

The most useful point of departure for examining the "deeper" reasons for French interwar stagnation is Charles P. Kindleberger's summary of the literature.[29] Kindleberger divides the main explanations into: 1) insufficient natural resources; 2) population and the labor supply; 3) insufficient capital for domestic investment; 4) inefficient and "Malthusian" practices of the all-important family firm, in a situation where operating business units (especially retail stores) were too small and markets too dominated by cartels; 5) the overriding preoccupation with social antagonisms; 6) an unfortunately wide acceptance of aristocratic tastes for high quality, high

[28] Charles P. Kindleberger, "The Postwar Resurgence of the French Economy," in Stanley Hoffman, *et al., In Search of France* (New York, 1963), p. 143.

[29] *Ibid.,* pp. 118–58; and Kindleberger, *Economic Growth in France and Britain, 1851–1950* (Cambridge, Mass., 1964).

cost products rather than mass-produced goods; 7) an overly bureaucratic and too highly centralized government, prone to preserve the "stalemate society" (Hoffman) and thus providing a shield for economic incompetence. For our purposes we can rearrange all these arguments into three large categories: resources, values, and institutions.

Can such "structural" considerations be applied to so short a period as the 1930s? Kindleberger, to be sure, uses them primarily for the purpose of explaining change in the long run.[30] The very definition of "long run," after all, is a period different enough, structurally speaking, to establish a contrast with other periods. Certainly the impact of those governmental policy and "random" factors we have been examining seems more important or at least more immediate, though (as Kindleberger sadly observes toward the end of his *Economic Development in France and Britain*) we have as yet no way to weight the relative importance of any of our "independent variables." And how can we speak of the depressive effect of resources, values, and institutions that also were features of the prosperous 1920s? Perhaps all we can say here is that the depressive potentials of these longer-run considerations may have been overborne by the upward pressures of cyclical and other forces during the 1920s and only came into full play when the pressures were running in the other direction.

During the 1950s, at the time of our debate over the role of entrepreneurs in French economic growth, it became a standard joke in the Economic History Association that we were dividing into the "rôle men" and the "coal men." [31] The "coal men" stressed France's slow rate of population growth, her small proportion of liquid capital going into productive investment at home rather than into foreign bonds (or into *bas de laine*), and particularly her relatively poor natural equipment for rapid industrialization, and her lack of abundant coking coal. These arguments, especially when added to other geographical considerations such as optimum

[30] In his book cited, the comparison is between France and Britain over the whole span of the nineteenth and early twentieth centuries; in his essay, the purpose is to demonstrate reasons for progress after 1950 in view of stagnation beforehand.

[31] Alexander Gerschenkron and Rondo E. Cameron are considered the foremost proponents of the latter view. For Cameron, see "Economic Growth and Stagnation in France, 1815–1914," *The Journal of Modern History*, XXX, no. 1 (March, 1958).

location of industrial centers and markets, do make some sense in explaining nineteenth-century contrasts with Britain. And until the 1950s France's need to import much of her fuels weakened her economic drive. But all in all the "poor resources" argument adds only slightly to our understanding of interwar stagnation. Nature has endowed France with such marvelous gifts of minerals (especially once Alsace and Lorraine were recovered), fertile lands, climate, and topography that most of us today would hesitate to link such factors with stagnation. Furthermore, economists today like to point out that, especially in the medium run, economic growth tends to produce new natural resources rather than the other way around; France's present natural gas industry is taken as a good example.

When we include population and the labor force in the concept of "resources," however, some links with stagnation do appear. In an advanced economy, most of us would say, a growing population means higher aggregate demand, higher output, and thus a cushion for marginally efficient firms. It also encourages technological improvements as new and expanding firms equip themselves with better machinery. In the interwar era French business did not enjoy this cushion; there were just about one half of one percent more people in 1938 than in 1913, compared to between 10 and 40 percent more for the rest of Western Europe.[32] It is true France experienced population growth of a kind between 1919 and 1931, but this was only because the terrible loss caused by the First World War and low birth rates was made up in part by immigration. Then in the 1930s the "labor safety valve" was screwed down, and about half a million more foreign workers were encouraged to leave than were admitted,[33] so that between 1929 and 1938 France was the only industrial nation to show an actual decline in its population of working age.[34]

The special situation of the foreign labor supply in France seems quite tightly related to stagnation in the 1930s. France possessed a mighty instrument for exporting unemployment, that is, the refusal to renew immigrant work visas whenever jobs became scarce for Frenchmen. This helps to account for the fact that even in

[32] Maddison, *Economic Growth*, pp. 205–6.
[33] Lorwin, *French Labor Movement*, pp. 67–68.
[34] Maddison, *Economic Growth*, Appendix C.

1932 and 1933 the number of unemployed on relief rolls was tiny—perhaps 2 or 3 percent, compared to about 25 percent in Germany and the U.S.A. Another factor in reducing unemployment, it is true, is that French enterprises followed a policy of "short time" —spreading the work by allowing each laborer only four or five days of work per week.[35] All this would today be recognized as a mixed blessing, since a pressing need for large unemployment benefits might have forced the government into large-scale deficit financing, an important counter-depression factor. Equally important, the loss of large numbers of foreign workers, coming as it did just when the country was beginning its slight recovery in 1932, may have helped choke off that recovery by shrinking domestic demand.

The arguments that the family firm, likewise, had a bad effect in the medium as well as the long run, seem quite convincing. The impersonally efficient "managerial" corporation in interwar France was comparatively rare. The pace therefore was set by firms which were run by and for families. This meant that the French business community was comparatively undynamic. Family firms characteristically avoid risky ventures, tend to be content with a small steady turnover, retain as managers men whose main qualification is a blood or marriage relationship (or who are loyal family retainers), and channel off profits as a sort of family annuity rather than as investible capital. Furthermore, they are hampered by empathy with other family firms which makes them reluctant to undercut and absorb weak rivals. This fusing of family interests and business activities was one of the reasons the unit size of French firms—including her farms—was so small, preventing her from enjoying the returns to scale so important in other countries.[36] One of the more famous demonstrations of the regard of the French for small firms is the laws passed during the Popular Front régime making it difficult for chain stores such as Prisunic to expand. It seems clear that there was an inefficiency feedback circuit in French business life which kept costs high during the depression; in turn this damped down domestic and foreign demand and lowered investment opportunities. Many good things can be said for the

[35] Shepard B. Clough, *France: A History of National Economics, 1789–1939* (New York, 1939), p. 486, n. 178.

[36] The notion that French production these years was dominated by huge cartels is completely erroneous.

family firm, including the fact that it tended to be loyal to employees and to use "short time" rather than dismiss its people. But the indictment stands that this institution made it difficult for France to adapt her economy to the world the depression made.

Other institutional deficiencies hampering France in the 1930s include the relatively scanty use of her scientific genius by her industrialists; the "powder" of retail stores (David Landes) struggling along on pitifully few sales per day; and other factors purporting to demonstrate that France was "the paradise of the inefficient." Less convincing are the claims that the banking institutions themselves were structured so that France was hampered in her recovery efforts. It is true that it was only comparatively recently, in the 1920s for the most part, that the large deposit banks began to allow their regional affiliates the power to lend to local manufacturers. But by the 1930s the old timidity concerning this sort of loan was disappearing. And in fact the volume of liquid capital in France at least until 1934 seemed to remain much higher than in other countries; in this land of *rentiers* the problem seemed to be much more the inducement to invest than the availability of plentiful funds.[37]

"Ultimately what was responsible [for retardation] was the nature of the French bourgeoisie—its beliefs, its attitudes, its way of life . . ." This is the conclusion of Stanley Hoffman, a political scientist and one of our most penetrating and influential analysts of French society.[38] This approach views institutions—as well as less formal patterns of action—as explainable by beliefs and attitudes; thus Jesse Pitts, a sociologist, explains the French family firm as an "institutional incarnation" of bourgeois values. This is certainly the most popular interpretation of our problem among historians, most of whom have been brought up in the Dilthey–Croce–Collingwood "idea of history" tradition: that when we contemplate great historical changes we should look for causes in changing patterns of thought. Let us for the moment put aside

[37] But see Charles Morazé, who sees the causal lines going from "psychologie de crainte" to "richesse inerte," that is, a greater proportion of savings went into state bonds (rather than into risky shares) thus shrinking the "capital base" on which industry could progress. *La France bourgeoise*, pp. 197–202. Sauvy apparently agrees. *Histoire économique*, p. 37.

[38] "Paradoxes of the French Political Community," in Stanley Hoffman, *et al.*, *In Search of France*, p. 6.

objections we might have to this view and its assumptions and sketch out what such a "values" approach has to offer us.

We must agree that the values in France often called "deep social fissures" (John Sawyer) had much to do with the failure of the Popular Front. One of the central features of this approach is that the moderate recovery policies of the Blum régime were the sort of measures that did produce at least some good results elsewhere, and that they could have been expected to produce a recovery in France if large segments of the upper and middle classes had not been so committed to the belief that the Popular Front *should* not succeed. The amazing refusal of the French business community to be stimulated by higher prices at home and by the potential improvement in export markets when the franc was devalued came in part from rejection of Blum as a man and from distrust of Popular Front intentions towards business leaders. The notion of a "sit-down strike of capital," often used by scholars as well as by politicians and journalists of the 1930s, is, of course, a "values" argument and apparently an important one.[39] Though much concerning the failure of the Popular Front remains a problem for scholarly investigation, we understand it well enough to see in it proof of the need for a "growth consensus" for a modern society in deep economic difficulties. Little can be done, within the framework of our capitalist system, to jar a country out of a depression when the leaders of the business community are cutting back their inventories, making do with their old plants, and refusing to bestir themselves in the interest of enlarging their markets—even while they berate the government for not producing recovery. The rich and the *rentiers* believed that Blum intended to hurt them, and nothing he could do or say convinced them otherwise. In February, 1937, when Blum announced his famous "pause" in the interest of mollifying business leaders, he showed he understood this dilemma. Even the introduction of compulsory labor arbitration is best interpreted as an assurance to business leaders that the government was doing what it could to protect France against further sit-down strikes, and not as an attack on free enterprise.[40] When recovery still was not forthcoming, and Blum in

[39] Joel Colton shows Blum using the "sit-down strike of capital" concept. See Colton, *Léon Blum* (New York, 1966), p. 271.

[40] Joel Colton, *Compulsory Labor Arbitration in France, 1936–1939* (New York, 1951), esp. ch. 4.

despair moved towards sterner controls, the upper classes turned him out easily—to their own great astonishment.

It is not necessary to see France in the 1930s as "two armed camps" (Stanley Hoffman)—this exaggerates the amount of tension, class unity, and class hatred.[41] But records of the era do show us a society shot through with corrosive dissatisfactions and suspicions, feeling sharpened by French wit in journals and French eloquence in parliaments. Certainly the peasants and the workers felt increasingly alienated from the rich. But given that before 1936 government was not responsive to lower-class grievances, worker–peasant dissatisfactions could have had only a small part in causing bad economic policy. There is no good evidence that social hatred made the French worker less efficient at his job or that hours lost due to strikes (before mid-1936) were an especially serious factor. The most we can say here is that displays of syndicalist propaganda and other manifestations of hostility (as Sauvy puts it: a "permanent indignation") had indirect effects in that they further increased the timidity of the business community.

One of the concepts recently offered to social scientists is that the Third Republic was a "stalemate society." [42] This is an attempt to picture *immobilisme* as the triumph of French bourgeois views concerning proper relations between individuals and the state, views sharply limiting structural change while rewarding individual achievements within rather rigid lines, and keeping the state as a guardian of the delicate balance of social forces rather than allowing it to become an instrument of general progress. And the concept seems very useful when we try to understand the Laval deflation. This immense and perverse effort was accepted by ruling government and business circles, we might say, because it seemed to promise to make French products competitive in world markets without devaluation and so to preserve for the *rentiers* the full gold value of their investments. The "stalemate society" concept explains both the perverted direction of the Laval deflation and, considering the desperate circumstances of 1935, its intensity.[43] Why

[41] Ehrmann shows that "bourgeois mentality" actually handicapped the concentration and organization of French business groups. *Organized Business*, pp. 15–28, 40.

[42] Hoffmann, "Paradoxes of the French Political Community," p. 3 and *passim*.

[43] But Hoffman is wrong (p. 22) when he says the Laval régime decided in favor of "freezing the economy at a low level"; these men certainly wanted recovery, but of course on their own terms.

did France develop practically no hydroelectric power projects in the interwar era? Possibly because the coal mine operators, through their influence in government and finance, managed to choke off competitive investment.[44]

When considered from the supply side, perhaps the single most favored argument for explaining French stagnation through values is the "aristocratic tastes" concept. Though France was one of the world's great industrial powers, her output was to a surprisingly large extent that of high-quality custom and artisan fabrication rather than inexpensive standardized commodities of the sort that can be mass produced. We think that such craftlike output was the result not of any special mix of resource and location factors but because aristocrats had dominated French fashion for so long, including most of the nineteenth century.[45] While from the last quarter of the nineteenth century France was a democracy, by then the bourgeoisie and even the middle-middle and lower-middle classes had so absorbed aristocratic preferences for individualized, aesthetically pleasing commodities—and France's foreign trade was so successful with such goods—that the French "powder" in the distribution system was matched by a "powder" of tiny artisan shops with four or five workers, hardly larger than their medieval counterparts. Even French workers, we are told, participated in such values, since many craftsmen liked to identify with the product of their labor.[46] To be sure, there were many large, modern, and exceedingly efficient factories in France, but presumably such units would have accounted for a larger percentage of total French production if it had not been for "aristocratic tastes." To the extent that this factor was important it acted to make French production less efficient than it might have been and less capable of adapting to the new conditions brought about by the Great Depression.[47] In addition, the fact that French manufacturing was not pointed at

[44] Svennilson, *Growth and Stagnation*, p. 116.

[45] There was of course a perfectly good reason why manufacturers should respond to such demands, since they promised great profits per unit of output and since there was a large foreign demand for high-fashion goods, for example, in fabrics. See David S. Landes in *The Cambridge Economic History of Europe*, vol. VI, part 1, pp. 392–93.

[46] André Siegfried, in Earle, *Modern France*, pp. 8–9.

[47] Mass-production consumer and capital goods industries, of course, are more capable of a technological "transformation" than artisan-type consumer goods industries. Svennilson, *Growth and Stagnation*, p. 21.

a mass market harmed the demand side of the economy by hampering the "swing into high mass consumption."

This last notion, of course, is a facet of W. W. Rostow's famous "take-off into sustained growth." [48] With our superior (hindsight) knowledge we can see that in 1931–32, when foreign trade and tourism fell off drastically, the government should have responded more energetically to build up the home market and particularly the purchasing power of the lower classes. But because of basic features in the nature of the demand side of the economy, it might not have responded so well to such stimuli even had they been massive and capably designed. As we remarked above, France suffered only moderate unemployment, so that the purchasing power of a French worker, in years when prices were falling, probably was only slightly less than in the late 1920s. Suppose the government could have made up the deficiency in demand caused by the forced emigration of foreign workers. Would expenditures have increased in proportion? We know that the lower and lower-middle classes bought relatively few goods such as small inexpensive automobiles, clothes, and housewares compared to their American counterparts; in addition, they added not at all to the demand for new suburban housing that was so important in beginning the era of "high mass consumption" in the U.S.A.[49] In this segment of French society there was little conspicuous consumption and almost no buying on time.

Rostow situates the arrival at the state of "economic maturity"— that is, advanced industrialization—at around 1910 in France, or about the same period as for the U.S.A.; but he believes the next stage, of "high mass consumption," did not begin for France until after the Second World War, or some 25 years later than in the United States. In this gap the French masses continued to demonstrate they were not yet anxious to acquire the sort of goods until then found mainly in middle-class homes. The astonishingly high proportion of their incomes they continued to devote to food and drink was one reason the percentage of the French occupied popu-

[48] W. W. Rostow, *The Stages of Economic Growth* (Cambridge, 1963).

[49] In France the number of passenger cars in the 1930s never recovered the level of 1929; in Britian, Germany, and Italy the figure for 1938 was about double that for 1929. Likewise, the construction of dwellings in France in the 1930s fell steadily, in sharp contrast to the gratifying upturn in Britain and Germany. Svennilson, *Growth and Stagnation*, pp. 51, 81, 149.

lation still in agriculture continued to be so high.[50] France was deprived of a powerful motor of economic progress partly because a confident drive for better goods was not yet part of the expectations of her lower classes. There is evidence of faint stirring towards such new demand patterns in the 1920s. But then the Great Depression came and caught France with her propensities unchanged. In other words, if in the 1930s the lower classes had had the same demand patterns they do today, the slight recovery in the autumn of 1936 (at a time when lower-class purchasing power was rising) might have encouraged a much more significant upturn.

The final category of values-oriented explanations for French interwar stagnation can be headed "flabby entrepreneurship." This is the argument the "rôle men" among us favored in the 1950s. They thought of French business as relatively pessimistic, timid, less driven by the capitalistic *ethos* Sombart speaks of. To use a favorite French expression, "Malthusianism" was thought to dominate French business leaders; convinced that total demand must shrink, the French business community was supposed to have been obsessed with building up cash reserves for rainy days, with forming agreements to avoid competition, with hanging on to old plant and equipment, and with being too much in a hurry to retire at an age young enough as to be able to enjoy the great aesthetic pleasures of French living. Certainly these charges against French businessmen do seem to fit the picture of the 1930s. There remains the question as to whether poor business performance should be ascribed to the decay of demand or the other way around. Indeed, because of downward cyclical pressures in the 1930s and other factors we have discussed, "flabby entrepreneurship" investigations really should be limited to periods of stability or prosperity rather than to the 1930s.

It is tempting to think that "underlying forces" in French society made inevitable the particular government policies, random events, and cyclical pressures we discussed—or at least made them much more likely. But these underlying forces, powerful though they may have been, did not devalue the pound sterling in 1931. Neither can one be certain that, given the "basic characteristics" of French soci-

---

[50] The decline in percent of the occupied population in agriculture in France was lower than that for any European country with the exception of Ireland. Svennilson, *Ibid.*, p. 71.

ety, the government was bound, for example, to respond to outside pressures with such vigorous and continued deflation. This response, we have seen, was at least in part conditioned by misinterpretation of the "golden afterglow"; and this lag in turn came about in part because of chance factors such as the timing of the 1926–28 devaluation and the beneficial effects of the undervalued franc. Therefore we can say that at times the causal lines seem to run from fortuitous to structural rather than the other way around; but of course the total picture is much more complex.

Many of the analytical procedures and concepts worked out in the 1950s to tackle such problems were developed by specialists in business history who were deeply influenced by the sociological methods of Talcott Parsons. While the value of such an approach is far from exhausted, obviously it is not powerful enough to bear the entire weight of the question: "What is the significance of French interwar stagnation?" I have tried to suggest some of the directions in which an effort to improve our over-all view of this problem might proceed. Of course every approach carries its own methodological worries. The factors I chose for reasons of exposition to call structural or fortuitous are figments of our scholarly imagination, cross-sectional abstractions from the discrete time periods in which "real life" factors—some of which we know and others we do not—continually modify each other in a fashion too bewildering for our present analytical abilities.

At this point, we must say, our answer to the "character or *conjoncture?*" question must be an emphatic "both"—followed immediately by a regretful admission that as yet we have no way of knowing which set of factors was more important. We seem even farther from being able to assign weights to single factors, and very far removed indeed from mapping both sets with connecting causal lines.

But for our topic it is important to advertise how little we know, since there are signs that a new error, erected on the foundations of the deterministic-stagnation error we made in the 1950s, is appearing. Why has the French economy been so progressive very recently? The answer, says Kindleberger, is "new men and new attitudes," that is, a massive reversal of the structural features of the bad old days.[51] But is the economy of today really so different from

[51] Kindleberger, "Postwar Resurgence," pp. 156–58.

that of the 1930s? And is it correct to imply that the poor performance before the 1950s was caused by "old men and old attitudes"? It is my belief that scholars working on the significance of recent changes in French growth must be warned that these problems are far from solved.

Even in 1935, her worst year, France possessed a very rich and highly complex economy. Theories of economic growth, which of necessity focus on the direction of changes in income rather than on the absolute level of income and wealth, tend to disguise this fact. In a very rich economy relatively slight factors can bring about a change in the direction of economic growth. Such a situation demands that we ask: Stagnation in relation to what? to other countries, to past performance, to potential (that is, in relation to how we feel the French economy *should* have performed)? Much of our discussion in the 1950s, it now seems clear, was colored by this last or normative consideration. In part, then, this problem of French interwar stagnation is a problem of definition.

We *know* that France is rich (by any definition); and we know that while at certain times (as during 1897–1913, 1924–30, and 1952–63) her wealth was increasing as rapidly as or faster than that of most rich nations, at other times (as during 1882–96 and 1931–52) she was lagging behind. We can *speculate*, more or less productively, about these periods of relative or absolute stagnation. But should they surprise us? Given the fact that, as Western capitalism changes, the "mix" required for rapid economic progress changes, too, and given all the variables that a nation must take into account in responding successfully to such challenges, lags and leads appear as a perfectly ordinary part of nineteenth- and twentieth-century economic history. Today's headlines remind us that even richer economies can falter.

Politics and Economics in the 1930s:
The Balance Sheets of
the "Blum New Deal"

JOEL COLTON

DUKE UNIVERSITY

On November 8, 1936, on the morrow of Franklin D. Roosevelt's reelection for a second term, William L. Bullitt, Roosevelt's ambassador in Paris, wrote to his chief:

Blum came personally to express his congratulations. That is unheard of. If you could have seen the manner of his coming, it would have done you good. He entered the front door, flung his broadbrimmed black hat to the butler, his coat to the footman, leaped the three steps to the point where I was standing, seized me and kissed me violently! I staggered slightly, but having been kissed by Stalin, I am now immune to any form of osculation and I listened without batting an eye to as genuine an outpouring of enthusiasm as I have ever heard. . . . Blum himself said to me that he felt his position had been greatly strengthened because he is attempting in his way to do what you have done in America. . . .[1]

On what Roosevelt was attempting to do in America there is now a vast and growing literature which cannot be examined here. But over thirty years have passed since the Blum Popular Front experiment in France, and appraisals of this, too, have been multiplying, adding to a substantial literature already in existence. One of the

[1] President's Secretary's File, France, B-5, Roosevelt Library, Hyde Park, New York.

most ambitious efforts at collective assessment was a colloquium organized in Paris in March, 1965, under the auspices of the Fondation Nationale des Sciences Politiques. Papers were read on selected topics by Gilbert Ziebura, Jean Touchard, and Louis Bodin (the coeditors, incidentally, of the anthology *Front Populaire* [Paris, 1961] which so successfully samples the color and excitement of the era), René Rémond, Georges Dupeux, Antoine Prost, J. M. Jeanneney, Pierre Renouvin, Charles-André Julien, and a number of other scholars, and there were oral "interventions" by individuals who had themselves in some way participated in the events.[2] That same year there appeared the first full-scale attempt at an impartial synthesis of the Popular Front by the indefatigable Georges Lefranc (*Histoire du Front Populaire, 1934–1938* [Paris, 1965]). Lefranc is the author of over a score of books dealing with the history of the French labor and socialist movements; unfortunately, he cannot conceal his impatience with his own Socialist party and with the Popular Front for failing to adopt the CGT Plan of 1934–35 of which he was one of the coauthors. In 1966 *Le Mouvement Social*, the quarterly review of the Institut Français d'Histoire Sociale, devoted its January–March issue to the Popular Front; and that same year the entire July–August issue of *Les Cahiers de l'Histoire* was taken up with a highly competent narrative account of the Popular Front years by Serge Bernstein. Antoine Prost, who contributed to some of the collaborative studies, has also written a valuable statistical analysis of the vicissitudes of the CGT at the time of the Popular Front: *La CGT á l'époque du Front Populaire: essai de description numérique* (Paris, 1964). There are "older" studies as well, in French, English, and German, that have not been superseded by the explorations of the 1960s[3] and there are a number of monographs for which early publication is projected in the United States (including a study of the French Communist party in the Popular Front years, based in part on Russian sources, by Daniel Brower, and of the left-wing Socialists in these same years, one by Donald Baker and another by Nathanael Greene).

A generation has passed and the reappraisals are under way.

[2] The proceedings have been published as *Léon Blum, chef de gouvernement, 1936–1937* (Cahiers de la Fondation Nationale des Sciences Politiques No. 155; Paris, 1967).

[3] See the bibliographies in my *Léon Blum: Humanist in Politics* (New York, 1966), pp. 495–512, and in Bodin and Touchard, *Front Populaire*, pp. 272–91.

Unfortunately, scholars will still have to wait almost two decades before the public archives are opened: the police records for the events of February 6, 1934, will not be available until—*absit omen!* —the year 1984. Hundreds of cartons of materials on the sitdown strikes of May–June, 1936, await the investigator. The memoirs, the private papers, the official documents remain sparse. Many private papers disappeared during the war and during the German occupation, but, for the most part, French political leaders in the 1930s did not commit themselves to writing. Léon Blum would have considered it improper (except when a wartime prisoner) to set down in some secret diary his innermost feelings. There is nothing comparable, therefore, to the diaries of Henry Morgenthau and Harold Ickes, or the papers of Harry Hopkins, or the Hyde Park archives, for the student of the French New Deal. The memoirs and occasional reminiscences are themselves of very uneven quality, self-exculpatory, and in some instances repetitious; if Paul Reynaud had written less and Edouard Daladier more, scholars would have reason to be grateful.

Without lingering over the accumulating bibliography, what phases of the Popular Front deserve attention and what conclusions are being reached?

Understandably, considerable attention is still being given to the riots of February 6, 1934, the prelude to the formation of the Popular Front. "Was there a 'sixth of February'?" is still being asked. There are those who see a concerted effort by the Rightist leagues to storm the Chamber, overthrow the Third Republic, and proclaim a new authoritarian regime. The parliamentary investigation after the war concluded that the riots were "un attentat contre le régime." [4] But the consensus among scholars is that there was no concerted or unified design to seize power and that the leagues lacked the coherence, unity, or leadership to accomplish such an end. Against the "plot" theory Max Beloff has rendered the Scottish verdict "not proven"; and René Rémond, the foremost authority on the French Right, concludes that the sixth of February was not "a *Putsch*," not even an uprising (*émeute*), but a "street demonstration" that history would have forgotten if it had not turned out tragically and if subsequent events had not clothed it retro-

---

[4] *Les événements survenus en France de 1933 à 1945: Témoignages et documents* (9 vols.); *Rapport* (2 vols.) (Paris, 1947–54), *Rapport*, I, 13.

spectively with greater significance.[5] The rioters were demonstrating, in the midst of the depression, against an inept, ineffectual parliament with a Left majority, some of whose Radical leaders were tainted by the Stavisky scandal. On the other hand, the pamphlets of some of the demonstrators (e.g., the Jeunesses Patriotes) had an insurrectionist ring to them; as Lefranc and others remind us, no one knows what the outcome would have been if the demonstrators had crashed the police barrier and reached the Palais Bourbon.

Lack of precise knowledge about the expectations and goals of the rioters cannot obscure the fact that 17 persons died and over 2,300 were injured that night, and that the Radical premier Edouard Daladier felt compelled to resign in response to street pressure. The Left was alarmed. The shots at the Concorde bridge, if not exactly heard round the world, were distinctly heard by the French Left. The myth of February sixth became reality and led to a "reflex of instinctive defense . . . against the perils that threatened the republic." [6] A successful counterdemonstration was quickly organized by the CGT and, after much negotiation and difficulties, there came into being eighteen months later the Rassemblement Populaire, the technically correct name for the Popular Front—a broad coalition of Socialists, Communists, middle-class Radicals, and organized labor who collectively took an oath of unity on July 14, 1935, in the Stade Buffalo and resolved to defend democratic liberties, combat the ravages of the depression, and work for peace. The complex negotiations that led to the formation of the Rassemblement Populaire cannot detain us here but it must be noted that a key element was the new "line" adopted by the Communists, directly related to the needs of Soviet foreign policy after the emergence of Hitler as a threat, which crystallized in the signing of the Franco-Soviet pact in May, 1935. The Soviets required a strong united republican France as an ally; the proletarian revolution in France, and elsewhere, could wait. Maurice Thorez displayed remarkable agility in translating the new orientation into French terms and was applauded for his accomplishments in the

[5] Beloff, "The Sixth of February," in James Joll, ed., *The Decline of the Third Republic* (London, 1959), p. 35; René Rémond, *La droite en France* (Paris, 1963), p. 217.

[6] Blum, testimony at Riom trial in 1942, *L'Oeuvre de Léon Blum* (Paris, 1954–   ), V (1940–1945), 233.

C G T ?

summer of 1935 by Georgi Dmitrov at the seventh world congress of the Comintern. The French example became a model for the world's Communist parties.

By January, 1936, an electoral program had been hammered out for the coming general elections by the coalition; the program promised to curb the fascist leagues, combat the depression, introduce social, economic, and fiscal reforms, and work toward collective security (that most ambiguous of terms in the 1930s).[7] In retrospect we can see the Popular Front platform and the oratory connected with it as essentially negative rather than positive—*against* the "two hundred families," "*against* the fascist leagues," *against* the "merchants of death," *against* the spokesmen for retrenchment and deflation. Moreover, it was a catalogue of electoral promises rather than a comprehensive plan for the transformation of the French economy and society as, for instance, the CGT Plan of 1934–35 had been. No measures to nationalize key industries or the credit structure of the country were included, the Communists siding with the Radicals to prevent any sectarian measures that would alienate the middle classes. Differences were glossed over in order to establish a least common denominator of political accord. The program spoke of ending the deflationary and retrenchment policies of previous governments without mentioning the need for devaluation of the overpriced franc; of curbing the flight of capital and decline in the gold reserves without mentioning exchange controls; of reforming the Bank of France without mentioning the overhauling of the antiquated credit system; of checking external aggression without raising the indelicate question of rearmament. Yet it was a document that hinted at a new life and quickened the pulse of working-class militants, trade unionists, intellectuals, and liberals in France and elsewhere.

We know now, as a result of the minute scrutiny by Georges Dupeux of the election returns of April 26–May 3, 1936,[8] that the Left popular vote was not as spectacular in comparison to 1932 as it was generally acclaimed to be. It was a victory but "not a tidal

---

[7] The Popular Front program has been reproduced in many places, most recently in Lefranc, *Front Populaire*, pp. 441–45.

[8] *Le Front Populaire et les élections de 1936* (Paris, 1959), published in the series "Partis et Elections" by the Fondation Nationale des Sciences Politiques. The Dupeux volume is a model case study in electoral sociology and electoral geography.

wave." The total Right vote declined only slightly from its 1932 figure (by 74,000 votes, or less than 2 percent). The Left vote totaled 5,421,000 as against a Right vote of 4,224,000. The Left vote, moreover, included 1,745,000 Radical votes—a clear reminder that the "proletarian parties," with 3,676,000 votes, were in a distinct minority in the country and that no mandate had issued from the electorate for any profound structural reforms. The Communists, biting into both Socialist and Radical strength, were the big winners, with 1,469,000 votes, almost doubling their popular vote of 1932 (783,000), and increasing their representation in the Chamber from 11 to 72 deputies. Their emergence from the narrow sectarianism of the 1920s had paid off; the slogan that Communism was the Jacobinism of the twentieth century gained supporters in the 1930s—and later.

Even if the Popular Front rallied only 46 percent of the total electorate, the results were nonetheless a decisive parliamentary victory in the Chamber for the Left coalition: the Popular Front could count on some 380 seats as against some 220 for the opposition. It was a comfortable margin; one had only to bear in mind that if the Radicals abandoned the coalition they could shift the majority to the Right (as would happen in the same Chamber in the autumn of 1938), and that the government's majority in the Senate, where the last partial elections had taken place in 1935, was much less secure and almost wholly dependent on Radical strength.

Unlike the Left cartels of 1924 and 1932, the new majority had a common program. There could be no quick disintegration as in 1924 or 1932—or so one believed. The key party was that of the Socialists. They had overcome the damage done by the secession of the *neos* in November, 1933, outstripped the Radicals, and for the first time in history been returned as the leading party in the Chamber and of the Left majority.

Blum, who for years had steered a middle course in his party between neo-Guesdist purists like Paul Faure, who opposed Socialist entry in any bourgeois cabinet, and reformists who saw a need to integrate the party fully into the parliamentary life of the republic, was premier-designate. He himself had insisted that, save for emergencies, when "participation in power" or an "occupation of power" would be justified, the party must enter a cabinet only if it were strong enough to form and direct one. Now that these conditions had come to pass, Blum formed the first Socialist-directed coalition cabinet in the country's history, the Socialists sharing ministerial posts with the Radicals but ostensibly remaining directors of policy. The CGT and the Communists each declined to join the cabinet but pledged to support it, the Communists somewhat disingenuously contending that their presence would "sow panic" in the country and weaken the cabinet's support;[9] the suspicion could not be dismissed that they were bent on preserving their freedom of action. Blum's Popular Front government, a Socialist "exercise of power" but not "socialism," seeking to provide the maximum welfare for the country within the existing political and economic framework, pledged to combat the depression and restore prosperity by elevating purchasing power, was launched on June 4, 1936. As Blum told Bullitt, and as he several times openly proclaimed, it was a conscious effort to follow the example of the American New Deal, "adapting it," as he said, "to the conditions and resources of our country." [10]

Programs, coalitions, electoral victories are one thing; unforeseeable events, inevitable in the life of any great nation, are something else again. The first of the contingencies that confronted the new government was the great rash of sit-down strikes that burst upon the country a week after the Popular Front election victory, during the interregnum between the elections and Blum's assumption of office. Many efforts have been made, by participants and by scholars, to explain this social explosion—the "great fear" of 1936. It seems to have been compounded of a sense of elation at the Popular Front election victory, bitterness at the suffering of the depression years, resentment at the authoritarianism of French industry, and an unwillingness to rely on parliamentary processes alone. Most serious investigators are convinced that the strikes were spontaneous. There were left-wing militants, to be sure, who fanned the flames: Trotskyites, whose *Lutte Ouvrière* was banned by the government when it became too incendiary; revolutionary syndicalists—Pierre Monatte's *Révolution Prolétarienne* had no use for any kind of politicians, especially those of the Left; and other splinter groups.

[9] Thorez's reply of May 14, 1936, to Blum's invitation is reproduced in Bodin and Touchard, *Front Populaire*, pp. 72–73.
[10] See, e.g., his speech to the American Club in Paris, February 22, 1937, *Le Populaire*, February 23, 1937.

But certainly neither the Communists nor the left-wing Socialists in Blum's own party, the Gauche Révolutionnaire led by Marceau Pivert, were responsible for initiating the strikes. Pivert, to be sure, tried to press Blum to transform the strike movement into revolutionary channels with his inflammatory article of May 24 in *Le Populaire*, "Tout est possible," but he himself (for a time) even accepted a post in the government. Significantly, it was the Communists who replied to Pivert with the decisive refutation, "Tout n'est pas possible." And it was Thorez's words on June 11, "Il faut savoir terminer une grève," that really cooled things off. There is convincing evidence that the CGT and the Communists, far from inciting the strikes, found themselves outstripped by events and had difficulty in regaining control of the militant rank and file.[11]

Were the strikes "revolutionary"? There is little evidence that they were, except in Trotsky's definition of "the Revolution" (for some reason cited approvingly by Lefranc[12]) as "the direct intervention of the masses in historic events." There was no hint of revolutionary goals, political or economic, on the part of the strikers. The workers "occupied" the factories and sought satisfaction of their demands—wage increases, collective contracts, paid vacations, a shorter work week, redress of specific factory grievances—but manifested no intention of expropriating the plants or of pressing the Popular Front government in such a direction. In many instances, as Simone Weil's perceptive and sensitive essays written at the time reveal, the strikes were something of a lark—a holiday. A sense of exhilaration prevailed at having taken over the plants; one took good care of the machinery; one sang and danced. The workers were less soldiers in battle, she could write, than "soldiers on furlough" who knew they would soon have to return to less pleasant chores and duties.[13] (From some descriptions the events that spring resembled what a later generation would call a "happening.") Blum, faithful to his notion of "exercising power" within the existing

---

[11] There is a good detailed reconstruction of these days in Jacques Danos and Marcel Gibelin, *Juin 36* (Paris, 1952). Although well documented, the book is written from a left, almost syndicalist, point of view and needs to be used with care.

[12] *Front Populaire*, p. 137.

[13] Simone Weil's articles at the time in *La Révolution Prolétarienne* were later collected and published posthumously in *La condition ouvrière* (Paris, 1951); the quotation, from her article of June 10, 1936, is on p. 170.

political and economic structure, and scrupulously aware of the limitations of his electoral mandate, would not even consider sounding a revolutionary clarion; moreover, revolution was not on the agenda either for the CGT or for the Communists. The contention that Blum, in order to preserve his own image of personal integrity and moral scrupulousness, "betrayed the Revolution" in June, 1936, the substance of Colette Audry's conclusions in her searching but tendentious and essentially wrong-headed book *Léon Blum ou la politique du juste: essai* (Paris, 1955) holds no weight.

In the face of the strikes, industry looked to Blum as a providential figure who could talk the language of the workers and persuade them to behave. If Blum did not lead a revolution, he concretized the demands of the workers. From industry, he extracted the now famous Matignon agreement, as much a Magna Carta for French labor as Article 7A of the National Industrial Recovery Act in the United States was for American workers. Employers pledged themselves to practice collective bargaining, remove all impediments to union organizing, and grant a blanket wage increase ranging from 7 to 15 percent (and averaging 12 percent). Second, Blum obtained from the new Chamber and a somewhat more reluctant Senate passage of the principal reforms demanded by the strikers: a collective bargaining law to codify the concessions made at Matignon, a paid vacations law which had been moldering in the Senate committee files since 1931 (but which had not been part of the Popular Front program), and a law establishing a forty-hour week; the shortened work week was justified not only as a reform in itself but as a means of spreading work among the unemployed in order to raise purchasing power. In all instances, despite later criticisms, the bills were adopted in both houses with few opposing votes. The momentous strike movement in which some two million workers were involved conditioned the entire Blum experiment even if some later critics—and especially the Vichy prosecution at Blum's wartime trial at Riom—deliberately overlooked this.

The strikes did not push Blum and his government in some undesired direction but they undoubtedly pushed him faster and farther than he would otherwise have gone. The labor laws were enacted and the nationwide wage increases inaugurated within a fortnight of Blum's taking office. Neither the opposition in the Chamber and Senate nor industry would have sanctioned the adoption of the labor laws had it not been for the sense of panic, the feeling that something resembling civil strife was in the air. For the employers, as Blum later wrote, it was the "ransom that had to be paid to avoid civil war." [14] Not only the three major labor laws but a whole series of additional reforms were quickly adopted: a national wheat office to curb speculation and help farm prices rise, the first step in the nationalization of the arms industry, the raising of the age for compulsory school attendance from 13 to 14, the restoration of pay cuts to government workers; and more reforms were promised. Never had the French legislative process moved so quickly.

The immediate impact of the Popular Front reforms was intoxicating. With wage increases, paid vacations, collective contracts, shop representation, and a sympathetic government, labor thought it saw the dawn of the long-awaited social republic—1792, 1848, and all that. Above all, that summer of 1936, workers enjoyed the first paid vacations in their history. At the same time the Popular Front reforms were not designed for labor alone but for the middle classes, farmers, and government workers as well, and the reforms fitted into an over-all economic attack on the depression. Through wage increases, a shorter work week, a public works program, and travel and vacation expenditures, it was anticipated that purchasing power and consumer demand would be raised, industry would increase production to meet the rising demand (thereby easily absorbing the increased labor costs), and the depression would be overcome.

Despite the note of triumphant self-confidence and the pledges of continued innovation, the initial breath-taking pace of legislative action during the ten "heroic" weeks from June to August was not maintained. The history of the Popular Front government was one of buoyant expectations, spectacular speed in initial accomplishment, and then, a grinding to a virtual standstill. Not a single important new reform was adopted after the first exciting weeks; a "pause" that became official in February, 1937, had already set in by August, 1936. The labor *élan* itself was checked once the strikes subsided. The Minister of the Interior, cornered, to be sure, in de-

[14] *A l'échelle humaine,* his wartime essay completed in December, 1941, *L'Oeuvre de Léon Blum,* V (1940–1945), 460.

bate by a reactionary senator, as early as July 7 even announced that if the sitdown strikes were resumed the government would end them "by all appropriate means." [15] (At the end of the year a compulsory arbitration system was inaugurated to forestall labor difficulties.)

The government found itself on the defensive, overwhelmed by the legacy it had received from its predecessors. "I was more a receiver in bankruptcy," Blum's Finance Minister, Vincent Auriol, later wrote, "than an executor of an estate." [16] (Not much less could be said of Yvon Delbos, Minister of Foreign Affairs, only a few months after the Hoare-Laval agreements and the March 7 remilitarization of the Rhineland.) By the end of the summer the government was struggling with currency and Treasury problems— refusing to devalue the franc even though devaluation was long overdue—the flight of private capital, a counteroffensive launched against the labor laws by industry, the hostility of financial circles, renewed labor unrest, an economy that refused to revive, and, above all, sharply rising international tension. "By some malicious conspiracy of fate," Blum later said of his government, "all kinds of difficulties, foreseeable and unforeseeable, accumulated—and all at the same moment." [17]

The sit-down strikes had scarcely subsided when on July 18, 1936, the second of the great unforeseen emergencies, the Spanish Civil War, broke out. The story of Blum's reversal of his initial impulse to aid the Spanish Republic is a complex and tragic one. To this day it remains unproven, as Pierre Renouvin notes, that any *direct démarche* by the British was responsible for the reversal, or for the subsequent nonintervention pact, although there has been a suggestion (without documentary proof) of a "warning" by Stanley Baldwin to President Albert Lebrun that bypassed Blum.[18] The nonintervention policy seems to have been initiated by the

[15] The debate is reproduced in Danos and Gibelin, *Juin 36*, pp. 217–18.

[16] *Hier . . . Demain*, I (Paris, 1945), 36.

[17] Speech to 34th national congress, Marseilles, July, 1937, *L'Oeuvre de Léon Blum*, IV, part 2 (1937–1940), p. 43.

[18] Professor Renouvin discusses this in his contribution to the 1965 colloquium, *Léon Blum, chef de gouvernement*, "La politique extérieure du premier ministère Léon Blum," p. 340. The suggestion that there was a direct *démarche* from Baldwin comes from the Spanish Socialist minister Luis Jiminez de Asua, who claims he heard it from Blum on July 25.

French Ministry of Foreign Affairs with the wholehearted encouragement of the British, and accepted by Blum.[19] Unwilling to act against the wishes of Baldwin and Eden (who had unofficially warned the French premier against giving aid to the Spanish Republic), aware of Radical opposition to any policy of intervention, fearful of a general European war, and concerned over the profound divisions in his own country that might culminate in civil war, Blum refused to obey the dictates of his heart and conscience, resigned himself to the nonintervention policy, and then made it his own. He convinced himself—and for the moment he convinced even the workers he addressed at Luna Park in his memorable speech of September 6 shortly after the fall of Irún—that in open competition Franco could get more aid than could the Republic, that men and arms would inevitably follow the shipment of supplies, and that a very real threat of European war existed. Once the egregious violations of the pact by Germany and Italy (and then, as a riposte, by the USSR) became known, he contented himself with a policy of surreptitious, clandestine aid, a relaxed surveillance at the frontiers which made possible a trickle of aid, but no more. His cruel dilemma was that he did not believe that he could save the Spanish Republic and the peace of Europe at the same time. The policy weighed heavily on him even though he stoutly maintained that it had saved the peace of Europe on "at least two" separate occasions in 1936–37.[20] The nonintervention policy broke the *élan* of the Popular Front, demoralized his own party, turned the Communists irrevocably against him, alienated Léon Jouhaux and the CGT, and deepened internal divisions in the country as a whole.

In August, 1936—it would be difficult to categorize this as a "foreseeable" or "unforeseeable" emergency—Hitler announced the extension of German military service to two years. The French government had no choice but to assume a heavy rearmament program. Blum did not permit the antimilitarism of his party nor his lifelong devotion to disarmament (disarmament as a path to international

[19] For the sources and an extended treatment of Spain and of Blum's foreign policy see my *Blum: Humanist in Politics*, pp. 198–269.

[20] See Blum's testimony before the postwar parliamentary investigating committee, July 23, 1947, *Les événements survenus en France: Témoignages*, I, 219 Lefranc publishes an interesting memoir-note drawn up in 1964 by André Blumel, Blum's 1936 *chef de cabinet*, but it adds no new information; *Front Populaire*, pp. 460–66.

peace and even national security does not seem quite so strange to a later generation confronted with nuclear armaments) to interfere with the material rearming of the country. Ironically, the anti-militarist Popular Front government with a pacifist-minded Socialist as premier, voted larger sums for rearmament than any previous ministry of the interwar years and launched the country on an extensive, although fatally belated, national defense program. If Blum did not defer to the advice of a certain tall, fervent young lieutenant colonel who sought him out at the Matignon Palace in the fall of 1936 to press the need for tanks that could be massed in armored divisions and not scattered throughout the infantry, he was not alone in ignoring that advice.[21] Blum deferred to General Maurice Gamelin and the military on strategy and doctrine and left the details to his Minister of National Defense, Edouard Daladier. Perhaps, as Joseph Paul-Boncour has astutely noted in his memoirs, Blum and the men of the Left needed a better record of devotion to the military if they were to overcome the routine and inertia of the General Staff: "Too long mistrustful of the military, they were too timid to control it when in power." [22]

Around the failure of the economy to revive (until after the passing of the Popular Front), some of the liveliest controversy in the recent literature has centered.[23] A number of economists like Alfred Sauvy and J.-M. Jeanneney have scored the Blum government for the lack of economic expertise of its advisers and for its ignorance of the relevant economic data. They criticize the failure to devalue more rapidly and more effectively, the mistakes made in introducing the forty-hour week, and the inability to understand or sympathize with the capitalist mechanism with which the government was dealing. Others, including Pierre Mendès-France, have

[21] For Charles de Gaulle's account of this interview see *Mémoires de guerre* (3 vols.; Paris, 1954–59), I, 18–20.

[22] *Entre deux guerres: souvenirs sur la IIIᵉ République* (3 vols.; Paris, 1945–46), II, 268.

[23] See, e.g., Alfred Sauvy, *Histoire économique de la France entre les deux guerres,* II (Paris, 1967), 279–307, and Jean-Marcel Jeanneney, "La politique économique de Léon Blum," in *Léon Blum, chef de gouvernement,* pp. 208–40. For a debate between Jeanneney and Pierre Mendès-France, see Jean Bouvier, "Un débat toujours ouvert: la politique économique du Front Populaire," *Le Mouvement Social,* January–March, 1966, No. 54, pp. 175–81; and see also Georges Boris, "A propos d'une polémique sur Léon Blum et son gouvernement de 1936," *Cahiers de la République,* September–October, 1960, No. 27, pp. 7–10, reproduced in Boris, *Servir la République: Textes et témoignages* (Paris, 1963), pp. 201–3.

entered the lists in defense of the government, conceding some errors, but pointing to the state of economic theory at the time and the circumstances in which the government was compelled to act. In almost all instances one overriding consideration is overlooked. Despite all unforeseeable contingencies, the economy, given time, might have revived and all of the new social reforms have been absorbed and even extended, but time was a commodity that the Blum government did not possess in the unstable political system of the Third Republic, an instability only momentarily obscured by the Left victory at the polls and the existence of the Left coalition. There was no set period for experimentation, like a four-year term of office in the United States, but almost a daily battle against forces that sought to bring down the government once they had recovered from their initial setbacks. It cannot be forgotten that, in all, the Blum government lasted a little less than 13 months.

Most observers see the experiment as going through three phases. From June to late September, 1936, the hope was that recovery could be achieved without devaluation, but the anticipated recovery did not materialize. After the inevitable but belated devaluation in September, in the second phase, which lasted from October, 1936, to January, 1937, some recovery took place. On the other hand, the balance of payments remained unfavorable, Treasury difficulties persisted, and the forty-hour week began to emerge as an obstacle to production. The third and final phase ran from the "pause" in February—a pledge to postpone further reform and to retrench—to the fall of the government on June 21, 1937.

Everyone agrees that the initial attempt to stimulate recovery without devaluing the franc proved singularly unsuccessful. The index of industrial production (1928 = 100), which had been 87 in May, 1936, dropped still further, to 81 in September.[24] Wage costs burdened total costs without increasing production. The lag in production made impossible the absorption of the reforms by the spread of costs over a greater volume of production, as Blum and his advisers had hoped. Heavier production costs hurt still further the export trade already suffering from the overvalued franc. Blum staved off devaluation as long as he could even though as early as

---

[24] Jeanneney summarizes these statistics; see also *Mouvement économique en France de 1929 à 1939* (Paris, 1941); and the statistical appendices in Sauvy, *Histoire économique*, II, 482–592.

June he knew of its necessity and had already initiated conversations in Washington and London so that it would not be effected unilaterally.[25] Everyone in France (or almost everyone—Paul Reynaud was an outstanding exception), Left, Right, and Center, from the Communists to the most conservative banking circles, opposed "tampering" with the currency; they had not forgotten the currency crises of 1925–26. Yet after the devaluation of the British pound in 1931 and of the American dollar in 1934 a devaluation of the franc was inevitable. When the step was finally taken in late September, 1936—under the face-saving device of a tripartite monetary accord with Great Britain and the United States—it occurred *à chaud,* under the pressure of renewed speculation and gold losses. The government lost many of the advantages that an earlier deliberate devaluation might have brought. Several technical errors were also made which need not be recounted here. Suffice it to say that the devaluation of 30 percent would have been inadequate in June and was therefore that much more inadequate in September. The effort to attract gold was also bungled by not offering the proper inducements until too late, and the Treasury, in addition, failed to derive the kind of legitimate "profit" that the United States and other countries had enjoyed when they had devalued.

Ineptly handled though it was, the devaluation did help French products to compete on the world market. From October, 1936, to March, 1937, there was a revival of economic activity. The index of industrial production rose steadily from 81 in September, 1936, to 93 in February, 1937, but the recovery was uneven and was accompanied by an aggravated deficit in the balance of payments and by continuing Treasury difficulties that undermined confidence in the franc; moreover, in this second phase, the decrees establishing the forty-hour week began to appear.

The errors connected with the introduction of the forty-hour week and its impact on the economy have given rise to more heated controversy than any other topic. (I leave aside any question of interference with military production.) There seems to be clear evidence that the government lacked adequate statistical and other economic documentation in connection with the forty-hour week.

[25] For these conversations conducted by Emmanuel Monick see John Morton Blum, ed., *From the Morgenthau Diaries,* vol. I, *Years of crisis, 1928–1938* (Boston, 1959), pp. 145, 156–58.

For one thing, there was the erroneous notion, which Blum shared, that the major plants were working fewer than forty hours a week because of the depression.[26] Actually, the work week in major plants —those employing over 100 workers—was 44.5 hours; and though workers in these plants were in a minority (40 percent of the total labor force), the industries involved were the key ones of the economy. The American example was misleading because in the United States the average work week had actually fallen below 40 hours, from 46.2 in 1929 to 33.8 in 1933.[27] Second, there seems to have been a distortion and misunderstanding of the unemployment problem. At its highest, the official unemployment figure ran to about 500,000, or no more than 2 to 3 percent of the active population; even if the figure were set at 800,000 (because of the low official estimates), it was still a far lower percentage than in Germany, Great Britain, or the United States. As Asselin has demonstrated, even if all the unemployed could have been rehired, the expanded labor force would not have been adequate to compensate for a ten percent decline in the length of the work week.[28] Moreover, most of the unemployed were unskilled; to absorb them one needed a certain number of skilled workers, who were distinctly unavailable.

Further damage was done by the rigidity with which the law was applied. The government would have preferred a more flexible application of the work week but the unions insisted on a five-day week in order to secure its proper enforcement. The system adopted meant a forty-hour plant week with men and machinery idle over the long weekend, even when orders were beginning to accumulate. (Here, too, there was a contrast with the American forty-hour week, which was conceived of as a norm beyond which overtime was to be paid—"a norm for wages rather than a limitation on work" in Professor Laufenburger's words[29]—not as a legal maximum on hours with exemptions difficult to secure.) The more rigid work week made it impossible to absorb the unemployed since there were not enough skilled workers to create additional shifts; they

[26] See his testimony at the Riom trial in 1942, *L'Oeuvre de Léon Blum,* V (1940–1945), 268.

[27] On the American example see Henri Laufenburger, "Expérience Roosevelt et expérience Blum," *Revue Économique Internationale,* XXIX (June, 1937), 442–44, 448–50.

[28] See Jean-Charles Asselin, "La semaine de 40 heures, le chomage et l'emploi," *Le Mouvement Social,* January–March, 1966, No. 54, pp. 184–204.

[29] Laufenburger, "Expérience Roosevelt et expérience Blum," p. 448.

could not, of course, be hired only for Saturdays, as Jeanneney sarcastically notes. Of course, the system might have worked if there had been increased productivity and a renewal of equipment through expanded investment, but this was the last thing that industry was willing to undertake under a Popular Front government.

Finally, the forty-hour week was introduced more brusquely and more rapidly than the government had anticipated. The first decrees appeared in October, 1936, and the system was almost universal by May, 1937. The rapidity was obviously at labor's insistence; the unions recalled industry's grudging acceptance of the eight-hour day in 1919 and did not want to repeat that experience. We know from Jouhaux's biographer that when the question of a more gradual introduction was broached in the autumn of 1936 the CGT leader's retort was: "The forty-hour week for everyone, and right away!" [30] The added costs of production, the difficulty of absorbing unskilled workers without available skilled workers, the rigidity with which the system was applied, all proved to be additional barriers to production and to satisfying the increased demand that was emerging. Sauvy maintains that the decision to introduce the forty-hour week was taken "in darkness" and that the Popular Front which, after devaluation, "held economic victory in its hand" lost it "through ignorance." [31] Any hope that the French national product could be increased by the necessary 40 percent to the level of 1929, when the index of industrial production had been 109, was doomed.

In that second phase, in the winter of 1936–37, rising costs and the forty-hour week appear to have destroyed the advantage gained by devaluation. The prospect of growing budgetary deficits, augmented by rearmament expenditures, and the state of the hard-pressed Treasury contributed to a new round of currency instability. The United States government, despite the good wishes of Roosevelt and Morgenthau, was of little help to the Treasury.

[30] Bernard Georges, "Le CGT et le gouvernement Léon Blum," *Le Mouvement Social*, January–March, 1966, No. 54, cited on pp. 52–53. The article is drawn from the projected second volume of Bernard Georges, Marie-Anne Renauld, and Denise Tintant, *Léon Jouhaux: Cinquante ans de syndicalisme;* volume I has the subtitle: *Des origines à 1921* (Paris, 1962).

[31] Sauvy, "Information, clef de la démocratie," *Revue Française de science politique,* 1951, p. 30; and cf. *Le pouvoir et l'opinion* (Paris, 1949), pp. 100–10. Sauvy's over-all judgment on Blum is worth citing: "un grand homme mal informé," *Histoire économique,* II, 307.

(French scholars have not to date caught up with this incidental information!) Vetoing an advance from the American Stabilization Fund, Morgenthau remarked confidentially that it would be "just flowing money into the Atlantic Ocean." One wonders what Blum would have thought if he could have heard Morgenthau state that they could do no more than "patch up" the French situation every so often, that the United States could not "really help" the French because of the "constant increased percentage of their budget going for war purposes." [32] It made Blum sound very military indeed.

In February, 1937, Blum was compelled to embark on a new course, the "pause." In the interests of stabilizing the public credit, he barred new reforms and additional expenditures. Works projects that had been authorized but not yet begun were canceled. From the beginning the Keynesian-type program of deficit financing and pump priming through public works projects had been slight, and now it abruptly ended. As some writers have correctly noted, Keynesian ideas were still unknown in France. Georges Boris, economist and journalist, friend of Blum's, and author of a book on the American New Deal (*La Révolution Roosevelt* [Paris, 1934]), did not read the *General Theory*, which had appeared in 1936, until some time in the summer of 1937.[33] He later helped Blum incorporate Keynesian ideas into the proposals advanced at the time of Blum's *second* government in March, 1938, when he and Mendès-France served as financial aides to Blum. (A bold program of government expenditures on rearmament and public works was then intended to serve as the basis for reviving the economy. The proposals were rejected by the Senate in April, 1938, and nothing came of them.)[34] At the time of his first Popular Front government Blum remained fearful that large budgetary deficits would lead to increased flights of capital. Not unnaturally, he had to take into

[32] J. M. Blum, ed., *From the Morgenthau Diaries*, I, 456, 458, 460.

[33] For some reason Lefranc (*Front Populaire*, p. 125) implies that it was available in French as early as February, 1936. Boris notes that he read it in English and that it did not appear in a French translation until several years later (*Servir la République*, p. 203).

[34] The *exposé des motifs* of the bill that would have conferred decree powers on the government to execute the Keynesian program is reproduced in Boris, *Servir la République*, pp. 191–99. Mendès-France called it "le premier document official français qui soit inspiré de la 'Théorie génerale' et de la théorie du 'circuit monétaire'" (*Ibid.*, p. 191).

account the psychological reactions of investment circles which were then convinced that government expenditures could lead only to inflation and currency instability. Falling between two stools, the Popular Front government succeeded neither in stimulating the economy by government spending nor in inspiring confidence in private investors by keeping the budgetary deficit down. Given the state of economic thought at the time, no one would have tolerated or dared to undertake deficit financing on a large scale. Perhaps, as Joseph Caillaux scathingly remarked in the Senate on June 16, 1936, the Blum New Deal was "Rooseveltism for Lilliputians."

For a short time the pause helped improve the situation. But episodes of political and economic unrest continued, including the Clichy episode in which a demonstration organized by Popular Front supporters clashed with the police under circumstances still not clear, taking a toll of five dead and 200 wounded. Clichy and continued strikes contributed to economic instability. In the final phase of the experiment, from March to May, 1937, the limited economic recovery ended abruptly—in contrast to world economic recovery at the very same time. The French index fell from 94 in March to 89 in May and June. The French economic decline then merged with the world recession of the winter of 1937–38, which further hurt French exports and tourism. France, Robert Marjolin noted in *Economica* that year, was "the only country to have passed from one period of depression to another without enjoying an interval of prosperity in the meantime." [35]

Can the failure of the economy to revive be attributed to the special economic problem which the Blum government insisted it had to face: the existence of an "enormous internal hoarding" of capital and the continued flight of French capital abroad? The needs of the Treasury and the security of the nation's gold reserves were undoubtedly dependent upon the return to circulation of the hoarded and *émigré* private capital. With typical, and mistaken, optimism Blum believed that he could create an atmosphere of confidence and that the problem could be solved. Again and again he repeated his assurances that his government was committed to a reform program within the strict bounds of existing political and economic institutions. He spoke of his government as "practicing eco-

[35] "Reflections on the Blum Experiment," *Economica*, V (May, 1938), 177.

nomic liberalism more faithfully than any other government in the past," [36] by which he meant that exchange controls were not being introduced. But the repeated protestations of moderation, authentic though they were, fell on deaf ears. The sit-down strike of capital, which outlasted the sit-down strikes of labor, in the long run proved decisive in the failure of the Blum experiment. Jeanneney's argument that Blum misunderstood the causes of the flight of capital, that there was nothing deliberate or hostile about it, that it was a natural reaction of the capitalist mechanism itself to the state of the French economy omits too much of the political climate to be convincing.

Another fatal weakness of the experiment was the failure to overhaul the banking and credit structure of the nation. The plan to nationalize the Bank of France and transform it into a publicly controlled credit agency for the nation had to be scrapped during the negotiations on the Popular Front program because of the apprehension of both Radicals and Communists that nationalization would antagonize middle-class voters. In addition, the unanimous recommendation for nationalization made by the advisory committee appointed to draft a reform bill was also discarded "at the request of the Premier's office." [37] The emasculated bill that passed did little more than democratize control over the Bank and reorganize its governing structure; it failed to alter the unsatisfactory credit system of the country. The changes in the Bank served to irritate the financial community without effectively making it a servant of the national interest.

Thus the Blum experiment was caught in a vicious circle. The revival of the economy could have made possible the absorption of the social reforms of June, 1936, but the revival did not materialize, in large measure because of the absence of investment capital and of adequate credit facilities—factors quite beyond the ability of the Popular Front government, given its self-imposed limitations, to control. Jeanneney contends, however, that the experiment was flawed from the beginning. An adequate immediate devaluation, linked to an effort to reduce costs, he maintains, would have per-

[36] New Year's Eve radio broadcast, December 31, 1936, *L'Oeuvre de Léon Blum*, IV, part 1 (1934–1937), p. 473.

[37] A. Dauphin-Meunier, *La Banque de France* (Paris, 1937), p. 199. Dauphin-Meunier was a member of the advisory committee.

mitted competition on the world market and would have stimulated production. The model that one could have hoped for he schematizes as follows: "Devaluation $\longrightarrow$ restored prospects of profits $\longrightarrow$ decisions to invest $\longrightarrow$ increase in industrial orders $\longrightarrow$ increase in production and total wages paid out $\longrightarrow$ lowering of unit costs $\longrightarrow$ increase in hourly wages $\longrightarrow$ increase in domestic comsumption." [38] The Blum experiment, of course, pinned its hopes on a reverse model, beginning with wage increases. For it to have succeeded, industry would have had to accept the added labor costs of June, 1936, agreeing, as an act of faith, to increase production and to expand plant and equipment even though increased wage costs were for the moment reducing profits.

Jeanneney and other critics correctly observe that Blum did not have solid economic training, experienced economic advisers, economic theories with some pragmatic testing behind them, or sufficiently detailed and precise statistical documentation for guidance. But, alas, even if he had had all these assets, like any other statesman, he could not have operated in a vacuum. In the hectic days of June, 1936 with the labor reforms a necessity to avoid civil strife, with near-unanimous hostility to devaluation, with rearmament imposed by circumstances, with the antagonism of industry toward the government, Blum could not coolly assess the economic situation. Of all the economic policies possible he chose that which corresponded best to his optimism and the prevailing liberal notion that labor reforms and a better distribution of purchasing power would set the economy to rights again; circumstances over which he had little control did the rest.

Georges Boris, shortly before his death in 1960, made a judicious observation:

Twenty-five years ago one knew very little about the treatment of economic crises. . . . Since then we have learned a great deal. That it would have been necessary to begin with a devaluation would have shocked the minds of many. . . . It is unjust to impute to Léon Blum [and] to his government a supposedly wrong orientation given to the French economy in 1936; the economy was undergoing at the time a crisis which was not at all the result of any labor legislation, but of a

[38] For the model and discussion see Jeanneney, "La politique économique de Léon Blum," in *Léon Blum, chef de gouvernement*, pp. 228–29.

policy of money, credit, and investment. In those matters, if Léon Blum had then known what modern economics teaches today, he would have undoubtedly immediately taken the necessary measures.[39]

In June, 1937, came the end of the Blum government; the government's financial difficulties proved to be the Achilles' heel of the whole experiment. A run on the gold reserves in May reduced the reserve to a level endangering the national security. To meet the crisis the government requested temporary decree powers to enact measures it deemed necessary to save the situation. The Senate, including conservative-minded Radical Senators like Joseph Caillaux, nominally supporters of the government, saw its opportunity for revenge on the Popular Front and imposed a long list of restrictions that would have curtailed the government's freedom of action. Blum received renewed support from the Chamber but the Senate was adamant, and on June 21 Blum resigned.

Dupeux in a challenging but unconvincing article has suggested that, instead of resigning, Blum could easily have remained in office and even tamed the Senate.[40] He could have demanded that the President of the Republic dissolve the Chamber and call for general elections—even though there had been no such dissolution since Marshal MacMahon's in 1877. With a new mandate, he argues, Blum might have pushed through legislation curbing the Senate's power to interfere with legislation. There is, however, a major weakness in Dupeux's argument. The consent of the Senate would have been necessary for a dissolution of the Chamber; and the Radical members of the cabinet, we have it on Auriol's authority, would not have accepted an all-out fight against the Senate.[41] All that can be said is that the opposition of the Radicals confirmed Blum's inherent unwillingness to tamper with the constitutional

[39] Boris, "A propos d'une polémique sur Léon Blum," *Servir la République*, pp. 201–2.

[40] "L'échec du premier gouvernement Léon Blum," *Revue d'histoire moderne et contemporaine*, X (1963), 35–44. Dupeux argues that Blum could have won the political fight "without much difficulty" but gave up because he faced a "bourgeoisie" incapable of understanding that he offered them a "transformation without revolution of the social and economic structure of the France of 1937." One must agree with Lefranc (*Front Populaire*, pp. 251–53) that (1) Blum had no intention of any profound transformation of French society and (2) there would have been many difficulties in resisting the Senate even if it would have been worth the try. On the other hand, Lefranc's intimation that Blum welcomed resignation because of the illness of his second wife who died in January, 1938 (p. 253, n. 1) is utterly unconvincing.

[41] See Auriol's letter on the episode in *L'Express*, September 21, 1961.

structure he had sworn to uphold: one of his chief weaknesses always was that he identified the defense of the republic with the parliamentary régime of the Third Republic. Politically, there was no guarantee in June, 1937, after so many issues had risen to divide the Popular Front, that a newly united Center-Right majority might not have swept the elections. Jean Zyromski and Marceau Pivert, the left-wing Socialists in Blum's party, also had their proposal: a few thousand demonstrators in the Luxembourg Gardens might give the Senators reason to reconsider their vote; but Blum would not accept the consequences of unleashing mass turbulence.[42]

In any event, the financial and political emergency coincided with rising international tension (as every emergency did in those days): the Germans, retaliating for an attack on one of their ships, had just bombarded Almería on the Spanish coast. Uncertain of Communist support, aware of the Radical opposition to any all-out fight with the Senate and to extreme economic measures such as exchange controls, and unwilling to aggravate the financial or the political crisis in the midst of the troubled foreign situation, Blum, after one of his famous *examens de conscience*, resigned and called upon the supporters of the Popular Front to facilitate a peaceful transition to a new government.

The experiment was over. Budgetary, currency, and Treasury difficulties, inherited from previous cabinets but aggravated by the hostility of financial circles, had overwhelmed the government and brought it down. And it went down before the opposition of the Senate without a fight. Apathy and disillusionment followed the heroic days of June, 1936. For eighteen months after the fall of the Blum government the Popular Front was in a slow death agony— the Chautemps-Blum government of June, 1937–January, 1938; the Chautemps government (without the Socialists) of January, 1938– March, 1938; a brief, feverish, four-week revival under the second Blum government in March–April, 1938, beset by new strikes; the Daladier government from April, 1938, on into the war. The Radicals withdrew from the Popular Front in October, 1938, but the coalition ended when Daladier, once the Radical darling of the

---

[42] Blum discussed this in his speech to the 34th congress of the Socialist party at Marseilles in July, 1937; see *L'Oeuvre de Léon Blum*, IV, part 2 (1937–1940), pp. 53–55, 59–61.

Popular Front, moved against the "week of two Sundays." The *coup de grâce* came (after Munich and after the Reynaud financial decree laws) with the crushing of the general strike of November 30, 1938. Union membership crumbled, the Socialist party was hopelessly divided over foreign policy, and labor was as alienated from the national community as it had ever been.

Judged by a variety of criteria, the year in office emerges as only a qualified success. Strongly on the credit side, the pattern of industrial relations was revolutionized by the collective bargaining legislation and by the enormous growth in trade union strength that followed. Here perhaps was the closest resemblance to the American New Deal: the day of the open shop, of divine-right rule by the factory magnate, was over. Even if collective bargaining did not flourish without excessive governmental intervention and even if the trade union growth was temporary, a model was initiated for the future. Second, the paid vacations law became a permanent feature of French life; twenty years later, Blum's two weeks were extended to three, and steps were being taken to extend it to four. (In the economy of the 1950s and 1960s paid vacations did not interfere with the expansion of French production.) While some of these labor reforms were not as spectacular as the Popular Front insisted and simply involved "catching up" with other industrial countries, they were substantial as well as symbolic and not lightly to be dismissed. Given the relative backwardness of French social legislation under the Third Republic and the isolation of the French workers from the national community, the collective bargaining and paid vacations reforms were long overdue. As to the forty-hour law, by a twist of irony, a social reform designed to cope with the ravages of the depression and to satisfy the long-postponed promise of a better life had to be introduced at a time when the country's defense needs were increasingly urgent. The many miscalculations and errors made in its application to the economy were faults shared by labor, government, and industry.

On the other hand, no significant economic recovery took place under the Blum government. The index of production in 1937 was still 20 percent below the 1929 figure. Inflation eroded labor's wage increases—the 12 percent average wage increase under the Matignon agreement and the subsequent gains won by the collective contracts and arbitration awards were consumed by rising prices. Labor had won a battle in June, 1936, but lost a war. The promised public works program was postponed indefinitely. No attempt was made to transform the credit structure of the country or the economic base. Little was accomplished to democratize the higher administrative echelons even if a few replacements were made. The Blum-Viollette measure to extend the suffrage to several thousand Arabs in Algeria never came to a vote because of the hostility of the *colons* and their friends in Paris. The fascist-type organizations remained a lurking source of danger, as the bomb explosions in the Etoile area in September, 1937, made apparent. Roger Salengro, Blum's Minister of the Interior, was hounded to suicide by the calumnies of the Rightist journal *Gringoire*; a press law to prevent a repetition of such occurrences was completely emasculated. In foreign affairs the nonintervention policy in Spain turned into a diplomatic fiasco. The ties with England and the United States were strengthened but neither nation had France's obligations to the countries of central and eastern Europe. Nothing was done to implement the military clauses of the Franco-Soviet pact. And little was accomplished to shake the military out of its inertia so that the country might have an army commensurate with its responsibilities in Europe.

The social reforms, introduced with excessive rapidity under the pressure of circumstances beyond anyone's control, imposed a burden on an economy unable to free itself from the grip of the depression and on industries with antiquated machinery, whose costs were already among the highest in the world. Lack of confidence and outright political animosity dried up investment capital. The government, in turn, could do little to assist the economy because of the state of public finances and an understandable timidity towards deficit financing; the burden of rearmament added to the difficulties. The country possessed neither the elastic credit facilities of the United States, American self-sufficiency in natural resources, nor American technology; it shouldered from the beginning a public debt relatively much greater than that of the United States and it depended heavily on its exports for its balance of payments. Nor did the French industrial classes display the resiliency that their American counterparts did in making possible the absorption of the labor changes. Political passions in the United States, intense though they were in the age of Roosevelt, also cannot be compared to those in France. The animosities there fade into insignificance in comparison with the hatreds directed toward Blum as a Socialist and as leader of the Popular Front, and they were compounded with anti-Semitism. (In February, 1936, Blum had been attacked and almost lynched in the streets of Paris by Camelots du Roi ruffians.) The French New Deal was tried under vastly different circumstances from the American. And an American President had four years at least—in Roosevelt's case more than twelve—in which to try out his program, back and fill, shift gears, take detours, creep along, or, if he wished, exceed the speed limit.

In his wartime essay, *À l'échelle humaine,* Blum scathingly reproved the bourgeoisie for failure to modernize the productive apparatus of the country. It had displayed "no reserves of energy, no imaginative resources, no capacity for renovation and reconstruction in order to overcome the economic depression." [43] The indictment was justified, yet it underscored the failure of his own government to recognize these inadequacies and launch a determined assault upon them. Twenty years later a Socialist writer admitted that few in the government at the time fully recognized the retardation of French industry. "Insufficiently aware of this defect, one overestimated in 1936 the ability of the national economy to increase its productive output and to compensate thus for the additional burden that was added to costs by the raising of wages and for the forty-hour week. . . ." Of Blum he wrote: "Believing, like all his contemporaries, that the French economic machine was healthy, that French production had simply slowed down because of the unsatisfactory and unjust distribution of income, he thought that a better distribution . . . would revive production at the same time that it would satisfy justice." [44] The analysis is accurate. A program of true innovation had to await another day. Briefly returning to political life after his wartime ordeal as prisoner of the Nazis and of Vichy, Blum, as provisional

---

[43] *L'Oeuvre de Léon Blum,* V (1940–1945), 440–41.

[44] Étienne Weill-Raynal, "Les obstacles économiques à l'expérience Blum," *La Revue Socialiste,* No. 98 (June, 1956), p. 54. Jeanneney notes that there was an incorrect emphasis on "overproduction" as a basic cause of the depression because of the highly dramatized oversupply of certain agricultural products ("La politique économique," in *Léon Blum, chef de gouvernement,* p. 229).

head of the government in 1947, presided over the inauguration of the Monnet Plan—he himself had had no direct part in it— and noted that France was moving forward to build the industrial base which "she lacked in so markedly tragic a manner in 1940." [45] The Monnet Plan made possible a far more extensive transformation of the structure of French industry than the Popular Front distributive reforms of 1936.

Like all political leaders, Blum himself must be held responsible for the balance sheets of his government. Many elements, conscious and unconscious, combined to undermine the kind of leadership that Blum gave to his government and to limit his freedom of action—the need to respect scrupulously the conditions for "exercising power" within the existing economic and constitutional framework, to keep faith with the Popular Front program and with his middle-class Radical allies, to build the closest diplomatic ties with Great Britain and the United States, to work for national unity in the face of foreign danger, to create an atmosphere of confidence that would revive the ailing economy, to demonstrate that the country would be "safe" under its first Socialist (and first Jewish) premier. They made it impossible for him to apply the bolder measures that were required, to take some of the risks that were necessary, to exercise the political flexibility that the exigencies of economic life and international affairs demanded. His sense of political morality made him the prisoner and not the master of the coalition which he headed. The results of the Popular Front experiment were limited by the compromise program of January, 1936, to which Blum committed himself totally; by the circumstances, domestic and foreign, in which it was launched; by the inadequate technical and statistical data and economic theory available to the Popular Front theoreticians; and by the personality —the very integrity—of the man who presided over it.

In August, 1942, from a Vichy prison cell, Blum called upon the Resistance in France and in London to help educate General de Gaulle to the need for political parties in a democracy and to help the general formulate a sound program for postwar France: "I am thinking naturally—it is impossible that the memory not return to one's mind—of the preparation of the program of the

[45] Radio speech, January 7, 1947, *L'Oeuvre de Léon Blum,* VI (1945–1947), 359.

'Popular Front,' and it is a democracy of the same kind that I envisage." [46] Despite its limitations, economic and otherwise, the inspiration of the Popular Front—the defense of democratic liberties, the quest for social and economic democracy, the search for peace—lived on long after June, 1937. Perhaps the final balance may best be found in the judgment of one commentator, Jean Bouvier: "short-range failure and long-range success." [47] In the minds of the young workers in France of the post-1945 generation the memory of 1936 has faded, but, in Georges Lefranc's haunting phrase, "Frenchmen lived it as a great adventure." [48]

[46] " 'Schéma d'une sorte d'instruction pour mes amis,' Paris–Londres," August 28, 1942, *L'oeuvre de Léon Blum*, V (1940–1945), 368.

[47] Bouvier, "Un débat toujours ouvert," *Le Mouvement Social*, No. 54, p. 180.

[48] *Front Populaire*, p. 9; for testimony that the memory of 1936 was fading, see Michelle Perrot, "Les ouvriers français et la culture," report of a survey conducted in 1958–61, in *Annales, économies, sociétés, civilisations*, November–December, 1964, pp. 1145–46.

Bibliography of
Shepard B. Clough

(in chronological order)

Making Fascists, with Herbert W. Schneider. Chicago, University of Chicago Press, 1929.

A History of the Flemish Movement in Belgium: A Study in Nationalism. New York, Richard R. Smith, 1930; reprint, New York, Octagon Books, 1968.

"Education under the New Régime in Italy," *University of Pennsylvania Bulletin, Eighteenth Annual Schoolmen's Week Proceedings,* March, 1931.

"The Evolution of Fascist Economic Practice and Theory, 1926–1930," *Harvard Business Review,* April, 1932.

Visual Outline of Modern European History. 2 vols. New York, Longmans, Green and Co., 1933.

"Present Trends in French Historical Writing," *Columbia University Quarterly,* XXVI, No. 2 (June, 1934).

"The Objectives of Education in Fascist Italy," in Rexford G. Tugwell and L. H. Keyserling, *Redirecting Education,* Volume II. New York, Columbia University Press, 1935.

"The Literature of World History, 1934," with Charles W. Cole. *The Social Studies,* XXVI, No. 6 (1935).

"Esquisses d'un projet pour une histoire de l'économie nationale de la France depuis 1789," *Revue d'histoire moderne,* March–April, 1936.

"The Literature of European History, April 1935–April 1936," *The Social Studies,* August, 1936.

"Recent Literature of Economic History," *Social Education,* March, 1938.

France: A History of National Economics, 1789–1939. New York, Scribners, 1939; reprint, New York, Octagon Books, 1964.

Economic History of Europe, with Charles W. Cole. Boston, D. C. Heath and Co., 1941; revised editions, 1946 and 1952.

America Insures Itself: A History of the Mutual Life Insurance Company of New York, 1843–1943. Privately reproduced for company use.

"The House that Pétain Built," *Political Science Quarterly,* January, 1944.

"What About Reparations this Time?" *Political Science Quarterly,* June, 1944.

"La cuestion de las reparaciones," *Moneda y Crédito* (Madrid), September, 1944.

A Century of American Life Insurance: A History of the Mutual Life Insurance Company of New York, 1843–1943. New York, Columbia University Press, 1946.

"The Crisis in French Economy at the Beginning of the Revolution," *The Journal of Economic History,* VI (1946).

"Retardative Factors in French Economic Development," *The Journal of Economic History,* Supplement VI (1946).

"Economics and History," *Social Education,* XIV, No. I (January, 1950).

"Toward European Economic Organization," New York, The Academy of Political Science, Columbia University, 1950.

"Prolegomenon to the Economic History of Civilization," in *Studi in Onore di Gino Luzzatto.* Milan, Giuffrè, 1950.

The Rise and Fall of Civilization. New York, McGraw-Hill, 1951; revised edition, New York, Columbia University Press, 1957; reprint, New York, Columbia Paperback, 1961; German translation, *Kultur und Wirtschaft,* Frankfurt, Humboldt Verlag, 1954.

Histoire économique des Etats-Unis, 1865–1952. Paris, Presses universitaires de France, 1953.

The American Way: The Economic Basis of our Civilization. New York, Thomas Y. Crowell Co., 1953. Translated into Korean, Arabic, Burmese, German, and Spanish, 1955.

"Strategic Factors in Economic Growth," *Political Science Quarterly,* March, 1955.

"Economic Growth in Italy: An Analysis of the Uneven Development of North and South," with Carlo Livi, *The Journal of Economic History,* September, 1956.

"Economic Planning in a Capitalist Society: France from Monnet to Hirsch," *Political Science Quarterly,* December, 1956.

"The Diffusion of Industry in the Last Century and a Half," in *Studi in Onore di Armando Sapori,* Volume II. Milan, Cisalpino, 1957.

The Economic Development of Western Civilization. New York, McGraw-Hill, 1959. Second edition under title: *European Economic*

History. The Economic Development of Western Civilization. New York, McGraw-Hill, 1968.

The Basic Values of Western Civilization. New York, Columbia University Press, 1960.

"Philanthropy and the Welfare State in Europe," *Political Science Quarterly*, March, 1960.

Contributor to: The American Historical Association. *Guide to Historical Literature.* New York, Macmillan, 1961.

An Economic History of Modern Italy, 1861–1963. New York, Columbia University Press, 1964; Italian translation: *Storia dell'Economia Italiana dal 1861 ad oggi,* Bologna, Cappelli, 1965.

The European Past, with Peter Gay and Charles K. Warner. 2 vols. New York, Macmillan, 1964.

A History of the Western World, with several collaborators. Boston, D. C. Heath, 1964.

European Economic History: Documents and Readings, with Carol Gayle Moodie. Princeton, Van Nostrand, 1965.

"Estratto della Storia dell'Economia Italiana dal 1861 ad oggi," *Rivista Italiana di Storia Economica e Sociale,* IV, Part 3 (1965).

"French Social Structure, Social Values, and Economic Growth," in Evelyn M. Acomb and Marvin L. Brown, Jr., eds., *French Society and Culture Since the Old Regime* (Eleutherian Mills Colloquium, 1964, of Society for French Historical Studies and the Société d' Histoire Moderne). New York, Holt, Rinehart and Winston, 1966.

"Financing Italian Industrial Development—Examples of the State's Role," *South Atlantic Quarterly*, LV, No. 1 (Winter, 1966).

Contributor to: Melvin Kranzberg and Carroll W. Pursell, Jr., eds., *Technology in Western Civilization.* New York, Oxford University Press, 1967.

The Economic Basis of American Civilization, with Theodore Marburg. New York, Thomas Y. Crowell, 1968.

Economic History of Europe: 20th Century, with Thomas and Carol G. Moodie. New York, Harper & Row (Torchbooks), 1968.